FEAR OF SUCCESS, RELIGIOSITY AND WELLBEING

FEAR OF SUCCESS, RELIGIOSITY AND WELLBEING

By
Roshan Lal Zinta
Upasna Kataik

Neha Publishers & Distributors
4832/24, Prahlad Lane, S-207 Ansari Raod, Daryaganj, New Delhi-110002

Published by
Neha Publishers & Distributors
4832/24, Prahlad Lane, S-207 Ansari Raod, Daryaganj,
New Delhi-110002
Tel.: 011-43570976, 23278261
Email-nehapubdistributors@gmail.com

First Edition : 2013

ISBN : 978-93-80318- 49-3

Price : 895/-

Laser Typesetting by : Vinod Bhardwaj

Printed at: Vikas Computers, Delhi

Preface

Most enduring pursuits of humanity on the planet is to attain La Dolce Vita an Epicurian philosophy of attaining Hedonism through Eudiamonism, optimal experience and functioning by applying their brain processes. In this world, some people pursue towards sensual pleasure; some for love and intimate relationships, some for self-actualization, while some significant others search for the peace of mind through contemplative spirituality. In many cultures, religious beliefs and practices provide a forum for the expression of spirituality and serve several psychological functions, such as providing a system of shared meaning and social practices and protecting people from the social conflicts, dominance, social discrimination, terror of death, good health, longevity, social fame, wealth, power, status , self-esteem and safety from natural catastrophes. Religion is metaphysical in nature whose expression may be intrinsic and extrinsic. The Hinduism incorporates many gods and sects for showing their faith. Some practices *Manism* (worshipping of ghost); some *animism* (worshiping of spirit); some other as *polytheism* (worshipping of god) whereas some significant other practices *Monotheism* (worshipping of supreme beings for escaping from fear and guilt.

Famous philosopher Karl Marx viewed religion as the sign of the oppressed creature, the heart of a heartless world, just as it is the spirit of a spiritless situation. Mark Twain pointed out that the religion involves set of things which the average man thinks he believes and wishes he was certain of. Famous psychologist Freud stated that it is an illusion and strength falls in instinctual desires. Generally religiosity deals with ideological, intellectual, ritualistic, experiential, and consequential dimension that connotes specific behavioural, social, doctrinal, and denominational characteristics. The Himalayas with long chains of mountains is rich in religious believes, customs, traditions and cultures. Studies in Hinduism generally commence with classical text like those dedicated to the description of mythologies (Puranas), hymns and liturgies (Vedas), classical epics (Mahabharatas), dietary and customary prescription or normative ideals for proper social behaivour (Caraka Samhita, Manava dharma Sastra etc.) treaties is a spiritual discipline and enlightenment (Upnishad & Yogasutras of Patanjali).

India being culturally a very rich country has always cultivated a seed of religiosity in which Himachal Pradesh has also kept its indelible impression by considering as Dev-Bhumi a place for 330 million mythological gods, Rishis, Munis or Sadhu and Santa. The people here have their specific deities and village deities those spread their positive vibration to specific territory through Gurism, Maali foresee their grief, ailment, suffering and future as well and promote their community health. The deities in Himachal Pradesh are the expression form of Brahma, Vishnu, and Mahesha those serve as to fulfill Dharma, Artha, Kama, and Moksha. From the Vedic period Agni, and Vayu were famous. Beside this, the Yama, Sarasawati, Durga, Lakshmi, Krishna, Buddha, Chaitanaya, Kamadeva, and Ganesha were some other prominent those still are pleased through *dhoop, agarbati , and other heaven* related material like presentation of roat, atta, gur, halwa-puri, ganthi-daan, handa and Bakra, lamb, cock as well gold and silver jewellery so as to escape from calamities. The "big idea theory" also consider such people as full of illusion. **Some theologians and philosophers argued for the reverse that human moral reasoning points to the existence of God as moral law-giver.** Within Hinduism a large number of personal gods are worshipped as murtis those are depicted in humanoid, partially humanoid and complex iconographic in nature. Approximately 330 thousand deities in Hindu traditions have their illustration. Explanation of Kama and Cupid, Vishwakarma and Vulcan and Indra and Zeus portray the similarity of Hindu mythology to Greek mythology. Ancient Alien theory states that the Aliens created realities.

When we are faced with betrayal, hurt, anger or disappointment we then expect a moment of calm that is only possible with God's grace. It is believed that the deities prevent us from goblins, gnomes, ghouls, vampires, witches, imps, werewolves and pishachas as well as wild spirit. Scientist in the present scenario told that god is not proved objectively then the question arises what is proved objectively; the electron, neutron or proton because nobody have seen them.

The dedication, devotion and immutable beliefs of people in deities led some highly status people to become their administrator in the form of Kardar, Motmein, Kothari, etc. Some other people are highly involved in construction of wooden and cemented temple, brass, silver and gold faces of deities known as Mohras, precious dresses like ghaghris, big palanquin and sorts of precious gifts, money, celebrating fair and festivals for pleasing them so as to overcome their fear of success. Guru or Malis of Devta seems to follow path of dharma those cultivate dharti (tantra), kshama (forgiveness), damah (control) asteya (steal anything physically and mentally), shaocha (external and internal cleanliness), indriyanigraha (controller or patriarch), dhi (benevolent intellect), vidya (internal assimilation of external objectivities), satyam (truth) and akrodha (non-anger) and make local community more religious by pushing them towards humility.

The Purvaj Syndrome (Ouch) is also common in Himachal Pradesh that is considered as misfortune in the family due to suffering of dead recent family member's soul that could not obtain Sadgati, liberation or rebirth, want solace, recognition, importance and institutionalization (sthapna). In Himachal Pradesh it is called Paap, Newa, Chhua, Mashani and Ouch those causes psychosomatic disorder. The deities alleviate such suffering and promote wellbeing. Therefore, the local deities helps in becoming people more religious, solve situational and emotional conflicts; provides a sense of power and control through association with an omnipotent force; promotes social cohesion; offers a sense of identity, satisfies the need for belonging, and unites people around shared understandings. The devi and devta in this state govern all social, cultural, moral, economic, religious and political life of the village folk. As a result they are pleased by singing various music, *dhol, nagaras, baam, kansal, guju, bhana, tali, dhokoli, ransingha, karnali, tali, damru, Khanjar and chimtas, fairs and festivals. In Himachal Pradesh there are separate devis and devtas in various caste. The scheduled castes devta are generally Kilbalu, Rajput and Thakurs Devta as Mahsu(Chalda or Botha Mahsu/Pabasi, Khantu (Jhangru), Lankda Veer,Nageshwar, Narain, Bondra, Shirgul, Golinaag, Dhounlu, Kiran, Klau, Ektanga, Kimshu, Shimniaon, Mashan, Vir/ Cholbeer, and Kandralu etc.* With the advent of science and technology and attainment of higher education the belief in deities remained status quo. The fear of success seems to be significant factor behind deities customary practices. So in the present manuscript a pioneer attempt has been made to study fear of success, religiosity and wellbeing among the people of hilly areas.

Dr. Roshan Lal Zinta
Upasna Kataik

CONTENTS

INTRODUCTION

Happiness is neither within us only,
nor without us;
it is the union of ourselves with God."

– Blaise Pascal

One of the most enduring pursuits throughout the entire history of humanity has been the search for well-being, happiness,. and good life. It takes only a minor excursion into human history to realize that the answers to this question have been extraordinarily diverse. Some people have pursued towards sensual pleasure; others have sought love, the joys of intimate relationships and still others have worked toward the actualization of their potentials, while some significant others have searched for the peace of contemplative spirituality (Compton, 2005; Shrivastava, 2012; Sethi, 2012; Khan, 2012). It is hard to find a man who has desire for what he has not tasted universally. The person on the planet mostly had craved for seeking pleasure and freedom and seems very hard to find a man who craves for nothing with open mind, which neither seeks nor shuns wealth, duty, life or death .We generally crave with the help of unfulfilled desires through our word and sound that desires according to Rabindranath Tagore is to exist. But it is not possible to accomplish the instinctual desire of being, belonging and becoming all the time. At the same time, the individual is firm to accomplish the same for their pleasure in general and their family in particular. Therefore, the human being, most of the time sublimate and surrender their intense desire to the God in general and goddesses in particular for the sake of gratification. It seems that the human being consider themselves as weak, believes in external and spiritual power and totally surrender to the supreme being so as to overcome his fear on the one hand and gratify their need on the other(Kamat, 2012).

India being culturally a very rich country has always cultivated a seed of religiosity in which Himachal Pradesh has also kept its indelible impression by considering as Dev-Bhumi. They have steak belief in them and the forecasting, decision and order as well as justice made by the people are smoothly followed without any revolt. The people here have their specific deities and village deities those spread their positive vibration to specific territory and foresee their grief, ailment, suffering and future as well and promote their health (Dhaleta, 2012). With the emergence of men as conscious animal, the concept of health may include mind and body as a major concern whose concept date backs to Yoga and Ayurveda who talks about mind, body and spirit interaction for lively survival. Based on the theories of Ayurveda, Siddha and Unani, the traditional health system in India comprises of two stream namely local health belief and the practice relying on instantaneous available local resources and the codified knowledge. Organized relationship between modern and traditional medicine came into four ways. Monolithic, tolerant, parallel and integrated factors. Amchi also has been incorporated in health system which is a Tibetan system (Bhasin, 1997). Official health system deals with Western science and technology which is medically based required doctor. But the people living in hilly area still believe in their traditional local institution of deities in general and Gurism particular promoting health of the community (Ashwini, 2012).

The Himalayas with long chains of mountains is rich in religious believes, customs, traditions and cultures. The myths, ritual and trusty behaviours of Himalayan people, functions as a conceptual apparatus in the life of the community members. A large number of rituals are performed with a view to achieve some goal or end. The end may be physical like good health, longevity, social like fame, wealth, fame, power, and status and natural life safety from flood, droughts etc. The religious beliefs are intermingled in the Psyche of Himalayan people in such a way that it has become the way of life. The traditional religious believes therefore play vital role in physical, social, psychological and cultural life of the people. The people believes in institutions of deities, priests, old customs, possessions and practices as well as rituals and is said to govern human behavior and help them to adapt in better way in their environment. Therefore the people of India seems to be happiest on the planet (Poll by global research company).

According to Vastu Sastra, the world comprises five basic elements known as the *pancha maha bhoota* known as Earth (Bhumi), Water(jala), Air(Vayu), Fire (Agni) and Space(Akash) built by Purusha an energy, power, soul or cosmic man. Therefore, Brahma is considered as the creator of the universe (Desire). There are four goals of human being named as Dharma, Artha, Kama, and Moksha. Dharma occupies the first place in the four categories of human goals because the pursuit of security (Artha) and pleasures (Kama) needs to be governed by ethical standards. Artha striving for security comes second because it is the foremost desire of everyone. Given basic security, everyone wants to live happily and pursue what they think will give pleasure. The last category is that of liberation or Moksha as a direct pursuit only after one has realized the limitations inherent in the first three pursuits. So these five basic elements have intermingled in the life of the human being at every chokepoint of life. The religiosity also evolves from it.

In psychology, a famous psychologist William James also attempted to integrate religion and psychology as early in 1902. In his book, he talked about varieties of religious experiences such has supernatural phenomenon and emphatically told that the faith can affect both physical health and disease processes (James, 1902). So question arises how religion and faith may affect our thoughts, emotional processes and behaviour. Its answer seems to be that most of us are driven to be successful, whether in our careers, social lives, families or other dimensions of human existence. It is very true that in this world something is bound to be happen and the human being intends to achieve success in every stage of life. At the same time he fears to accomplish certain things important for him. A low level of fear can be inspiring, but a higher level of fear can become a full-blown phobia that may cripple their progress.

The fear therefore is considered as a powerful and primitive human emotion that alerts us about the presence of danger. It seems that fear is the basis of the whole thing. Most important fear in life is the — fear of the mysterious, fear of defeat, and fear of death. In today's driven society; failure is often seen as unacceptable. We are encouraged to innovate but avoid "wasting" time or money. When we fail, we may be threatened or even punished by employers, spouses and parents. Some individuals fear that outside forces may take away their success. Sometime the human being fear that higher we climb in life, the further we're going to fall. For example the success will bring – for example, loneliness, new enemies, being isolated from our family, longer working hours, or being asked for favors or money; added work, responsibilities, or criticism that we face. Our relationships will suffer friends and family will react with jealousy and cynicism. In the words of Sigmund Freud, those wrecked by success occasionally fall ill precisely when a deeply-rooted and long-cherished wish has come to fulfillment.

For overcoming their fear, the people seem to generalize and connect their inner self to the spirituality and religion so as to find appropriate solution of certain fear to promote their wellbeing. We generally fear that accomplishing our goals, and realizing that we have the power to be successful, may actually cause an intense regret. Therefore, we went into the shelter of God and goddesses. They consider religious believes in general and institutions of local deities as an important for promoting their mental health. As a result the people in India in general and in Himachal Pradesh in particular believes in God, goddesses or devi and devtas in Himachal Pradesh by performing various prayers, holy spirits, incantation, and worship in their respect, although may their own fear to follow them and their assumption for the seem may be to reducing psychological suffering and preventing natural, physical and social calamities. The psychologists in India also have realized that the inner religious believes may also play crucial role in real life that may exert profound influence on the wellbeing (Broota, 1987). The belief in supernatural element and power is not only prevalent in India but it is prevalent in Western countries as well (Kamat, 2012). For example the US poll 2005 found

88% Americans as religious whereas in India every people seem to follow this path.

In this manner, there are various myths, rituals, superstitious and traditions those may play very important role in social, cultural and religious life of a persons in terms of adaptation patterns. It seems that when religious people think about the fear of death, their religious beliefs appear to be strengthened at both conscious and unconscious levels. Negative affect from guilt and fear associated with religious beliefs is an important topic that has received little research attention. Ellis (1980) uses guilt as the foundation of their arguments that religion is neurotic. Thus, the supernatural belief in spirit in the present scenario has commanding importance (Thakur, 1997). Similarly, Walter Houston Clark (1958) in his book "Psychology of Religion" found that the religion sometime become very superficial and laughable. He told that the religion require a balance between activity and passivity, between the life urge and death urge. Sometime it may provide comfort, security, adventuresome, courage, imagination and creative spiritual insight. In primitive societies, the religion aroused and gave expression to the consciousness in community and its members. It later becomes a customs, traditions or religious systems across the country. The religious beliefs provide a mean to establish social order, challenged by death and crisis in order to survive best in the environment. The rituals do also assure validate people's beliefs, experiences and values (Srivastava, 1992). Most probably the ritual of believing in local deities and devta in India in general and Himachal Pradesh in particular have been playing a key role in their development.

There are approximately, 330 million mythological gods whose sovereignty takes in two specific forms in Himachal

Pradesh. Wilkins (1972) gave three classification of Vedic gods named as Agni whose place is on earth; Vayu or Indra whose place is in air and Surya whose dwelling is in the sky. They have been receiving many appellations in consequences of their greatness, or the diversity of their functioning. Beside this there are Yama, Sarasawati, Shiva, Durga, Lakshmi, Krishna, Buddha, Chaitanaya, Kamadeva, and Ganesha and some other prominent deities who are honored by everyone for promoting their universal brotherhood. So the belief in the God in general and god and goddess in particular especially in Himachal Pradesh people have played an important role in maintaining their quality of life.

In this state the individual have their own family deities, village deities and whole valley deities. The village god is considered to rule over encapsulated territories, the largest of which includes the territories of subordinate gods. A village god is perceived as a king over his territory and receives regular tributes (nazrana) from those who live within his jurisdiction. He exercises his sovereignty through a set of various representatives. Firstly he can be consulted directly by speaking through his own institutional medium, the Gur/Mali, who is gods receptacle possessed by means of ritual procedure. During consultation a dialogue is held between the god and the village who ask him to interpret their problem to give some advice and decision to them. Almost everywhere in India, spirit possession is described as means of social regulation and of conflict resolution through symbolic transformation. The family deities dwell in one corner especially on the small temple made on shelf of the house. The valley god is a god of all the villagers who in various ways celebrate his fair and festivals.

Almost everywhere in India, spirit possession is described as means of social regulation and conflict resolution process through symbolic transformation. It is found among Gaddis of western Himalayas in general and amongst the people of Shimla, Sirmour, Chamba and Kinnaur of Himachal Pradesh. Possession is generally a belief and a practice. The upper and lower caste people in Himachal have their own devi and devta at their family and village level. For them their deities help them in overcoming every fear and helplessness with the help of Gur or maali. Generally the low caste people use it for removing social oppression (Dhalela, 2012). Possession is practiced for yogic practices such as Samadhi wherein deities enters inside the body of the individual and take full control of thought, pattern, behaviour and feelings that is found in daily routine. Possession took place in open area in order to solve cross personal and village litigation (Cote, 2007) in general and asking tips for health, preventing enemies and getting employment in particular.

The people of India are very religious and almost in every village have their own local deities. They have firm belief in them and consider them as curator and protector. The cultures of Himalayan people are very unique and interesting. In 1835 Lord Macaulay announced to the British Parliament – *"I have traveled across the length and breadth of India and I have not seen one person who is a beggar, who is a thief, such wealth I have seen in this country, such high moral values, people of such high caliber, that I do not think we would ever conquer the country unless we break the very backbone of this nation which is her spiritual and cultural heritage...I propose that we replace her old and ancient education system, her culture for if the Indians think that all that is foreign and English is good and greater than their own they will lose their self esteem, their native culture and they will become what we want them, a truly dominated nation".*

The belief in God in general and the village deities in particular across India and Himachal Pradesh have therefore played a vital a role (Wilkins, 1972). The village deities come into existence when people began to settle in agricultural community. After applying the sedentary mode of life, the people of hilly area now believes in religiosity especially in Gram Devta and Sthan Devta to promote community life, for preventing natural calamities, troubles and mis-happening and at the same time foster prosperity and happiness among them. If we look the concept from various angels it seems that the person or community members sublimate their fear of success in god and goddess so as to achieve their goal in short period of life. The fear of success may be the factor behind religiosity that may compel the individual to go into the shelter of local god and goddesses. The concept of fear of success is as follows:

1.1 EPITOMIZING FEAR OF SUCCESS

There seems to be a fine distinction between fear of success and fear of failure. People who possess a dominant fear of failure will not subject themselves to achievement activities. They are unwilling to engage in activities where the outcome may be doubtful. Fear of failure happens when people have the feeling they will never achieve because of the impossible goals or that they will never measure up to the standards because they generally perform badly anyway. People with a dominant fear of success are achievement oriented, but when goal is probable, they begin to participate in self-defeating behavior designed to protect themselves from expectations. Generally, if individuals are about to succeed, they believe that untenable things may happen, thereof are conditioned to fear success, they actually inhibit the opportunity to succeed. To them, the outcome associated with the success is more stressful than a less-prized alternative.

In general, the fear of failure evokes refusal to participate, or perhaps a perfunctory performance, while fear of success motivates striving and participation with intensity, but substitute's self-imposed detours in response to stress. A distinguishing characteristic between the two forms of motivation is the perceived personal reason for repudiation of competence. The concept fear of success was first characterized by Martina Horner (1968, 1972) and grew out of an effort to define achievement for women. She believed that fear of success was acquired, inhibit performance, restrict level of aspiration, and is an expression consistent with the developed self-concept. Pappo offers a more formal definition by saying it as s "a psychological state which leads to withdrawal in the presence of a consciously understood, subjective or objective goal which is perceived by the individual in the moment of withdrawal (Pappo, 1972).

The person who fears from the success is in conflict over success and tends both to approach it and avoid it. Such a person adopts an intermediate distance from success rather than putting it as far away from himself /herself as possible. Sigmund Freud first discussed "Those Wrecked by Success" in one of his 1916 papers. He noticed the bewildering phenomena that "people occasionally fall ill precisely when a deeply-rooted and long-cherished wish has come to fulfillment." He wrote: it is not at all unusual for the ego to tolerate a wish as harmless so long as it exists in phantasy alone and seems remote from fulfillment, whereas the ego will defend itself hotly against such a wish as soon as it approaches fulfillment and threatens to become a reality. This set the stage for the psychoanalytic study of fear of success.

Fear of success or success phobia has been studied from classical and relational psychoanalysis to social and cognitive psychology. Psychoanalytic theories believe that the unconscious forces are at work in fear of success. Other explanations emphasize conscious and environmental influences. Three major groups that evoked the most interest were students, vocations, gender and sex. Top executive may develop a success neurosis because of the "loneliness of command" brought on by isolation at the top. Feminists argued that women are reacting to stereotypes that inhibit females. Eric Erikson's development model and rationality or a straightforward choice deals with alternative life styles. Social theories leave the family of origin out of the etiology but cultural theories embrace family expectations. Psychoanalytic theories contend that our activities are determined by the unconscious content of our minds, a process called psychic determinism. That means unconscious psychic motivations determine humans activities, not the rational conscious thinking process. While these processes are out of conscious awareness they influence actions in ways that are *metaphorically* consistent with past methods of coping with anxiety producing situations that in some individuals while reaching their potential abilities is called as the fear of one's own greatness" or "the running away from one's own best talent" (Belss, 1998).

The fear of success is a very unique issue that arises when you are genuinely creating change and moving forward in your life. Fears of success tend to cluster around several issues. One of the core fears that arise from change is that success will lead to <u>loneliness</u>. Women especially fear from success because they are afraid that being powerful enough to create the life they want will render them unlovable. Sometimes people with fear success realized that being attacked by enemies, or besieged by others wanting money or other things from them. Many women fear success at losing weight because becoming more attractive to others could jeopardize the love and the life they have or create situations they do not know how to handle. The issue of failure and success correlates to grief and loss in an interesting way, again by using the phrase, "In a crisis we go back to old beliefs and old behaviors." When we experience a major loss—death, divorce, health, career—we automatically summon whatever information we have stored in our minds on how to deal with the feelings that loss provokes. The stored information we have will either be helpful or not helpful, and as such, will either lead to success or failure in how well we adapt to the loss and whether or not we know what to do to be able to complete what the loss left emotionally incomplete for us. Fear of success is mainly observed in women who have a high desire for success but fewer capabilities (Farahani, 1999).Individuals from socio-economically disadvantaged backgrounds fear that, for them, success will lead to alienation from their community, and the loss of identity and loss of overall sense of belonging within their culture. In numerous situations, people claim to want success but distance themselves from it by slacking and refraining from actions lead to success because they feel undeserving that in other terms may be considered as fear of success (Bagget, 2000). There are times that an individual has an ability to succeed, but the changes that ensue make him/her anxious (August, 2000). Karabenick and Marshall believed that Horner's initial thoughts of such fears revolve around competition in the workforce, especially if it takes place among men. Some studies demonstrate that some women think that success and womanhood are incompatible and this is the reason behind their fear. Another reason is the belief that success is accompanied by aggressiveness, which is in contradiction to women's characteristics. Therefore, rewards of success in women may cause anxiety (Hide, 2001). Women mainly have fear success because the idea of possessing enough power to construct their lives to their own preferences will diminish their likeability. Success has threatened their current lives and created a situation in which they are unsure of how to behave (Marano, 2004).

More often than not, fear of success is accompanied by a lack of confidence and self-respect, and individuals with these characteristics often turn out to be what others expect them to be. Therefore, anxiousness is an indispensable part of their lives and the feeling of helplessness makes them reliant on others (Motaghi et al., 2004). It may be due to lack of self confidence to attain one's goals (Brooks, 2005). In rural area such fear of success may be among illiterate person believing ancient institutions of deities. It may be channelized and generalized among their forthcoming elite masses. The fear of success involves a mental pattern by which the individual thinks of different changes that may occur afterwards and that he/she may have to cope with (Rao, 2004). Research has shown that both conditions share many of the same symptoms. Both are marked by anxiety symptoms in certain situations. Both conditions can be crippling, leading the sufferer to take few risks and make only safe, conservative choices. Fear of success also appears to be related to the level of control that the sufferer feels in his or her own life. Those who feel that external forces are in control tend to be at a higher risk for fear of success. It could be that they do not feel that their success has been earned, or it could be that they fear outside forces may take away their success. Some people seem to fear both from success and failure simultaneously. This can be a very difficult situation to be in, as every choice that the person makes must be weighed against these fears. It is entirely possible for someone in this situation to become paralyzed with indecision, unable to make any choices at all.

1.2 NATURE OF RELIGIOSITY

Religion is metaphysical in nature because like science and philosophy it arises as a result of man's reflection upon his surroundings and upon the means he can adopt for the adjustment of his needs, physical, psychological, and spiritual to the environment in which he lives. In fact, it is the very necessity of the inevitable adjustment with his environment that makes man incurably religious. All major religion of the world like Hinduism, Christianity, Buddhism, Judaism, and Islam are the outcomes of these religious evolutions and belief systems. The Hinduism incorporates many gods and has many sects those the people follow according to their faith and need. According to William James religious people have three main characteristics. All religious people have life goal and strive positively for attaining it and live purposefully. Secondly they have an ability to overcome their unhappiness. Finally the religious people are healthy minded. They have conquering efficacy of courage, hope and trust as well as key to worry, fear and nervousness. It involves an eternal unanimity of men with god is the core characteristics.

Man is essentially a religious being (Vidyarthi, 1978). In many cultures, religious beliefs and practices provide a forum for the expression of spirituality and serve several psychological functions, such as providing a system of shared meaning and social practices, explaining the unknown and protecting people against the terror of death. In addition, religion is a source of support and guidance that can help to maintain and enhance character and mental health. Religion can be said a system of ideas, norms, and rites that satisfy a need that is rooted in human existence, the need for a system of orientation and an object of devotion. Religiousness has also been divided into intrinsic and extrinsic religion (Allport & Ross, 1967). Intrinsic religion refers to being religious for its own sake, whereas extrinsic religion refers to being religious for any benefit it may bring. Research has found that people with intrinsic religion is linked to well being while extrinsic religion adversely affects well being (Dein, 2007).

Srivastava (1992) defined four types of religiousness according to four types of objects. These are *Manism* (worshipping of ghost); *animism* (worshiping of spirit); *polytheism* (worshipping of god) and *Monotheism* (worshipping of supreme beings). These beliefs are applied by the human being in their life to escape from fear and guilt. According to *Penguin Dictionary,* the religiosity is a general term that is used to designate all concepts concerning the belief in god(s) and goddesses as well as other spiritual beings or transcendental ultimate concerns." *The encyclopedia of Britannica* defines it in context with the human beings' and their relation to that which they regard it as holy, sacred, spiritual, or divine." In the words of Philip Rousseau, "The religious response is a response to experience and is colored by the wish to provide a wider context for a fragile, short and turbulent life."

Famous philosopher Karl Marx viewed religion as the sigh of the oppressed creature, the heart of a heartless world, just as it is the spirit of a spiritless situation. It is the opiate of the people. Similarly, Peter Berger pointed out that the religion is the human attitude towards a sacred order that includes within it all being—human or otherwise—i.e., belief in a cosmos, the meaning of which both includes and transcends man." Ambrose Further, Bierce pointed out that the "Religion is the daughter of hope and fear, explaining to ignorance the nature of the unknowable. More appropriately a religion in the words of famous psychologist Emile Durkheim is a unified system of beliefs and practices relative to sacred things, that is to say, things set apart and forbidden—beliefs and practices which unite into one single moral community called a Church, all those who adhere to them.

Earlier, Mark Twain pointed out that the religion consists in a set of things which the average man thinks he believes and wishes he was certain of. Famous psychologist Freud stated that it is an illusion and it derives its strength from the fact that it falls in with our instinctual desires." Glock offered a five part definition of religiosity named as (i) ideological (the person's belief system); (ii) intellectual (knowledge about scriptures); (iii) ritualistic (overt institutional actions); (iv) experiential (direct knowledge of ultimate reality through religious experiences); (v) consequential (the secular effects of the above). Thouless in 1971 in his book "*An Introduction to Psychology of Religion*" classified the factors, which produce the religious attitude into four main groups named as social influences, experiences, need and processes of thoughts. He argued that psychoanalysis has much wider function to understand the forces behind religious behaviour, their explanations and the role of unconscious. Religiousness has specific behavioural, social, doctrinal, and denominational characteristics because it involves a system of worship and doctrine that is shared within a group. Spirituality is concerned with the transcendent, addressing ultimate questions about life's meaning, with the assumption that there is more to life than what we see or fully understand, while religions aim to foster and nourish the spiritual life– and spirituality is often a salient aspect of religious participation–it is possible to adopt the outward forms of religious worship and doctrine without having a strong relationship to the transcendent."(Fetzer Institute, National Institute on Aging Working Group (1999).

The study of Pargament (2005) assumed that religion can be reduced to more basic processes. There may be something unique about religion. By definition it has a distinctively meaningful point of reference, the sacred one. Empirical studies also suggest that religion may be a unique form of motivation; source of value and significance; contributor to mortality and health; source of coping as well as source of distress. These findings point to the need for: theory and research on the sacred; attention to the diverse religious beliefs and practices; evaluation of individual and social interventions that address spiritual problems and apply spiritual resources to their resolution; and collaboration between psychological and religious groups that draws on their unique identities and strengths.

In the words Emmons (2005) the religion invests human existence with meaning by establishing goals and value systems that potentially pertain to all aspects of a person's life. A goals approach provides a general unifying framework to capture the dynamic aspect of religion in people's lives.

Hungsberger (2005) identified a link between religion and prejudice by suggested that the religion can both reduce and exacerbate the prejudice. The four levels of meaning associated with religion-cognitive, motivational, societal, and intergroup-may both promote and attenuate prejudice. Generally, it as an *individual* preferences, emotions, beliefs, and actions that refer to an existing or self-made religion that in turn denotes the whole of cultural symbol-systems that respond to problems of meaning and contingency by alluding to a transcendent reality and influences everyday. Religious symbol-systems incorporate mythical, ethical and ritual elements as well as 'salvation goods'. Therefore the religion is a cultural phenomenon that deals with prayers, sacrifices, believes, loves or fears his god –then this is 'religiosity'.

1.3 CONCEPT OF WELLBEING

The well-being deals with optimal experience and functioning. The research on it has been derived from two general perspectives: the hedonic (happiness) and Eudaimonic (self-realization). The hedonic perspective defines well-being in terms of pleasure attainment and pain avoidance; and the eudaimonic one defines well-being in terms of the degree to which a person is fully functioning. These two perspectives have given rise to different research foci and a body of knowledge. New methodological developments concerning multilevel modeling and construct comparisons are also allowing researchers to formulate new questions for the field. This review of research from both the perspectives concerning the nature of well-being, its antecedents, and its stability across time and culture (Ryan & Deci, 2001).

More appropriately, the general well being may be defined as the subjective feeling of contentment, happiness, satisfaction with life experiences and its role in the world of work. The general well being may show some degree of positive correlation with quality of sense of achievement and negatively with neuroticism, psychoticism and other such related variables. In this manner, the well-being comprises of sense of achievement utility, belonging ness, and non-distress, dissatisfaction or worry etc. those in some extent are very difficult to evaluate objectively. As ***a noun it refers to the s***tate of being well, happy, and prosperous and welfare. Finally, the global well-being involves present life satisfaction, global self-esteem and self-efficacy.

Similarly, the psychological and subjective well being is the focus of intense research attention (Diener & Diener, 1995). It resides within the experience of the individual (Campbell et al, 1976) in terms of life satisfaction (cognitive evaluations) or affects (ongoing emotional reaction). The study of Diener and Diener (1995), however, held that little attention has been paid to the predictor of psychological well-being those differ in various cultures and influence peoples' evaluations. There involves the role of personality and social support in psychological well-being (Nathawat, 1988, Nathawat & Rathore, 1996). In the words of Diener et al (1989) people who are successful at attending frequent positive affect may be happy as compared to their counterpart. The concept of 'psychological well-being' is considered from the standpoint of George Kelly's personal construct theory (Kelly, 1955) who argued that the origin of psychological disorder lies in the difficulty in 'person construing', with particular reference to 'self-construing'. The psychological well-being ranges from positive and negative aspects of well-being to the global aspect of well-being.

The positive well-being involves positive affect pleasure on previous day and positive self-esteem. The negative well-being includes negative affect, trait on previous day, anxiety, depressed mood, probability of minor psychiatric disorder and negative self-esteem. Thus, psychological well being is a subjective term that means different, things to different people. From all of the research for this answer the terms is used throughout the health industry as kind of a catch-all phrase meaning contentment, satisfaction with all elements of life, self-actualization, one's role in the world of work, socioeconomic status, health, social support, mood, self-efficacy, non-distress, dissatisfaction, worry or anxiety, just peace, and happiness. Many researchers articulated "psychological well-being" as a happy and satisfied person that seems to be a rather non-technical definition. The construct should focus on an individual's mental health. There is possibility of individual and gender differences in the psychological wellbeing.

Recently Heintzman (2002) proposed a conceptual model of the relationship between leisure and spiritual wellbeing based on current theoretical speculation and empirical study. It is based on the assumption that leisure experiences may either consciously or unconsciously provide opportunities for "grounding" or "working through" spiritual difficulties as well as "sensitizing" one to the spiritual. Leisure experiences involve interplay of time, activity, motivation and setting can provide contexts in which the spirituality is explored rather than repressed, and spiritual preoccupation due to a spiritual emergency can be addressed. The leisure style provides repeated opportunities to translate leisure experiences of a spiritual nature into spiritual development. The spiritual wellbeing model incorporates a number of theories that suggest processes that may link leisure and spiritual wellbeing. Restorative environments theory is helpful in explaining how specific activities and settings may move a person toward spiritual wellbeing. The proposed model suggests that leisure may play both a positive and a negative role in spiritual wellbeing and development. According to Wiegand and Weiss (2006), recent understanding of subjective well-being suggests that it consists of global judgments of life satisfaction, hedonic experiences, and beliefs about facets of one's life. Traditionally, life satisfaction judgments have been the outcome of interest in studies examining the relationship between religiosity and well-being. Two studies were conducted to look at the interactive effects of personal religious beliefs, namely God images, and environmental stimuli, particularly priming the thought of "God". The first study examines hedonic experiences, which is one of the information sources when constructing a well-being judgment. A second study attempts to replicate the findings with life satisfaction ratings. Results of the first study showed that one's image of God as a controlling or non-controlling entity moderated the affective response to being primed to think about God. In particular, those who had a high controlling image of God had a negative affective reaction to the God prime. Results of the second study replicated the pattern of results using life satisfaction ratings as the dependent variable. Thus it may be stated that the religiosity is an important component of wellbeing of the individual whether living in rural or urban areas.

1.4 WELLBEING AMONG RELIGIOUS PEOPLE

Assessing wellbeing among religious people is a topic of great concern in the present scenario. Generally the religious institutions are well thought-out as an enduring attribute for cultivating cultural life among the people of rural areas of Himachal Pradesh. The people of this hilly state are very religious and are totally devoted to their local customary practices of worshipping deities. The village deities in Himachal Pradesh play important role in promoting wellbeing of the people. These deities are considered to bring prosperity and wellness for the people of hilly areas. There are different deities in different village here who themselves lives harmoniously with other deities. The Brahaman, Rajput, Thakur and Harijan in Himachal Pradesh have their own deities. All the people including educated and uneducated have unlimited faith in their local deities. The village deities symbolize the fact of village life, the way of construction of temple, statue of deities and material used depend on geography. The temple is generally constructed by wood in the middle of the village so as to reach all the member of the village community. The deities' institution symbolizes culture, tradition and faith of village people. Most surprising custom is that the children and women including boys and girls are not allowed inside the temple where actual place of their real deities are established especially in the hilly areas. So the customs and norms in the local institutions of deities are multifaced and complex in ature those play vital role in promoting socio-cultural life of the native people. Some other people also believe in Kali that was considered as earliest goddess (Whitehead, 1976). This female deity is considered as generative and agricultural deities thereof acquire a dominant figure in this hill state. The village head devta or deities is accompanied and supported by other smaller devta. It is considered that even the Trimurti (Braha, Vishnu and Shiva) when failed to stop the wrath of demon Maheshasura, to whom Kali slained and emerged as Shakti.

The village deity in Himachal Pradesh is considered to have a power to destruct enemies, increase the production of crop, remove and reduce physical and psychological ailment as well as protect the people from demon, devil and witches. At the same time these deities are considered to help the people in boosting their knowing, giving justice during clash of two communities and members, increase horticulture and agriculture produces, protect forest as well as generating revenue and fitting the individual in employment and vocations. They are considered. They are considered to protect individual from flood, drought, and other natural calamities like earthquake in general and help in promoting physical wellbeing and mental health. The villager used various means such as presentation of goat or lamb as well as Bhog to the goddess. The deity become delighted and showers her blessing to cope the people in difficult situations and time. This type of prevalent may vary across culture and village to village (Sharma, 1999).

Allport and Ross, 1967, pass beyond external behaviours into the realm of experience and motivation. They describe those who are 'extrinsically' motivated as opposed to those 'intrinsically' motivated. The extrinsically religious "uses" his religion for personal gain and holds his beliefs lightly and selectively. The intrinsically motivated, in contrast, "lives" his religion and integrates his beliefs into daily life. The religions and the prayer play important role in reducing mental tensions and promoting peace and tolerance of the mind of the native people. Bhagvad Gita also quoted the role of religion in promoting human wellbeing. Similarly Sudhir Kakkar (1982) provided in-depth insight on healing practices apart from psychoanalytic perspective for restoration of mental health. He gave the concept of Shaman, mystic, and doctors in faith healing practices. He emphasized on the cultural aspects of psychotherapy for its effectiveness and negated the role of western psychologists in psychological healing. He thereof gave holistic concept of healing based on particular socio-cultural contexts.

Similarly the study of Schumaker (1992) summarizes the arguments as proposed by various writers about the potential benefits and harms of religion to mental health. According to him the religion reduces anxiety by offering an explanatory sense of hope, meaning and purpose, resulting in emotional well-being; provides a reassuring fatalism enabling one to better withstand pain and suffering and solutions to situational and emotional conflicts. It may also resolve the problem of death through belief in an after-life; provides a sense of power and control through association with an omnipotent force; encourages service to self and to others and suppress self-destructive practices. It may promotes social cohesion; offers a sense of identity, satisfies the need for belonging, and unites people around shared understandings and provides a foundation for cathartic collectively enacted ritual. Beside this there are some harms of religion. It generates unhealthy levels of guilt and promotes low self-esteem by way of beliefs that devalue our fundamental nature. It further provides the foundation for the unhealthy repression of anger; creates fear and anxiety through threats of fear and punishment; discourages a sense of internal control, rather placing excessive reliance on external sources of control, and thus fostering dependency, conformity and suggestibility; inhibits sexual expression; promotes intolerance of 'sinners'; instills paranoia of malevolent forces by threatening one's moral integrity and interferes with rational and critical thought.

The available evidence suggests that religion can have both beneficial and detrimental effects on well-being. It is very surprising that the different aspects of religion and the conditions under which they occur have not yet been delineated in research. Several observers have reported anecdotal evidence that members of fundamentalist religions tend to have high levels of religious guilt and fear (e.g., Barr, 1980; Hartz & Everett, 1989; Strozier, 1994). The usual explanation is that guilt and fear of punishment result from an inability to meet the very high, perhaps unrealistically high, standards of conduct and thought set by the religion. However, as Hood, Spilka, Hunsberger, and Gorsuch (1996, p. 427) noted in their anecdotal reports pointed out that the religion may possibly provide mechanisms to counteract feelings of fear and guilt. Haber, Jacob and Spangler (2007) found seven key factors which is accounted for the majority of variation (61.5%) for religion and spirituality measures associated with health and well being research. The seven factors were: religious motivation, social support, existential wellbeing, extrinsic motivation, religious proscription, spirituality and self, transcendence.

Lee and Newberg (2005) found that religion and spirituality played significant roles in patient's health, decreased morbidity and mortality, health-improvement, feelings of well- being, and reduce suicide. At the same time it may provide greater meaning in people's lives and, in turn, help patient's better cope with their disease. Some study reveals that believing in god may block anxiety and minimize stress. Some other studies revealed that the religious people show fewer activities in anterior cingulated cortex as compared to their counterpart (Science Daily, march 4, 2009). Most of the researchers find that religious people, on average, report higher subjective well being and also have less psychosocial pathology such as domestic abuse and violence (Myers, 2011). Famous western psychologists such as William James and Robert H. Thouless and indigenous psychologists like Sudhir Kakar, Shastri and Srivastava emphatically talked about the role of religious practices in restoring and promoting wellbeing of the people. In his psychoanalytic conception Kakar considered Guru as a healer of emotional suffering and somatic manifestation of Chelas. Similarly the studies conducted by Prof. R. S. Pirta, Department of Psychology, Himachal Pradesh University and the students who completed M. Phil. under his guidance emphatically observed the role of religion especially the local deities play important role in promoting mental health (Pirta and Ranta, 2007; Pirta, Ranta, and Vashisht, 2008) of the native people. Generally the Himalayan people have firm belief and strong faith in local deities and their institutions which according to them play important role in their lives. More appropriately, the people of this hilly state are physically, socially and psychologically attached to the institutions of local deities and adore them in their everyday life. The devi and devta in this state govern all social, cultural, moral, economic, religious and political life of the village folk (Thakur, 1997). These deities according to them alleviate their suffering of any kind. The people in turn please their deities with the help of gift like goat and jewelleries like chhatar of gold and silvers and other ornament. Fair and festival are another means for pleasing these local deities. Beside this various means of singing and music instruments like *dhol, nagaras, baam, kansal, guju, bhana, tali, dhokoli, ransingha, karnali, tali, damru, and chimtas* are used as a means of music to please the local deities. Not only this the devi and devta are decorated by giving shapes, wearing clothes named as ghagri, mohras, baal (hairs) and wooden palanquin are made for them so that people may show it to other people. As a result these deities are used for recreational sources. Therefore the people believe that these devta and deities will remove their suffering including protection from bhoot and pret such as demon and witches like vampire or Chudel in local.

Abnormal psychology in past also talked about such demonological practices and possession; good spirit (gift of god) and evil spirit (demon) punishment of the god for wrong deeds and sins. The theory of demonology has its elements in the supernatural and magical contents. The decision as to whether the possession involved good spirit or evil spirit usually depends upon individual symptoms. If speech or behaviour appeared to have a religious or mystical significance, it was usually thought that the person was possessed by a good spirit and so such individual are often treated with respect to that they had supernatural powers. Most possession are considered as the work of evil of spirit particularly when the individual become excited and overactive and engaged in behaviour contrary to religious teaching and so such possession were thought to represent the wrath and punishment of the God. In primitive era if the spirit were good, their possessor was honored , if they were evil, then the god has to be placated and coaxed to withdraw the demons, or the demons has to be exorcised i.e. force to leave the body.

Like other forms of social support, religious support would appear to have a positive relationship to a person's well being. It may be associated with decreased depression and increased life satisfaction. The stronger the religious beliefs and practices, the greater will be the life satisfaction and well being (Australian Unity & Deakin University, 2008). The study of Dew, Daniel, Goldston, Kuchibhatla, Scheifler, Triplett and Koenig (2009) has consistently found that positive religious coping strategies are directly linked to improved well being while negative religious coping strategies have been linked to persons experiencing more emotional distress, increased difficulties coping with the challenges in their lives and worsening physical and mental health. At the same time Zinta (2006) observed that beside unprecedented benefit of the religious institutions like local deities, it also is the basis of social discrimination and social evils, restrict the path of the progress and economy and force the youth to waste their time and imbibe customary prejudices and stereotypes, thereof spread them in the society that generally harm the underprivileged society and their offspring's. It is believed that different people might have different opinion about the benefit and harm of local institutions of deities those are the means of religiosity in hilly area. The men and women including employed and unemployed as well as educated and un-educated people may differ in this respect. However, it is believed that the institutions of local devta as well as palanquin of these devta and their devotion are important for promoting wellbeing of the people.

1.5 PRESENT STUDY AND OBJECTIVES

From the above studies it is quite clear that in Himachal Pradesh people believes in the institutions of deities. According to them these deities and devta play vital role in their life for alleviate suffering. They prevent them from enmeshing diseases, promote their economies, bring success in employment, education and vocation as well as well as prevent them from natural calamities like drought, earthquake, fire, and flood. Beside this these deities are said to settle their village dispute related to land and other properties among real brothers during division as well help them with their neighbor. It may be said to restore community life especially are the shield for the poor and socially disadvantaged people including females to protect atrocities and social dominance. In this state these deities and devta worked as a judge whose judgment are silently acceptable by the local community whereas the local people may revolt against judiciary system. So the people fear from them that if they do not pray their local deities they may destruct their life in various way. In fear of success and fear of failure the local people felt that their deities may play important role. The belief in deities is quite firm or strong among all the castes including employed and unemployed people, educated and uneducated people, rural and urban people and men and women of Himachal Pradesh. Especially it seems that the local people have fear or phobia about these deities. Fear of success seems to be the important factor behind their religiousness. Probably, the religiosity according to most of the studies is associated with the promotion of wellbeing while fear of success may deteriorate the wellbeing. So, in the present study an attempt has been made to study employed and unemployed men and women of different castes (Brahmin, Rajput, Thakur and Harijan) in terms of fear of success, religiosity, and wellbeing on the aforesaid variables. Further, an attempt has been to see the relationship between fear of success, religiosity and wellbeing. In the final stage impact of fear of success and religiosity will be tested on the wellbeing. So the descriptions of detailed objectives are as follows:-

1. To study and compare the employed and the unemployed men and women of different caste on the measure of fear of success.

2. To study and compare the employed and the unemployed men and women of different caste on the measure of spiritual wellbeing.
3. To study and compare the employed and the unemployed men and women of different caste on the measure of wellbeing.
4. To find out the relationship in terms of magnitude and direction between fear of success, religiosity and wellbeing among employed and un-employed men and women of different caste.
5. To see the impact of fear of success and religiosity on the wellbeing of the people.

SOCIAL CONSTRUCTION OF HUMANITY

"When a man is freed of religion, he has a better chance to live a normal and wholesome life."

–Sigmund Freud

The research, it turns out, actually contradicts what Freud believed. There does indeed appear to be a link between religion and happiness. Several studies have been done and most of the studies consider religious people as happier. Psychology of religion offers a chance for an expansion of behavioural science into realms of importance to many people. Both development during adolescence and the implications of gender differences may be illuminated by a consideration of the role of religion in human life (Donelson & Elaine, 1999). Generally the question arises, are the religious people are happier than to the atheists? Freud did not believe so. He saw the religious person as a neurotic, creating guilt and suppressing sexuality. It is perhaps the fear of the human being that makes them religious and positive toward religiosity. In the recent years, positive psychology focuses on searching the psychological strengths of human beings rather than weaknesses therefore has emerged in the field of human sciences as a reaction to psychopathology-oriented view of human functioning. The concept of well-being is one of the core conceptions of the positive psychology movement. The study of Pyysiainen (2003) tried to explain the philosophy and psychology of religious belief. Although the phenomenon of religious belief has been much discussed in philosophy of religion, yet a prairie argumentation alone cannot establish what religious belief is like as a psychological attitude. Recent advances in the cognitive science of religion have paved the way for a new and natural philosophy of religion.

There are two paradigm shifts that play very important role in understandings individual and his relationship with the social environment. The first paradigm shift involves the acceptability of the social science of behaviour, and the second shift relates the changes within the behaviour therapy movement. These two paradigm shifts are, respectively, concerned with the evolution of social behaviour and the role of social factors in strengthening inner resources. For nearly 100 years the traditional non-evolutionary social science approach, the Standard Social Science Model (SSSM) dominated psychology. In recent years four new areas have developed which uses Darwin's evolutionary thinking. These four areas are: Ethology, sociobiology, behavioural ecology, and evolutionary psychology. All these four areas has challenged the SSSM, which was based on the assumption that human behaviour, particularly social behaviour, develops through learning, the biological factors are not important. The new paradigm in social behaviour takes into consideration innate and learned factors following evolutionary approach. A growing body of scientific research suggests connections between religion, spirituality, and both mental and physical health. The findings are particularly strong in patients with severe or chronic illnesses who are having stressful psychological and social changes, as well as existential struggles related to meaning and purpose. Recent studies indicate that religious beliefs influence medical decisions, such as the use of chemotherapy and other life-saving treatments, and at times may conflict with medical care (Koenig, 2004). The majority of well-conducted studies found that higher levels of religious involvement are positively associated with indicators of psychological well-being (life satisfaction, happiness, positive affect, and higher morale) and with less depression, suicidal thoughts and behavior, drug/alcohol use/abuse. Usually the positive impact of religious involvement on mental health is more robust among people under stressful circumstances.

It seems that the beginning of the ancient cradles of civilization started in Egypt, Mesopotamia, China, and India. The creation of mythological tales and philosophical meditations, saga, and destiny of the cosmos and humankind gave people a sense of meaning and purpose for their lives and all existence (David, 1999). Religion and myth provided conceptual and dramatic schemes for understanding reality and giving ethical direction to life. Although there are numerous and varied ancient religions and myths that dealt with past and future, and the values and goals yet it should guide and direct human action. There are two fundamental perspectives on time and the future coming out of these ancient traditions that dominate mainstream religious and spiritual thinking of the present scenario. These two views are the Eastern and Western those were inspired by the apocalyptic vision of Zoroaster, Judaic, Christian, and Islamic theories of the future. Judaism believes that Messiah would come that will lead the chosen people of God to victory over the evil forces in the world. Christianity and Islam, both believing that the ultimate prophet and “Messiah” has come, anticipate a great final world battle where God and the forces of good will triumph over Satan and the forces of evil. Further, both Christians and Muslims believe that those people who believe in God will be rewarded with eternal life and ultimate happiness in Heaven, while disbelievers will suffer eternal damnation in Hell. Within Christianity, many believe that Christ will return – a "Second Coming" - to lead the forces of good against a prophesized Anti-Christ and the forces of evil, and that Christ will reign over a thousand-year-long earthly paradise that will follow after the final battle before deserving souls ascend into Heaven.

This general theory of the future has provided the moral and metaphysical core of a general paradigm for life and the future. In the name of the beliefs, prophecies, and values of their respective doctrines and creeds, followers of Christianity and Islam have conquered, colonized, and ruled over countless nations and millions of other people worldwide in an attempt to convert non-believers to their religion. Though progressive in their view of the future - believing that life in the future will be better than today - the road to this better reality will involve great conflict, turmoil, war, and chaos. There is a passage through the darkness as a prelude to reaching the light. God and the forces of good will triumph. It is the individual destinies that are uncertain and contingent upon the choices and free will of humans. Still, in the final analysis, there are really only two possible future scenarios for each person, happiness and bliss in Heaven or misery and torture in Hell may be the main reason behind become religious. A vision of war and great destruction, as well as punishment and eternal damnation for those individuals who reject God. But then, there is a positive side. In Christianity, for example, there is an emphasis on love, forgiveness, and kindness as critical moral qualities in living one's life. It is through these positive qualities that a better future will be realized. Although life may be unfair, God will enact justice, rewarding those who live a good life and punishing those who lead an evil life. Finally, in spite of all our imperfections, failings, and times of unhappiness in our present mode of existence, there is a promise of eventual perfection and complete happiness once we ascend to Heaven.

As one final point, there is a decidedly other-worldly and metaphysical dimension to this theory of the future. The forces that will ultimately determine the future are supernatural and at a higher plane of existence than the natural world; these same forces were also responsible for the creation of the world, as well as the general plot, drama, and direction of events in the world. Humans existing on the material plane and within time cannot affect the overall outcome of things; we can only chose in which of the two predetermined metaphysical realms we spend eternity. Secondly, the ultimate future for humanity is therefore not something within the physical world of time, but in a metaphysical sphere (House, 2006). In contrast to Western linear thinking, both Taoist and Hindu views of reality involve a cyclic theory of time. Within Chinese Taoism, reality is described as an oscillation of the 64 complementary forces of Yin and Yang. Similarly, within Hindu cosmology, a common belief is that the God Shiva will bring worldly existence to a catastrophic and fiery ending, but then the God Vishnu will dream the world a new and a new cycle of creation and destruction will begin.

Temporal existence is ultimately an endless repetition of birth and death and this cycle of creation and destruction is often referred to as *"The Dance of Shiva."* There is, though, a progressive dimension within Hindu thinking, as well as in its philosophical offspring, Buddhism. The Hindu doctrine of *reincarnation* involves the notion that the souls of individuals who have died will return to an earthly and temporal existence incarnated in a new body. Yet, the new body and temporal existence of the soul will depend upon how ethical a life the soul led in the previous life. This is the theory of karma. A good life brings good karma and a better existence in the next life. An ethically bad life produces negative karma and leads to a lower existence in the next life. If, in its new incarnation, a soul can eliminate through ethical actions whatever bad karma it accrued in its past lives, the soul can ascend into Nirvana and break free of the cycle of life, death, and rebirth. Nirvana is a higher existential state – an eternal and spiritual state involving unity with the absolute oneness of Brahman, the ultimate source of all being. As can be seen in the Hindu ideas of reincarnation, karma, and Nirvana, the direction of the future is determined by ethics; positive moral behavior leads to a better future – negative moral behavior leads to a worse future. Further, cosmic justice determines the direction of the future. Good deeds are ultimately rewarded and bad deeds are punished. Finally, the positive future that awaits morally good individuals lies outside of the temporal and material realm, in the higher spiritual reality of Nirvana.

One significant difference, though, between Eastern and Western religious visions of the spiritual future can best be illustrated in the teachings of Buddhism. Within Buddhist philosophy, it is desire and an attachment to the individual ego that produce misery and unhappiness in the world. In fact, desire is a consequence of conscious attachment to an ego. The goal of enlightenment is to see beyond the ego. Once we achieve this enlightened state –

to see reality as a one without a separation of the ego and the world – we achieve Nirvana. Hence, while Western religions like Christianity and Islam promise individual immortality, Buddhism views Nirvana as precisely the lost of individuality. In Hinduism also, the emphasis is on achieving oneness with Brahman, rather than the preservation of an individual ego. These beliefs were prevalent in the past and even today these are quite prevalent in the society. So the question generally is that how the society play important role in one's life.

2.1 SOCIAL CONSTRUCTION OF HUMANITY

It is a well established fact that the society enters in their life of the people and constructs them socially. There are various ways in which society enters into the life of individual. These ways might be the search for food, shelter, work and other necessities of life as well as formations of rules and regulations of state, experiences and ethical and cultural values which by which the persons are influenced by the society. The radicalist's believed also emphatically realized the role of society as extremely important for maintaining their wellbeing of the individual. The mismatch of any kind result personal distress that in turn may affect mental health of the individual as well as members living in community.

The chief features of the social theory according to Banton, Clifford, Frosh, Lousada and Rosenthal (1985) is to understand how society enters into individual's life and construct him socially. According to this theory there are three linked practices important in this process named as economic, political and ideological practices. Economic practice is largely concerned with processes that threatened the physical and mental survival of individual. It alienates individual from, the product of his activity, the activity itself, his own essential nature, and, other men as well as community. The political practice involves the representation of the relation of power between classes and class fractions. It is here that the concept of power becomes extremely important for mental health. According to social theory, ideological practice deals with the way the contradictions of the social world. It has significance for mental health.

Although there are differences among socialists how the individual experiences these contradictions, a dominant view emphasizes lived relation between individual and the world. According to them external social contradictions become part of the unconscious of the individual through a process that escapes consciousness. Thus, ideology is the social access around which experience becomes organized. In other words, the contradictions of the social organization take the form of embodied material relations inside the individual. For example, caste system is institutionalized in various ways among Hindus in particular and in Indian society in general. A child does not just become conscious of the caste structure of the society and confuse it with a "natural" state of things (false consciousness), instead caste is experienced as a principle, defining a field of possible relationships in a particular social setting, e.g., "a village." Social theory considers this as the reality of the subject, in which the world is experienced. This aspect of social theory attracts our attention to the effect of ideological practice, as it is here that we try to understand individual as an autonomous entity constructed in the flux of contradictions originating in the social sphere. To understand this process of social construction, socialists use psychoanalytic concept because they also believe that for mental health it is important to make sense of the unconscious material, which is full of contradictions and fragmentary. Moreover, the social theory reveals that people are subject to economic, political and ideological forces, which are more powerful than other conscious factors affecting individuals. The starting point of social (radical) mental health practice is the resilience of the community. Problems mainly arise due to our failure to analyze the experiences related to powerlessness, apathy, isolation and self-destructiveness both at an organizational and subjective level. Socialist viewpoint of mental health is distinct from the other schools of psychotherapy. Since, it aims at to understand the process of marginalization of certain sections of communities and to suggest ways to resist oppression.

Social theory also distinguishes between *'remembered community'* and *'real community.'* It is through 'remembered community' that the contradictions and antagonisms develop inside the individual. The 'remembered community' reflects a paradigm of community life that is reinforced or strengthened through media politicians and welfare workers. When the individual views it in terms of his day-to-day experiences, the contradictions is devastating. The structure of the state also influences community in various ways. Distinctions of classifications are made between rich and poor, different classes or castes. The control of the state extends to an extent that there is virtually management of subjectivity through mental health industry. Social theory calls for development of real community alternative, which involves various processes of re-socialization. This process involves re-individualization, enabling them to have personal possessions, treating them as individuals with rights and abilities, offering them training in basic social skills. Furthermore, they emphasize possibilities for community activation through self-reliance and wisdom. Such re-socialization considers community self-control more important than by the state. They also emphasize the importance of conditions for creating resistance which is based upon knowledge. Thus, the mental health program need to provide knowledge to community that would help people n the search for alternative and refuse to bow to control. Socialist mental program struggles for: gender issues, racial discrimination, deprivation of certain sections of communities and all those conditions increasing distress in a population.

It seems that the society when enters into the life of the individual it may pose various threat to them. Thus psychological fear of various sorts may make the persons as vulnerable by influencing their inner belief process. As a result the people went into the shelter of God, thereof become religious and try to compensate their wellbeing. In the below mentioned sections various theories of fear especially fear of success have been given in order to understand how person become religious and promote their wellbeing.

2.2 FEAR OF SUCCESS IN A PSYCHOANALYTIC FRAMEWORK

Fear of success or success phobia has been studied from classical and relational psychoanalysis to social and cognitive psychology point of view. Psychoanalytic theories believe that the unconscious forces are at work behind the phobia. Other explanations emphasize conscious and environmental influences. Consistent with latter-day Zeitgeist shifts; multicultural issues have been looked at recently. Also, more interest has been shown in athletes. These later studies have not enhanced our theoretical understanding of the problem but reflect practical, political, and academic interests. Various, less popular, theories that have been put forth include considering students rebelling against parental authority when they flunk out of school. Manfred Kets de Vries, a psychoanalyst who has studied leadership and human dynamics, argued that the fear of success is really the fear of loss of affiliation. Top executive may develop a success neurosis because of the "loneliness of command" brought on by isolation at the top. Other theories incorporate Eric Erikson's development model and rationality or a straightforward choice between alternative life styles. The last two theories had less of a following, but gave interesting perspectives and insight into fear of success. Social theories leave the family of origin out of the etiology but cultural theories embrace family expectations. Psychoanalytic theories contend that our activities are determined by the unconscious content of our minds, a process called psychic determinism. That means unconscious psychic motivations determine humans activities, not the rational conscious thinking process. Description of psychoanalytic framework is as under:

> Good and bad experiences of the child leave unconscious memory traces that influence future attitudes that may not be explained by language. Many feelings stem from pre-verbal times. The re-experience or transference of childhood reactions and means of dealing with *metaphorically* triggered situations carries over to adulthood. Some psychoanalysts, however, further focused on the sexual nature of the intra-psychic conflict associated with success. Earlier Otto Fenichel identified many examples of the success fearing character logical group as having intense guilt from infantile sexual conflicts. To them success is something wrong and

unmerited. Fenichel considered work a substitute for instinctual needs, and a defense against them, in modern culture. Thus, some people who work hard never strive effectively to achieve. Conversely, the opposite effect is also possible. The conflict resolves itself as a counter phobic reaction in the other (dichotomous) extreme. Thus, humans vary; people are not simple cause and effect machines. A decade later, Daniel Schuster, in 1955, extended Fenichel's and Freud's work to those who accomplish less than their native talents would indicate they could, or who pay too great price for success in terms of anxiety. Schuster talks about tensions and struggles that comprise the oedipal problem and castration complex that is considered purely sexual. Oedipal conflicts represent the child's perception of the love-hate relationship with his or her parents. Castration represents the young and powerless child's fears of severe punishment when pitted against an all-powerful parent. Repressed Oedipal conflicts are not an antiquated idea relegated to ancient couch-oriented, long-term psychoanalytic technique.

2.3 ATTACHMENT RELATIONS AND TERROR MANAGEMENT

This theory was given by John Bowlby in 1969 which is based on the bond established between mother and infant. According to him care giving experiences are internalized as working models that not only serve as a prototype for future relationship with significant others but also provide unwritten rules for how one experience expresses and copes with distressing emotions. This theory is based on three tenets: proximity to other, proximity maintenance depends on the responsively of other person to ones attachment need and third is experience with significant other. Childs internalization of relationship with an attachment figure create a secure base of support and comfort in time of distress and facilitates the child's exploration of widest world. Recent theories have suggested this relational process as the circle of security (Marvin, Cooper, Hoffman & Powell, 2002) in which a Childs move from secure base to exploration and then back to safe heaven following a rupture. Contemporary theory and research recognize the interconnection between attachment, care giving, and exploration for adults (Freeney & Collins, 2004; George & Solomon, 1999). Similar to child's adult attachment system is activated in times stress or novelty and adult turn to their attachment figure to alleviate this distress and regulate their affect (Hazan, Gur-Yaish & Campa, 2004). Bowlby and Ainsworth further proposed that young children internalize early attachment processes as internal working models of attachment which serves as relational templates with continuity throughout the life span (Hesse, 1999; Fonagy, 2001). Ultimately adult navigates their relational world influenced by either secure or insecure internal working model developed in their early work. Secure adult attachment relations are characterized by the capacity to relate to others in mutual reciprocal manners to provide coherent narratives about relationships, and to sustain continuity of connections (Basham & Miehls, 2004; Hesse, 1999).

Further Fisher and Crandle (1977) suggest that couples who are securely attached "shift freely between the dependent and depended upon position" with an open expression of need for comfort and contact as well as an open reception of that contact. In other words the attachment system of secure adult partners can be appropriately activated and de-activated in a flexible manner depends on the emotional need of an individual at any given time. In contrast insecure individual may be dismissing, pre-occupied or unresolved/ disorganized in their state of mind about attachment (Hesse, 1999). It leads them towards bi-directionality, flexibility or mutuality common among secure partner. Recent research suggest that adult couples may create way of relating that are specific to the relationship and perhaps different from individuals global model of attachment or state of mind about early childhood attachment relationship. As the child become young then his mother attachment is generalized and converted to place attachment, land and house attachment as well as attachment to his friends. The place matter a long for the child. As the youth actualize their inner self, then he identifies his fear about success or to be succeeding in various fields that seems important for him. Therefore he starts believing in god so as to overcome his fear. The gods according to his or them help them in managing the terror as he experienced in his life.

The concept of attachment can be seen as the mode of being in the world, which is especially important with regard to private/individual and interpersonal construction of the world. Bowlby (1973) defined attachment as closely related to the fear of damage, illness, and death. Fear as a base for the development of the attachment styles by which personal mode of being in the world and others is defined is especially important with regard to feeling of safety and in-homeness. According to the attachment theory, thus, attachment system is the key determinant related with the threatening situations in adulthood: Adult personality is seen as a product of an individual's interactions with key figures during all his years of immaturity, especially of his interactions with attachment figures. Thus an individual who has been fortunate in having grown up in an ordinary good home with ordinarily affectionate parents has always known people from whom he can seek support, comfort, and protection, and where they are to be found. So deeply established are his expectations and so repeatedly had they been confirmed that, as an adult, he finds it difficult to imagine any other kind of world (Bowlby, 1973; p.208)."

Attachment, therefore, is a powerful personality dimension that determines one's reactions to all phenomena, in life whether personal or cultural. Attachment system as a personality characteristic which seems highly sensitive to the threatening situations, as mentioned by Bowlby above, defines the ways by which the individual will try to overcome the terror of death. Accordingly, taking the assumption that the attachment system is activated automatically in threatening situations as a base. Mikulincer et al. (2002) showed that threat contexts automatically activated cognitive representations of attachment figures. That is, representations of people who are the sources of comfort may be active and may influence mental process during the encounter with a threat, even when this threat is irrelevant to interpersonal relationships or to the frustration of attachment needs. Research additionally indicated that this activation system is changed according to the attachment style of the individual. Indeed, Bowlby (1973) clearly suggested that the attachment system is directly related to the growth of self-esteem. The research has already highlighted the importance of attachment to self-esteem. These investigations consistently suggested that the secure based attachment system is correlated with internalized self-worth. Moreover, there is evidence that the role of attachment on psychological health is primarily mediated by self-esteem. Recent research suggested that the attachment system is closely related to the variables that are especially important for worldview validation such as identification with social groups, and group processes, the concept of social identification can be seen as a type of attachment with regard to groups or more expanded evaluation of relationships. The authors called this phenomenon as attachment to groups. Stated more clearly, they argue that adult attachment theory may be able to shed light on the processes underlying people's identification with social groups as well. Thus, it is suspected that people also have internal working models of themselves as group members and internal working models of groups that in combination influence their thoughts, emotions, and behaviors.

Derived from Becker's assumptions, Terror Management Theory (TMT) is extended to involve many psychological phenomena such as identification with gender and ethnicity (Jonas & Fischer, 2006), intrinsic motivations of self, 17 stereotypic thinking, cognitive strategies concerning death, cognitive-experiential self theory, aggression, creativity, sex, identification with body, interpersonal distancing, and risk-taking behaviors. It appears that empirical research will extend the theory to almost all phenomena concerning human life. According to TMT, the inevitability of death is an ongoing source of concern, regardless of whether one is currently consciously focused on it or not, and a person's awareness of death is one of the most important motivations underlying one's distinct psychological motives. Conscious and unconscious processes result in two distinct set of defense mechanisms against death that is termed as dual-process theory which consists of proximal and distal defenses. TMT suggests that conscious thoughts of death are defended against by means of proximal defenses. The proximal defenses include attempts to suppress thoughts about death or to bias rational inferential processes by pushing the problem of death into the distant future.

The proximal defenses have already been investigated in the literature with regard to classical defense mechanisms. Unconscious thoughts of death, on the other hand, are defended against by distal defenses. The distal defenses address the problem of death in more indirect symbolic manner by modifying people's perceptions of themselves and of the world in which they are embedded, which is the main focus of the present research. Most TMT studies have focused on the distal defenses: the terror of death can be managed either by adherence to a 18cultural worldview or by enhancing self-esteem. The empirical support for the theory derived from the experimental research has been based on two main hypotheses. One is 'mortality salience' deriving its assumptions from the idea that individuals' will increase their psychological structure, whether it is self-esteem or worldview faith, when confronted with death. The second hypothesis of the TMT is the 'anxiety buffer hypothesis' stating that if individual's psychological structure protects them against anxiety, then strengthening that structure should decrease individual's anxiety whereas weakening the structure should increase individual's anxiety. To conclude, TMT points out that all human behaviors including self-actualization are the result of the terror of death. The main outcome of facing death is human beings' effort to enhance their psychological structure by cultural worldview validation and enhancing self-esteem. Self-esteem has been of much interest in psychology and the vast majority of psychological theories assume that self-esteem is a pervasive force in human motivation that is generally adaptive and associated with a broad range of desirable outcomes.

From an evolutionary perspective, TMT suggests that human beings have a cognitive complexity, which, in turn, results in the awareness that death is inevitable, compounded by the concurrent realization that one is perpetually vulnerable to permanent obliteration for reasons that can never be adequately anticipated or controlled. In the light of the negative correlation between anxiety and self-esteem and the framework of TMT, the anxiety buffer function of self-esteem was tested. The former indicated by three experiments during which subjects who received positive personality feedback reported less anxiety in response to a video about death than did neutral feedback subjects. In the other studies, it was hypothesized that increasing self-esteem would reduce anxiety among individuals anticipating painful shock. Consistent with the hypothesis, both 19 success and personality directed positive feedback reduced subjects' physiological arousal in response to subsequent threat of shock.

The latter research confirmed the hypothesis of TMT by showing that individuals with high self-esteem did not respond to mortality salience with increased worldview defense, whereas individuals with moderate self-esteem did. Moreover, the other experiment of the research indicated that high self-esteem facilitates the suppression of death constructs following mortality salience. Self-esteem acquires its anxiety buffer function by the socialization process as stated by Becker. Generally the people actively seek symbolic icons of powers toward which they might submit themselves. Therefore, the author claims, most people must draw upon the established categories of culture (public logic) for a personal sense of worth and forward movement. Life is a constant movement between establishing personal meaning and seeking confirmation of that meaning from the group.

Cultural worldview, in that respect, is considered as a prerequisite for one to feel self-worth from the TMT perspective. There is a vast majority of research indicated the relationship between fear of death and the indicators of cultural worldview. The most important conclusion of these investigations is that the awareness of mortality results in one's defense toward his or her group and cultural worldview against the threats.

Although the cultural worldview is hard to define empirically, operational definitions are closely related to interpersonal evaluations, judgments of moral transgressors, in-group bias, social consensus estimates, and conformity to cultural standards. Cultural worldview has been defined as criteria such as political bias, culturally intolerable facts such as prostitution, and cultural stereotypes concerning gender-role, 20which are situations in which subjects are supposed to react those who do or do not conform to the standards concerning the criterion. Some recent developments concerning the theory suggest that group identification is a general factor underlying the cultural worldview validation. According to the authors, group identifications play a major role in people's sense of who they are and how they feel about themselves. Thus, group identifications would be expected to play a significant role in how one manages the concerns about mortality.

According to the TMT to the degree that the groups with which one is affiliated are positively valued, these identifications reflect positively on the self and thus provide a useful buffer against existential fears. Derived from the social identity research, collective self-esteem is a way of determining the extent to which one's identification with groups such as race, ethnicity, religion, and the like. Social Identity Theory has a parallel presupposition with TMT with regard to the self-esteem enhancing effect of identification with groups. Social identities, in that respect, become important, because they embody the cultural worldviews. When confronted with a threat, people maintain a positive social identity by identifying or creating favorable comparisons between their own group(s) and out group(s). In a similar vein, the majority of the research on cultural worldview validation, the manipulations have been based on in-group/out-group distinction. Indeed, the research showed that collective self-esteem has an anxiety buffer function toward the terror of death created by the standard mortality salience effects.

Religiosity as a type of social identification is of special importance with regard to the transcendence needs against the terror of death. Religious and spiritual dimensions are the most efficient factors in the sense of making the symbolic immortality possible. According to the concept of a Creator God is obviously human beings' transference object. State that as a way of symbolic immortality spiritual and religious attainments are modes dealing with the possibility of transcending death. The main feature of this mode, according to the authors, is that it takes the form of a search for a higher plane or realm of existence, in which the self is allowed to transcend its physical finiteness. The recent conceptualizations suggest that the basic assumptions of TMT be reconsidered in the light of the other personality dimensions concerning the close relationships and interpersonal relationships. Thus, the fear of death seems to include interpersonal concerns. The recent developments concerning the fear of death are in line with the idea that the terror of death is a multidimensional construct including interpersonal dimensions in addition to personal ones. It proposed a multidimensional construct of fear of personal death, consisting of three psychological components: the intrapersonal, interpersonal, and transpersonal meanings of death. Fear of personal death is regarded as the consequences or impacts on these dimensions, which is weighted by personal preferences or inclinations. The results of the research indicated that early loss of a significant other is positively related to the interpersonal component of fear of death, which is clearly mentioned by Bowlby (1973).

2.4 WELLBEING PARADIGMS

The wellbeing is a very complex process that generally deals with hedonic (happiness) and Eudaimonic (self-realization) including functioning and optimal experience. The phrase *psychological well-being* arose in a regulatory, rather than scientific, context thereby is a hypothetical construct whose validity can be determined only in relation to a theory that defines its properties and relation to empirical data that address the fit between predicted and observed phenomena. We do not have a theory to guide thinking and research on well-being; the development of a coherent theory of psychological well-being is an obvious research need. Such a theory ought to incorporate cognitive, behavioral, and physiological characteristics of the organism in an integrated view of well-being. It also ought to encompass the possibility of species, age, sex, and individual differences in responsiveness to the same immediate environmental situation. Some of the work that has been done so far in this domain is based on notions of how humans behave and how they react to environmental situations. Thus most of the article refers to a person with "psychological well being "as a happy, satisfied person, "while seem to be a rather than technical definition, it seems to fit every instance to find. Its utility will depend upon this relationship and a network of relationship with other (Verma & Verma, 1989). Psychological well being seems to be whole array of biological and social, psychological changes with the passage of time and interaction with the environment, affecting its survival and adjustment potency. It is tremendously varied and complex field that involves four radical aspects of varying degrees of discreteness and overlap. These may be called the "biological" the "psychological", the "sociological", and the "socio- psychological" or behavioral". The descriptions are as follows:

(1) **Biological Aspect:** Biologist regards the normal psychological well being as a complex of changes in cellular composition such as neuromuscular system. According to the biological aspects the health is the crucial feature in the psychological well being of an individual that has its impact on the individual's Self-image and personality and the reaction of society.

(2) **Psychological Aspect:** It deals with_the changes in sensory processes, per up that capacities, psychomotor performance, mental functioning, and so on. Psychologists are also concerned with the changes in personality and behavior of the changing individual. Attention has been given to the external influences, such as cultural expectations and environmental factors.

(3) **Sociological Aspects:** It focuses on the changes in the individual that are characterized by changing situation of the individual as a member of the family, community and society. These include competition

of many roles like, social support, demand of society, role limitation, socio-economic status, income, etc. This social content encompasses the family and friends at the level, and the society or cultural another level. The social frame work determines the meaning of the psychological well being for the individual and social concepts, positive and negative affects.

(4) **Behavioral Aspect:** It is concerned with the meaning the individual ascribe to the changes and internal and external adjustments he makes to them. These include inner relation with regard to such matter as changing self image, feeling, mental being, and tolerance to stress. More appropriately the psychological well-being dealt with balanced positive and negative affects.

2.4.1 Affect Related Model of Psychological Well-being

A model of psychological wellbeing developed by Bradburn and Caplovitz (1965) deals with the individual position on two independent dimensions- one of the positive affect and the other is negative affect. The model specifies that an individual will be high in psychological well being in the degree to which he has an excess of positive over negative affect and will be low in well being in the degree to which negative affect predominated over positive affect. Thus in many respect, the model is similar to older pleasure pain or utility models that view an individual's happiness or well being in terms of the degree to which pleasure predominates over pain in his life experiences. This particular model stems from an empirical base. It suggests that there is a series of forces whose absence merely results in a lowering of absence of positive affect rather than any change in negative affect. On the other hand, there is also a series of different circumstances that contribute to the presence or absence of negative affect but have no influence on a person's positive affect. Since an individual's overall sense of well-being is dependent upon the relative balance of these two sets of forces, those contribute to either positive or negative affect in order to understand an individual's position along the resultant dimension of well-being.

The model proposed here for the understanding of psychological well-being is similar to one Herzberg, Mausner, and Snyderman work satisfaction model. They noted the existence of one group of factors that played a role as "dissatisfies" and another group that played a role as "satisfiers". The presence of such things as low pay, poor work conditions, and disagreement with the boss led to job satisfaction. Negative affect appears too related primarily to the variables that have been dealt with by the traditional "mental- illness" approaches as compared to the positive affects that is related to the positive approach. The fact that there are two independent dimensions then might well help us explain the differential effect of what appear to be equal amounts of stress on different individuals. Of the stress works toward changing the levels of negative affect, its total impact on well-being would be a differential function of the individual's level of positive affect. Since life is an ongoing, dynamic process, we would expect that factors affecting both positive and negative experiences are continually changing and that one's sense of well-being at any particular time might be thought of as a running average of the relative strength of positive and negative affect averaged out over the recent past.

One of the well-established findings in social science is that individuals of lower education and income are less likely to be involved in their environment and generally lead more restricted lives. Since environmental participation and variability appear to be highly related to the presence of positive affect, we would expect there to be less positive affect among lower socioeconomic groups and negative affect in the low socioeconomic status person. Of, in addition, there is a differential in terms of the difficulties in role adjustments related to negative affect, we would expect an even stronger relationship between socioeconomic status and overall well- being. It is important to note, however, that even without such differential difficulties in coping with problems; we would expect differences in well-being due to the restrictions on environmental variability and social participation that are characteristics of lower socioeconomic groups. The use of psychological well-being as the major dependent variable that focuses on interpersonal problems, negative affect, social participation, sociability, environmental variability, and factors that appears to be more related to positive affect and to be concern of those oriented toward positive mental health. This conception offers a model that enables each type of study to contribute to an understanding of the basic phenomenon of psychological well being .Generally the wellbeing deals with the being" (who one is), "belonging" (connection with ones environment), and "becoming" (Achieving personal goal, hope and aspiration) components the description as described by ***Brown, Friefeld, & Schiller (1993)*** is as follows:

Table 2.1 Being, Belonging, and Becoming Components of Wellbeing

Being	One who has
Physical Being	physical health, personal hygiene; nutrition; exercise; grooming and clothing, general physical appearance
Psychological Being	psychological health and adjustment; cognitions; feelings; self-esteem, self-concept and self-control;
Spiritual Being	personal values; personal standards of conduct; spiritual beliefs
Belonging	Connections with one's environments
Physical Belonging	❍ home, workplace/ school, neighbourhood, community
Social Belonging	❍ intimate others, family, friends ❍ co-workers, neighbourhood and community
Community Belonging	❍ adequate income, health and social services, employment, educational programs, recreational programs, community events and activities
Becoming	Achieving personal goals, hopes, and aspirations
Practical Becoming	❍ Domestic activities, paid work, school or volunteer activities, seeing to health or social needs.
Leisure Becoming	❍ activities that promote relaxation and stress reduction
Growth Becoming	❍ activities that promote the maintenance or improvement of knowledge skills and adapting to change

(Source: *Brown, Friefeld, & Schiller, 1993)*

2.4.2 Need Based Theory of Wellbeing

This theory starts from the hypothesis that satisfying individual needs is the prerequisite to wellbeing. Abraham Maslow, an American psychologist, in 1954 developed a hierarchy of needs in the form of a pyramid with primary (or vital) needs at the bottom and luxury or comfort needs at the top. The hierarchy of needs posits that physiological needs must be satisfied before protection needs (security). The satisfaction of security precedes love needs (belonging) which in turn precede the satisfaction of ego-esteem (recognition). Spiritual needs (self-transcendence) are placed at the top of the hierarchy. Inevitably, there is a connection between material affluence and the satisfaction of needs. The specification of a hierarchy of needs can serve geographers as a useful framework for comparative work on inequalities and spatial injustice as well as shaping priorities for policy. At the same time, geographers of health can combine a critical approach with empirical study to assess to what extent such values are held across time and space.

Wellbeing is treated here as a homogeneous utility, reflecting only consumption and the fulfillment of preferences that are defined prior to experience. This approach is associated with several related criticisms. First, expressed preferences may reflect an adaptation to long-term hardship. For example, Sen draws attention to the imprecise nature of individual interests and how, consequently, needs are relative once vital needs have been satisfied. He therefore asked that whether the people undergoing long-term hardship spend their time complaining or whether they adopt the position of taking pleasure in the little that is offered to them. Thus, while we can measure living conditions through objective indicators (e.g. levels of income, assets, access to basic primary services), this does not necessarily map onto a faithful reflection of wellbeing. Second, while it would seem to be undeniable that it is essential to satisfy primary needs, the hierarchical organization of secondary and tertiary needs will vary from one individual to another (Diener & Lucas, 2000).

Some authors go even further; cross-cultural work on defining poverty and needs in the global South using participatory approaches has indicated that what people consider to be basic needs may vary considerably. Chambers (1997) concluded that there is no inevitability in people's prioritizing of needs. This observation is also echoed in research from high income contexts where recorded variations in expressed needs and preferences are seen to depend on what is valued in a particular society or culture demonstrated that the correlation between the need for esteem and self-fulfillment and the individual perception of wellbeing is much lower in Germany than in the USA. This is certainly related to the importance accorded to individual values in these two societies. The challenge then is how to distinguish between universal needs and contextual needs.

2.4.3 Relative Standards Theory

It links wellbeing to individual happiness and conditioned by the individual's perception of the context in which he or she is living. As a result, its 'absolute' value (position felt and defined through comparison) has very little impact at the level of society. Geographical research on wellbeing drawing on a relative standards approach can build directly on a well-established engagement within the geographies of health with social construction approaches to health and ill-health. The relative standards theory tries to address some of the limitations in the theory of needs by explicitly treating the concept of wellbeing as relative and subjective. It proceeds from a construction that is both individual, through comparison with other individuals, and social, in that the standards for every individual are relative. Thus, it states that objective conditions, which the theory of needs tends to highlight, only affect wellbeing in comparison with other possible conditions. The standards of comparison vary from person to person and they too are subject to contextual effects (Layard, 2005). Consequently, from one person to another the same objective conditions may give rise to different levels of wellbeing: 'In short, the theory stipulates that happiness is relative and that a change in objective living conditions does not necessarily translate into a change in the level of happiness (Schyns, 1998).

This theory also has some limitations. First, by treating the level of wellbeing as subjective, the relative standards theory often effectively equates wellbeing with satisfaction and, despite the lack of contextual sensitivity to the basic needs approach; numerous researchers have argued that there is nonetheless something to human wellbeing that goes beyond individual satisfaction, including sustained good health. Second, whilst a relative definition of wellbeing can accommodate the criticisms of the basic needs theory by collecting people's own assessments, exploring how different groups define this, what influences their evaluations, and how to use the information to inform policy, are major challenges. Similar to other relative measures (e.g. satisfaction with health care –in this approach, the information cannot be used as a simple evaluation as many different variables including expectations will affect definition and evaluation (Atkinson, & Haran, 2005).

2.4.4 Capability Model

The capabilities approach, developed by the economist Amartya Sen, attempts to negotiate these conflicts between objective and subjective conceptualizations of wellbeing and their associated problems. Sen argues that we need a combination of substantive, objective descriptors for the dimensions of human wellbeing alongside a space for historical, cultural and personal specifications (Alkire & Black, 1997). Wellbeing is seen within a capabilities approach as the positive freedom to live a flourishing life. Lives are seen as combinations of functioning are making up the state of the person through a set of beings and doings (Quizilbash, 1997). Capabilities then are a range of attainable and valuable functioning's including sets of skills and power. A pattern of consumption is a means to provide the ability to do or be a range of things, not the end in itself. The geographical interest here lies in exploring the nature of settings that enable the translation of potential capabilities into attained functioning's.

The approach inevitably comes in for attack from both sides, by trying to combine some elements of the objective and subjective perspectives Gasper, (1997). He grappled with defining the entry points for policy by grouping capabilities into three types for operational purposes: (i) *O* capabilities, an opportunities set; (ii) *S* capabilities, set of skills; and (iii) *P* capabilities potential or latent. In this hierarchy, a potential capability can become an *S* capability through training, education and experience whilst suitable contextual circumstances are needed for this to translate into an *O* capability having real possibility for action. Others have tried to define a basic capability set.

2.4.5 PERMA Model

The PERMA Model was developed by positive psychologist, Martin Seligman, who widely published it in his influential 2011 book, "Flourish.""PERMA" stands for the five essential elements of well-being. These are positive emotion: deals with positive emotion of our lives. Any positive emotion like peace, gratitude, satisfaction, pleasure, inspiration, hope, curiosity, or love falls into this category. It is really important to enjoy life here and now. The engagement component deals with the situation, task, or project, we experience a state of flow time seems to stop, we lose our sense of self, and we concentrate intensely on the present. The more we experience this type of engagement, the more likely we are to experience well-being. Positive relationships is other component. As humans we are "social beings," and good relationships are core to our well-being. Time-and-again, we see that people who have meaningful, positive relationships with others are happier than to their counterpart. Relationships really do matter. The meaning comes from serving a cause bigger than ourselves. In meaning component a specific deity or religion, or a cause that helps humanity in some way need meaning in our lives to have a sense of well-being. Accomplishment and Achievement element deals with are striving in a better way, whether we're seeking to master a skill, achieve a valuable goal, or win in some competitive event. As such, accomplishment is another important thing that contributes to our ability to flourish. Therefore these components help us in promoting wellbeing.

2.5 GENDER CONJECTURE AND CONSTRUCTION

According to biologically-oriented theories, gender differences arising from the differential biological roles played by the males and females in reproduction underlie gender role development and differentiation. It explains gender development and differentiation on the basis of ancestrally programmed. According to evolutionary psychology, the biological basis of gender differentiation has changed little since the ancestral era. Kohlberg defined gender constancy as the realization that one's sex is a permanent attribute tied to underlying biological properties and does not depend on superficial characteristics such as hair length, style of clothing, or choice of play activities. There are three discrete levels of gender understanding comprises gender identity, stability, and consistency components of gender constancy.

Human evolution provides bodily structures and biological potentialities that permit a range of possibilities rather than dictate a fixed type of gender differentiation. People contribute to their self-development and bring about social changes that define and structure gender relationship through their agentic actions within the interrelated systems of influence (Bandura, 1993). Most psychological theories treat gender development as primarily a phenomenon of early childhood rather than one that operates throughout the life course. However, rules of gender role conduct vary to some degree across social contexts and at different periods in life. Psychoanalytic theory posited different processes to explain gender development in boys and girls especially focuses on identification processes that have its early influence. Psychological theories typically emphasize the cognitive construction of gender conceptions and styles of behaviour with the familial trans mission model. According to cognitive developmental theories the gender identity is postulated as the basis of organizer and regulator of children's gender learning (Kohlberg, 1968). Children develop the stereotypic conceptions of gender from what they see and hear around them. The social cognitive theory the gender role development and functioning specifies how gender conception are constructed from the complex mix of experiences and how they operate in concert with motivational and self-regulatory mechanisms to guide gender linked conduct throughout the life course. The theory integrates psychological and socio-structural determinants within a unified conceptual structure. In this theoretical perspective, gender conceptions and roles are the product of a broad network of social influences operating interdependently in a variety of societal subsystems. The Behaviorist theories have accorded prominence to parents in shaping and regulating gender linked conduct.

In social cognitive theory, gender development is promoted by three major modes of influence known as modeling (where great deal for gender linked information's exemplified by models in one's immediate environment such as parents and peers); enactive experience (discerning the gender linkage of conduct from the outcomes resulting from one's actions); vicarious experience (through direct tuition); and affective experience (emotional expression). Mastery experience, social modeling, social persuasion and physical and emotional states including their capabilities can develop people's beliefs in the efficacy. This theory extends the analysis of human agency to collective agency (Bandura, 1982). Personal and collective efficacy differs in the unit of agency but both forms of efficacy beliefs serve similar functions and operate through similar processes. The self-efficacy can play important role in the development and regulation of gender role conduct.

Peoples shared beliefs in their efficacy influences, the type of futures they seek to achieve collectively how much effort they put into their group endeavors. Social cognitive theory posits that through cognitive processing of direct and vicarious experiences, children come to categorize themselves as girls or boys, gain substantial knowledge of gender attributes and roles, and extract rules as to what types of behaviour are considered appropriate for their gender. The developmental changes posited by social cognitive theory are concerned not only with attributes and activities that get gendered but with the mechanism through which such conduct is regulated. Sociologically oriented theories emphasize social construction of gender role mainly at the institutional level. According to sociological theories, gender is a social construction rather than a biological given. The source of gender differentiation lies more in social and institutional practices than in fixed properties of the individual. The study of documents masterfully the social construction and perpetuation of stereotypic gender differentiation. Gender stereotypes shape the perception, evaluation and treatment of males and females in selectively gendered ways that beget the very patterns of behaviour and confirm the initial stereotypes. The sociological theories focus on socio-structural determinants of gender role development and functioning (Epstein, 1981). Moreover, socio-cultural and technological changes necessitate revision of pre-existing conceptions of what constitute appropriate gender conduct. Gender schema theory is centered upon individual difference in gender schematic processing of information. According to Davar (2001) gender has now become audible in professional circles where it was talking down attitude earlier. No significant effort in women empowerment seems to be effective in removing the oppressive and threatening situation that still exists in various forms of sexism and axiomatic disregard for the females.

FEAR OF SUCCESS AND RELIGIOSITY

Since the inception of planet earth the human being on it had tried to exploit the natural resources by maintain their contact to the community members through utilization of their inner processes and behavioral outcomes. Before the optimum use of science and technology the human being generally believes that their future and destiny is in the Supreme Being. All that happens in the environment as well as in the life of the individual is all predetermined and controlled by the supreme force. The people of pleistoscenic period were quire candid in their approach to believe in such supernatural forces. The people use to believe in nature and natural related products. As a result the Stone Age people use to worship sun, land, water, tree and some animal as well as flower. As the time passes the human being aspiration also started increasing. The advent of science and technology further fueled and accelerated that helped the people of Neolithic period in accomplishing a lot. In the present scenario the people are striving for the best and are trying to achieve more and more within a short period of time. But the environment all the time does not permit the person to exploit it resources and create hurdles. Further the individual or group that form society and culture also exert influence on the demand of the people. Therefore, some desire of the human being are repressed those are very important for them. Therefore, the human being generalize their unaccomplished feeling to the supreme being by keeping in view that the God/goddesses will help them in accomplishing the desired need in a stipulated time. In Himachal Pradesh the people considered their local devta and deities as the medium behind their unaccomplished motives. They are supposed to bring happiness and satisfaction in their life. So the people believe in these devta and deities. But according to the local people the local deities in turn expect fair treatment as well as gift from the people.

There is generally an apprehension among the people that the deities and devta need worship through *dhoop, agarbati , and other havan* related material including gift like goat, lamb, cock as well gold and silver jewellery. If the people will not adhere their instruction, then these deities can come in wrath and causes doom in the form of destruction of their crops, environmental hazards like earthquake, drought, and flood etc. So the fear occurs as a response to something which is perceived as being threatening, dangerous and harmful. It causes a person to be nervous, anxious, impair bodily function and exert its influence on ability and functioning. In the modern world, most people have chosen to balance religion with science, seeking interpretations of sections such as revelations that make sense against a larger frame of reference. However, many people believe that these sections are meant to be taken literally. It is easy to see how a belief in the literal interpretation of religious practices and writings could develop into a phobia. Doomsday phobias with a religious bent could be related to death phobias, particularly in those who are questioning their faith. Someone who is from a religious background but has begun to question its teachings could easily develop a phobia of finding out the truth through death. It can be difficult to differentiate a legitimate doomsday phobia from the effects of mass hysteria. "Groupthink" is a documented phenomenon that occurs when members of a group begin to conform to the majority opinion without critically evaluating information for them. In a panic situation, this can lead to an evolving hysteria. The effects on human society, institutions, and environment resulting from communication with an extraterrestrial civilization could include, among others, sweeping changes in science, technology, religion, politics, and ecosystems. The actual magnitudes and types of change resulting from contact could vary greatly, depending on such factors as the extraterrestrial civilization's benevolence or malevolence, how technologically advanced it is, and the level of mutual understanding between it and humanity. In nutshell, the fear of various sorts including fear of success seems to be important reason behind being religious.

3.1 FEAR OF SUCCESS AND RELIGIOSITY

There seems to be a very important relationship between fear of success and religiosity. The persons who have fear of failure as well as success both generalize their feeling and expectation of accomplishment to the god and goddess. It is prevalent across the world including western countries where the people might be religious provided they do not endorse it. In India religiousness and faith in God and local deities including evil spirit are quite prevalent. In the academic psychology's relationship, study on religious experiences was initiated by James in the late 19th century. His motion was that the core of religious life lay primarily within the inner recesses of the individual, and that in each of us is the essential link between normal everyday awareness and mystical states of religious awakening. Three major influences on James's thoughts were (a) academic scholarship in the history of comparative religions; (b) the rise of the metaphysical or mind-cure movement; and (c) the historical interest taken by academic psychologists such as Stanley Hall and Gordon Allport in the psychology of religion (Taylor, 1978). Kureshi, Khan and Singh (1980) tried to compare Indian and non-Indian subjects on fear of failure. The non-Indian sample was represented by male graduate students hailing from fifteen Afro-Asian countries and the Indian sample mainly by students from U.P. and Bihar studying at Aligarh. A thematic apperception test developed after Mc Clelland and Birney was used as the main tool. No significant difference was discovered between the Indian and non-Indian subjects. However, differences were found to exist between the Indian and non-Indian subjects on certain indices of fear of failure.

The study of Verma and Ghadially (1985) aimed at finding out whether children of mothers with modern and traditional attitudes differ from each other on n-Ach and on expectancy for success. A sample of 244 children and 122 mothers having a minimum of one son and one daughter were selected from Lucknow. Results confirmed that the children of modern mothers have higher n-Ach than the traditional mothers. The daughters and sons of modern mothers do not differ in n-Ach. Further the sons of traditional mothers have higher n-Ach than their daughters. Finally the expectancies for success also showed the same trends. The study of Dhawan and Sripat (1986) hypothesized that fear of death will differentially influence the n-Affiliation scores of individuals with high and low religiosity. Forty undergraduates students aged 18-20 years were divided into high and low religiosity groups and administered a one-dimensional measure of perception of threat. Subsequently, n-Affiliation was measured using Murray's TAT cards. Results indicated that individuals with induced fear of death obtain higher n-Affiliation scores. Religiosity and fear of death were most related and as such religious attitudes did not serve to moderate the effects of induced fear of death on n-Affiliation scores. Implications of the findings are discussed in terms of the importance of situational variables as influencing personality and afflictive behavior.

Further Singhal (1988) conducted a study on 360 boys and girls from two school systems in India were divided into six groups are interviewed to identify the types of explanations freely used by children to explain (a) the success and failure at school (b) the relative success and failure of one's own and of others on specific tasks. A question was also asked to examine the effects of the quality of schooling, age and sex on the explanations. Six achievement stories and school examination scores are used as materials. Fifteen categories are developed to classify the free explanations of children. Ability and effort related categories support the current model of attribution. Task difficulty and luck are unimportant. A partial support to the control dimension is found in two different categories, namely regularity and mood and physical state. The unexpected importance of the behavioural attributions suggests the need of a revision of the taxonomy of current models. The effects of the quality of schooling and age are significant. The study of Boisen (1994) encompasses 39 cases of mental disorders, 36 cases of religious experience, and 5 cases of the experiences of men of religious genius. A chart was developed to illustrate personality changes and upheavals arising out of the sense of personal failure of these subjects. This personal failure and sense of isolation led these subjects to reorganize their worlds and their modes of thought and judgment. The chart also documents their controlling desires; degree of awareness; reaction modes; and transition to their solution as a valid religious type, a normal persons, or a mentally ill person.

Kasek (1999) in his study adapted the fine-factor model of personality to investigate the personality correlates of religious constructs for 104 middle school students in Warsow. The Polish Adjutive List was used to assess the personality factors of neuroticism, extraversion, openness, and conscientiousness. The Polish version of the Swedish religious Orientation Scale was used to assess intrinsic, extrinsic, and quest religious orientations. The results found suggest that intrinsic and quest religious orientations correlate with the fine-factor model traits of conscientiousness, whereas extrinsic religiosity is associated with extraversion. Overall findings of hierarchical regression analyses suggest that fine-factor model domains explain 4% of variance in relationship with God, whereas religious orientation accounts for an additional 35% of variance in relationship with God. In their classic study, Neal, Chatters, Meltzer, Tina & Morgan, David (2000) tried to explore in their study the nature and personal meaning of prayer in late life. Here they presented the results from a series of focus groups. Eight focus groups were conducted consisting of 63 adults age 65 yrs and older. Three major themes associated with prayer emerged front the group discussions. First, study participants identified a number of beliefs about low and nature of answers to prayers. Second, some participants fill it was important to distinguish between group and individual prayers. In the process, they discussed several ways in which the nature and impact of group and individual prayers may differ. Third, participants in our focus groups helped clarify what initially appeared to be a rather passive approach to the use of prayer during difficult times.

The exploration of Powers (2003) argues that psychology wishes to study the place of religious phenomena in the individual thought, in cultural form, and in personal and common activity. Here, psychology promise is to focus (1) on the way one thinks and talks about these matters, in images and opinions of all kinds, and (2) on the foundations of religious attitudes prior to thought and speech that is, on the disposition toward project either of only personal interest and value or of communal interest and value. The author maintains that Individual psychology does this by attending to subjectivity under the heading of creativity and by seeing its products is fictions, more or less useful to perception and understanding, rather than as illusions, dismissed as pathological and misleading. Ghazal (2004) in his research tries to explain that it also seems that the family behaviour may mediate the influence of religion on women's labour force activity. Prior research on families has largely overloaded the role of religion in influencing women's labour force decisions, particularly at different stages of the life cycle. The analysis begins to address this gap by examining whether religious affiliation and religiosity have direct relationships to women's work behaviours, or whether they primarily operate through family behaviours at different phases of the life course. The results show that religiosity exerts a negative influence on women's labour force participation, but only when children are present in the home. Among women with no children, religiosity has no effect on employment.

Cohen (2005) gave the traditional interpretation of "intrinsic" religiousness has fostered an unchallenged assumption that normative and substantive religious motivation is inherently individual and personal. Social motives for religiousness and structured practices have been characterized as "extrinsic" and as lacking informative significance. We argue that this view is most applicable in American Protestant religions, and hence existing religious motivation scales reflect a distinctly American Protestant view. We then show that social motives and structured ritual practices are, in fact, as normative as individual motivations in several religious traditions. In particular, we describe the social practices and motives normative for Judaism and certain streams of Christianity. We than discuss the potential relevance of this analysis to emotion, collective identity, and moral judgment. Richard (2006) in his study used two factors communion and complaint to find the relationship with God. He attempted to find empirical connections between the attachment, object-relations, and triangular lane perspectives as they apply to relationship with God. Attachment to God and object relations perspectives on God has already been extensively investigated in the literature. In this study, it was observed that the triangular love model of Sternburg could also be applied to relationship with God. Using established instruments from each literature-attachment, object relations, triangular love-it was observed that two factors best explained the correlations among these instruments. The first factor, "communion" describes the degree of intimacy, closeness, dependency, and trust in the God-relationship. The second factor, "complaint" describes the degree of disappointment and/or frustration involved in the God-relationship. Because these two factors-communion and complaint are orthogonal, it is argued that the commingling of communion and complaint in the God-relationship is one in human love relationships.

In his study, Jonas (2006) made an attempt to find the relation between terror management and religion. Terror management theory suggests that people cope with awareness of death by investing in some kind of literal or symbolic immortality. Given the centrality of death transcendence beliefs in the life of most religions people, it is hypothesized that religious beliefs play a protective role in managing terror of deaths. He reported three studies suggesting that affirming intrinsic religiousness reduces both death-thought accessibility following mortality salience and the use of terror management defenses with regard to a secular belief system. Study 1 showed that after a naturally occurring reminder of mortality. People who scored high on intrinsic religiousness did not react with worldview defense, whereas people low on intrinsic religiousness did. Study 2 specified that religious intrinsic belief mitigated worldview defense only if participants had the opportunity to affirm their religious beliefs. Study 3 illustrated that affirmation of religious belief decreased death-thought accessibility following mortality salience only for those participants who scored high on the intrinsic religiousness scale. Taken as a whole, these results suggest that only those people who are intrinsically vested in their religion derive terror management benefits from religious beliefs. Study of Pirta and Ranta (2007) tried to bring out the role of reconciliation processes mediated by local deities through possession and solve the social conflicts. They discussed six case studies involving social conflicts over resource use between villages and on social issues within and between the families from three Tehsils of Shimla District, Himachal Pradesh. These conflicts become further complicated due to the mediation by the institutions of local deities. In some acute cases the affection ties are severed to appease the soul of the deceased person. However, attempts are made to re-establish the social bonds through various reconciliation strategies adopted by the community in accordance with the little and great traditions. The important part of breaking and making of these affectional bonds is the possession of persons by spirits and deities. Some hypotheses have been proposed to explain this behavioural phenomenon

In his classic study, Kay (2008) proposed that the high levels of support often observed for governmental and religious systems can be explained in part as a means of coping with the threat posed by chronically or situational fluctuating levels of perceived personal control. Three experiments demonstrated a casual relation between lowered perceptions of personal control and the defense of external systems including increased beliefs in the existence of a controlling God and defense of the overarching socio-political system. A 4th experiment showed the converse to be true: A challenge to the usefulness of external systems of control led to increased illusory perceptions of personal control. In addition, a cross-national data set demonstrated that lower levels of personal control are associated with higher support for governmental control. Each study identified theoretically consistent moderators and mediators of these effects. The implications of these results for understanding why a high percentage of the population believes in the existence of God and why people so often endorse and justify their socio-political systems are discussed. The study conducted in Himachal Pradesh by Kumari and Pirta (2009) explore God as a secure base following the model of John Bowlby. In *Study1* qualitative information collected from participants provided evidence on functional relationship with God as secure base. Conceptualizing attachment to God along two dimensions, anxiety and avoidance, but the distributions of scores obtained was not normal. The effect of priming on recall of memories related to God as a secure base. Priming significantly affected latency, number of memories recalled, and categories generated. The study provides evidence that God serves as a secure base, which is a generalization of primary infant-mother relationship.

Galinsky (2010) says that it has been recently proposed that people can flexibly rely on sources of control that are both internal and external to the self to satisfy the need to believe that their world is under control (i.e., that events do not unfold randomly or haphazardly). Consistent with this, past research demonstrates that, when personal control is threatened, people defend external systems of control, such as God and government. This theoretical perspective also suggests that belief in God and support for government system, although seemingly disparate, will exhibit a hydraulic relationship with one another. Using both experimental and longitudinal designs in eastern and western cultures, the authors demonstrate that experimental manipulations or naturally occurring events that lower faith in one of these external systems (e.g., the government lead to subsequent increases in faith in the other (e.g. God). In addition, mediation and moderation analyses suggest that specific concerns with order and structure underlie these specific concerns with order and structure underlie these hydraulic effects. Implications for the psychological, sociocultural, and sociopolitical underpinnings of religious faith, as well as system justification theory, are discussed.

Sasaki (2011) tries to look at the intersection of culture and religion for a cultural analysis of religion's implications for secondary control and social affiliation. Religion helps people maintain a sense of control, particularly secondary control- acceptance of and adjustment to difficult situations- and contributes to strengthening social relationships in a religious community. However, little is known about how culture may influence these effects. The current research examined the interaction of culture and religion on secondary control and social affiliation, comparing people from individualistic cultures (e.g. European American), who tend to be more motivated toward personal agency, and people from collectivistic cultures (e.g. East Asians), who tend to be more motivated to maintain social relationships. In study 1, an analysis of online church mission statements showed that U.S. websites contained more themes of social affiliation than did U.S. websites. Study 2 showed that experimental priming of religion led to acts of secondary control for European Americans but not Asian Americans. Using daily diary methodology, study 3 showed that religious coping predicted more secondary control for European Americans but not Koreans, and religious coping predicted more social affiliation for Koreans and European Americans. These findings suggest the importance of understanding socio-cultural moderators for the effects of religion.

3.2 FEAR OF SUCCESS AND WELLBEING

The fear of success and wellbeing is very important topic in the present scenario. The motive to avoid success is conceptualized within the framework of an expectancy-value theory of motivation. It is identified as an internal psychological representative of the dominant societal stereotype which views competence, independence, competition, and intellectual achievement as qualities basically inconsistent with femininity even though positively related to masculinity and mental health. The expectancy that success in achievement-related situations will be followed by negative consequences arouses fear of success in otherwise achievement-motivated women which then inhibits their performance and levels of aspiration. The incidence of fear of success is considered as a function of the age, sex, and educational and occupational level of subjects tested between 1964 and 1971. Impairment of the educational and interpersonal functioning of those high in fear of success is noted and consequences for both the individual and society are discussed (Horner, 1972).

The study of Jackaway and Teevan (1976) intends to explore fear of failure and success in school students. They used verbal leads to elicit TAT responses from 160 male and female high school seniors, under neutral and aroused conditions. These protocols were scored for fear of success (FOS) according to the 1973 revised scoring system developed by Homer, Tresemer, Berens, and Watson (Note 1) and also scored for fear of failure (FOF) according to the Hostile Press Scoring System developed by Bimey, Burdick, and Teevan (1969). Significant positive correlations between the two motive scores were obtained under both neutral and aroused conditions. The lack of independence between the FOS and FOF scores rejects theoretical similarities in the definitions of the motives, as well as considerable overlap in the scoring systems. It was hypothesized that for those people (especially women) who are afflictive and achievement needs are interrelated, FOF and FOS may be nearly equivalent, since fear of social rejection thus becomes tantamount to fear of failure.

Further, Kimball and Leahy (1976) studied fear of success in males and females students. Horner's "fear of success" test was administered to 303 children between the 4th and 12th grades. There was an increase of fear of success imagery between the 4th and 10th grades and a decrease between 10th and 12th grades. Fear of success was related to sex only during high school, where it was associated with the course of study pursued by students. Thus, in a high school secretarial course, females showed the lowest fear of success while 12th-grade college-prep females showed fear of success higher than secretarial course females and college-prep males. The findings were interpreted as indicating developmental changes in fear of success due to increasing peer affiliation (4th'-10th grades) and sex-linked competitive achievement. The study of Eme and Lawrence (1976) tried to examine relationship between fear of success and academic achievement. For this they conducted a study on Seventy-eight female and 63 male 9th-grade students. These students were analyzed by administering the revised Homer fantasy-based measure of fear of success. Result based on the point biserial correlation revealed non-significant correlation between fear of success and academic achievement was not significant.

Olsen and Willemsen (1978) tried to explore the facts and artifacts of fear of success among school students. They conducted a study on 240 high school juniors and seniors wrote stories in response to one of four variations of the story cues used by Matina Horner to measure what has been called "fear of success." These cues described either Ann or John achieving success in medical school in a situation in which either all of the protagonist's classmates were men or there were equal numbers of men and women. Six different consequences of the success were assessed.

Results indicated that male and female students perceived the depicted success in similar ways and that when the "deviance" aspect of Ann being alone in a class of men was removed, negative outcomes of success were lessened. The common interpretation of these stories as the writers' projection of their own personalities is challenged.

In their study, Zuckerman, Larrance, Porac, and Blanck, (1980) studied effects of fear of success on intrinsic motivation, causal attribution, and choice behavior. Subjects worked either on puzzles of their choice or puzzles that were assigned to them and were then informed that they had performed either better or worse than the majority of other subjects. Measures of intrinsic motivation and of attribution for performance were obtained. Subjects then indicated how much choice they wanted to have over similar tasks that they were going to perform. Finally, subjects completed a fear-of-success and a resultant achievement motivation measure. Results showed that following success, low fear-of-success subjects, showed higher intrinsic motivation, made more internal attributions, and wanted to have more choice if initially they had been given choice and less choice if initially they had been given no choice. There were no significant differences between low and high fear-of-success subjects following failure. These results were obtained for both males and females and could not be accounted for by resultant achievement motivation that was unrelated to fear of success. Implications of the construct of fear of success are discussed.

Further, Douglas and Milton (1986) tried to explain effects of fear of success by explaining two hypotheses: Tremeser's (1977) boundary maintenance theory and Stiver's (1976) sex-role prescription model. Fear of success is defined as performance suppression (a reduction in performance from a first task to a second) following knowledge regarding success level and sex role orientation of the task. For the study seventy-five female male college undergraduates served as subjects. Employing a behavioral measure, support for the hypotheses was not found. Analysis of data that reflected how invested the subjects were in performing well, however, showed significant results in a manner generally consistent with the positions of both Stiver and Tresemer. From these data, it seems that participation in what is perceived as sex role inappropriate behavior plays a role in the fear-of-success effect. Since the power of the success feedback was limited, the importance of this variable to the fear-of-success effect could not be clearly determined. No overall sex differences were found using the task performance behavioral measure; data from the current study do suggest that men and women react differentially to some of the variables involved in the fear-of-success effect.

In the words of Piedmont (1988) over the past 20 years, research on Fear of Success has generated many inconsistent and contradictory results. Horner's theory regarding the motivational dynamics underlying the performance of males and females is reviewed and contrasted with later interpretations. Based on Horner's formulations, a model of FOS articulated by Piedmont accommodates previous research and provides also provides a framework for guiding future research. Perhaps one of the more theoretically engaging areas of motivation research concerned the construct fear of success and its relationship with achievement. Although much investigative effort was devoted to it, the research process was plagued with numerous theoretical and technical problems, not the least of which was a consistent inability to discriminate the construct from other related variables such as fear of failure and test anxiety. Piedmont (1995) in his report argued that the empirical overlap among these variables suggested the presence of larger motivational constructs. To evaluate this hypothesis, 263 predominantly Caucasian college women completed measures of fear of success, test anxiety, achievement motivation, and fear of failure. Scores on each variable were correlated with markers of the five-factor model of personality that revealed that these scales were factor ally complex. A regression analysis showed that it was the personality domains of neuroticism and conscientiousness that were most relevant to these performance-related variables. A preliminary model of motivation was proposed that was based on these two personality domains.

Victor, (1997) in this study examined the association between the loss of significant others and fear of personal death, using a group of 86 adults who dad experienced a significant loss in childhood or adolescence and a matched group of 86 subjects who had not experienced any early loss. Subjects in each group were further divided according to the experience of a significant loss during the previous two years and completed a multidimensional scale measuring fear of personal death. Whereas early loss was positively related to the interpersonal component of fear of death, recent loss was positively related to the intrapersonal and transpersonal components of this fear. These associations were found to be moderated by the identity of the lost person, the age of the subject at the time of the early loss, and subject's gender. McKinney, Paul and McKinsey, Kathleen (1999) in their study tried to find out importance of prayer in the lives of people in their late adolescents. Although prayer is a lulaniar that is performed by most people at least at some time yet social scientists appear to have neglected this concept. Seventy seven college students (aged 18-32 yrs) were interviewed, given the objective measure of Ego Identity Status, and asked to keep seven day diaries about their prayer activities, whether spontaneous or formal. Co relational analyses revealed a relationship between identity status and commitment of religion. A qualitative analysis of the diary data suggested that prayer may be a revealing approaches to the psychosocial lives of late adolescents, including their central concerns, temporal orientation, and the social bounds of their definition of self.

The study of Pyszczynski, et al. (2003) says that by specifying how the defense motives emphasized by terror management theory (TMT) and the acquisitive motives emphasized by self-determination theory (SDT) interact, a more comprehensive and well-rounded understanding of human behavior can be achieved. Although these two motive systems operate according to different principles, and sometimes orient the individual toward different goals, human behavior results from the dialectic interplay between them. To elucidate this interplay, the authors outline the conceptualization of the workings of these 2 systems, consider how each system can facilitate and interfere with the other, and discuss ways in which defensive needs can be served while allowing the individuals to optimize their creative potential and freedom. Hart, (2005) on the basis of prior work integrating attachment theory and terror management theory, the authors propose a model of a tripartite security system consisting of dynamically interrelated attachment, self esteem, and worldview processes. Four studies are presented that, combined with existing evidence; support the prediction derived from the model that threat to one component of the security system result in compensatory defensive activation of other components. Further, the authors predicted and found that individual differences in attachment style moderate the defenses. In studies 1&2, attachment threats motivated worldview defense among anxiously attached participants and motivated self-enhancement (especially among avoidant participants), effects similar to those caused by mortality salience. In studies 3 & 4, a worldview threat and a self-esteem threat caused attachment-related proximity seeking among fearful participants and avoidance of proximity among dismissing participants. The author's model provides an overarching framework within which to study attachment, self-esteem, and worldviews.

Assessment of Hossein, and Pishe, (2008) on fear of success revealed lack of trust and confidence in one's own personality. In this concept they tried to investigate the relationship between fear of success and burnout among working women in Iranian public schools. The results reveal that fear of success and burnout in women working in public schools are correlated; but there are no significant differences in levels of fear of success and/or burnout relative to demographic factors. Vess et al. (2009) in his four studies tries to see the role of extrinsic esteem contingencies in adjusting to shifting health- relevant standards when managing existential fears was examined. Study 1 demonstrated that after reminders of death, higher dispositional focus on extrinsic self-esteem contingencies predicted greater interest in tanning. Using a more domain-specific approach, study 2 showed that, after being reminded of death, the more individuals smoke for social esteem reasons, the more compelling they find an antismoking commercial that exposes adverse social consequences of smoking. Study 3 explored how situational factors (i.e.

priming a contingent relational schema) that implicate extrinsic contingencies facilitated the impact of shifting standard primes on tanning intentions after mortality salience. Finally study 4 found that mortality salience led to increased endorsement of exercise as a basis of self-worth when participants who derive self-esteem from extrinsic sources visualized someone who exercises. Together, these studies demonstrate that reminders of death interact with prevalent social standards to influence everyday health decisions.

Zou, (2010) proposed that both inflated and deflated self-assessments of performance maybe linked to an increased likelihood of practicing self-handicapping and having relatively poor performance in future tasks. Consistent with this proposal, we found that irrespective of the level of actual performance, compared with accurate self-assessment, both inflated and deflated self-assessments of task performance are associated with a greater tendency to self-handicapping and withhold preparatory effort perform relatively poorly in a subsequent, low academic achievement and low level of subjective wellbeing. The study of Ivers and Downes, (2011) concluded that fear of success is the key dimension of social class. It was hypothesized that individuals from socio-economically disadvantaged backgrounds fear that, for them, success will lead to alienation from their community, and the loss of identity and loss of overall sense of belonging within their culture. Eleven participants took part in the study, three males and eight females. Two-phase qualitative interviewing was employed as the primary source of data collection in an attempt to gain a deeper understanding of the constructions and experiences of the participants in relation to success. The majority of participants believed that they would have to make vast life changes, in order to facilitate their views of desired success. The participants' fear was rooted in what they perceived as the "consequences of success". These participants occupied a "trade-off mindset"; for these people, success meant leaving their family, friends, community and culture behind. The thought of losing this "connection" and sense of belonging was expressed with noticeable anxiety.

3.3 RELIGIOSITY AND WELLBEING

Most of the studies as quoted by different philosophers and psychologists reveals that the religious person is physically, socially and psychological better as compared to their counterpart. The study of Duhrssen (1978) described similarities between religious practices and psychotherapeutic methods. For example, the Jewish religion asks all members to be strictly obedient to the accepted laws and orders of God so that the alliance with God will not be jeopardized. This is similar to psychoanalysis in that patients are expected to do their best for their own mental health, but are also asked to accept special rules and laws of the therapy in order to maintain the working alliance with the analyst. Meadow, (1979) reported the views of five scholars, given at a symposium during the annual convention of the American Psychological Association in Toronto, Ontario, August 1978, on the relationships between religious ministry and various schools of psychotherapy, on training for psychotherapists and clergy who will engage in counseling, on defining areas of expertness of the two groups, and on related issues. Pertinent considerations for therapists and clergy alike are suggested in dealing with religious matters in the treatment of souls.

Study of Victor (1983) in his study beginning with P.O.Machean's model of the triune brain, the present article explores the question of whether creative processes result from co adaptation, in ritual, of genetic and cultural information. Also examined are the division of labor between the right and left cerebral hemispheres and its implications for play. It is suggested that play, intimately related to ritual, functions in the social construction of reality in a way that is analogous to that of mutation and variation in organic evolution. How brain functioning accords with the distinctive features of dominant religious systems is discussed. McLatchie and Draguns, (1984) tested mental health concepts of 47 members of strongly evangelical churches, 33 members of middle-continuum churches, 33 members of self-defined liberal churches, and 39 undergraduates by administering questionnaires. Measures of religious orthodoxy and of modernity served as independent variables. Dependent variables were attitudes toward seeking mental health services, opinions about mental illness, and tendencies to view mental health problems as spiritual. Results indicate that evangelicals were prepared to use professional help, although they were concerned about the beliefs and values of the mental health practitioner and expressed fears that secular therapists might try to alter their beliefs and values. They preferred religious advisers. They also appeared to have characteristic ideas about mental illness that need to be addressed in any attempt to counsel such clients.

The study of De Vas and Suarez-Orozeo (1987) tried to examine power as it relates to the ritual interaction of sacrifice to explore how the human capacity for coping is psychologically socialized around the inner experience of mechanical and intentional causality. It is suggested that these coping mechanisms are involved in the development of self- consciousness. Psychosexual development and the experience of power (from the aspects of psychophysiology and a religious sense of intentionality) are explored.). An attempt was made by Pandey (1988) study the relationship between religious beliefs (intrinsic and extrinsic) and social innovativeness. The subjects were 224 adult male Hindu cultivators of Bhagalpur district (Bihar). The sample was stratified on the basis of caste (upper and lower) and education (high and low). The results showed that intrinsic aspects of religious beliefs were negatively correlated with the extrinsic religious beliefs and positively correlated with social innovativeness. Caste and education were found to have significant relationship with extrinsic belief and social innovativeness. Education was found to have significant relationship with intrinsic beliefs.

Scott, Smith, and Davis (1989) investigated the relationship between religious beliefs (RB), personality and mental health in 36 female and 13 male. 19-57 year old Mormon psychotherapy clients (MPC's) and 30 female and 21 male, 21-64 year old Mormon non clients (MNC's). Measures included the Religious Orientation Scale and Defining Issues Test. An analysis of covariance (ANCOVA) revealed that MPC's scored higher on shame and lower on existential well-being. Female MNC's scored higher on guilt, and female MPC's scored higher on shame. Subjects preferred stage four moral reasoning, and 92% were intrinsically motivated in religious worship. Although MPC's, RB's and motivations appeared functional, psychological issues were manifested that could predispose them to unhealthy reactions to some of the doctrines and influences of their religion. The study of Umoren (1990) examined the relationship between African traditional religion and both the explanation and treatment of one type of mental illness, through an analysis of the case of an Annang man in Nigeria. Illness explanations and treatment are related to a worldview that can best be described as strongly religious. Two classes of religious explanations for mental illness among the Annang, possession and non-possession, were identified in the sociocultural process of the people. The nonpossessional process was selected to describe the treatment, which was directly related to the religious explanation for the mental disorder. The traditional healer's treatment was divided into 2 treatment modalities: the religio-psychotherapeutic (including relaxation, suggestion, and manipulation), and the religio-physiologic.

Jacobsson and Merdasa (1991) interviewed patients, health workers, and traditional healers show 3 traditional cultural influences existed in western Ethiopia before the 1974 revolution. These were traditional Oromo thinking, the Coptic Church, and the Islamic culture. In the traditional Oromo society, the Kallu was the religious leader who, through an ecstatic ritual technique, could investigate the causes of the disorder and advise what to do. The Coptic church looked on mental disorders as possession by evil spirits, which were treated by specially gifted priests and monks by praying and giving holy water or by exhortation. According to Islamic teaching in the area, mental disorders were caused by evil spirits sent by God to punish the unfaithful people. Some Muslim sheiks treated mental cases with prayers, but herbal remedies were also used. Peteet (1994) offered a conceptual framework for clinicians who must decide how to approach, within the psychotherapeutic context, patients who present spiritual and religions problems. A range of choices available to clinicians is detailed that includes the following: (1) acknowledging the problem but focusing exclusively on its psychological dimension; (2) clarifying and suggesting resources for addressing religious or spiritual problems elsewhere; (3) addressing the problems indirectly by using the patients spiritual perspective to foster greater integration of his spiritual and emotional life; and (4) addressing the spiritual problem directly within the framework of treatment through use of a shared religious or spiritual orientation. Considerations relevant to choosing among these treatment options are discussed.

In his article Bill, (1996) showed that the challenge offered to psychiatry by religions and spiritual values is one encountered by modern society. Blomfield comments suggests that it may be possible to advance the inquiry further, into value-patterns not covered by the block descriptions "scientific/secular" or "religious/spiritual". The study of Christopher and Jeffrey (1998) deals with religion-health connection that have increased markedly in recent years. This interest in the complex relationships between religion and mental and physical health is being fueled by energetic and innovative research programs in several fields, including sociology, psychology, health behavior and health education, psychiatry, gerontology, and social epidemiology. This article has three main objectives: (1) to briefly review the medical and epidemiologic research on religious factors and both physical health and mental health; (2) to identify the most promising explanatory mechanisms for religious effects on health, giving particular attention to the relationships between religious factors and the central constructs of the life stress paradigm, which guides most current social and behavioral research on health outcomes; and (3) to critique previous work on religion and health, pointing out limitations and promising new research directions. Controlled intervention studies offer considerable promise to better understand relationships and possible mechanisms between spiritual and religious factors and health.

Studies examining spiritually augmented cognitive–behavioral therapies, forgiveness interventions, different meditation approaches, 12-step fellowships, and prayer have provided some evidence, albeit modest, of efficacy in improving health under specific conditions. Researchers need to describe spiritual and religious factors more clearly and precisely, as well as demonstrate that such factors independently influence treatment efficacy. Inclusion of potential moderating and mediating variables (e.g. extent of religious commitment, intrinsic religiousness, and specific religious coping strategy) in intervention designs could help explain relationships and outcomes. Using a variety of research designs (e.g. randomized clinical trials, single-subject experimental designs) and assessment methods (e.g. daily self-monitoring, ambulatory physiological measures, in-depth structured interviews) would avoid current limitations of short-term studies using only questionnaires (Harris, Thoresen, Mccullough & Larson, 1999).

The study of Alex, Carl, Michael, and David (1999) gave the controlled intervention studies offer considerable promise to better understand relationships and possible mechanisms between spiritual and religious factors and health. Studies examining spiritually augmented cognitive–behavioral therapies, forgiveness interventions, different meditation approaches, 12-step fellowships, and prayer have provided some evidence, albeit modest, of efficacy in improving health under specific conditions. Researchers need to describe spiritual and religious factors more clearly and precisely, as well as demonstrate that such factors independently influence treatment efficacy. Inclusion of potential moderating and mediating variables (e.g. extent of religious commitment, intrinsic religiousness, and specific religious coping strategy) in intervention designs could help explain relationships and outcomes. Using a variety of research designs (e.g. randomized clinical trials, single-subject experimental designs) and assessment methods (e.g. daily self-monitoring, ambulatory physiological measures, and in-depth structured interviews) would avoid current limitations of short-term studies using only questionnaires.

Similarly, Watson (1999) in his study said Cognitive-Experimental Self-Theory (CEST) differentiates an emotional experiential from a rational system of the personality. CEST further hypothesizes that religion can express adaptive experiential potentials. A Constructive Thinking Inventory (CTI) has been devised for recording a healthy functioning of the experimental system. In the present project, the CTI was administered to a sample of college students to test the hypothesized linkage between religion and the experimental system. The intrinsic scale and type largely predicted constructive thinking among college students, whereas the extrinsic and quest scales and the extrinsic type were largely associated with destructive thinking. Quest also correlated inversely with a personal interest in religion, and a number of findings suggested concerns about the basic validity of the Quest scales. Most importantly, these data confirmed that CEST offers an empirically useful interpretation of religious commitment. The research of Cheston (2000) tries to explore the Adlerian practice of encouragement from a spiritual and holistic perspective. Emphasis was given to the physical, psychological, and spiritual impact on clients. Adler only alluded to spirituality in his writings and interviews. Because Adler's view of spiritual development primarily involved support of religious activity and commitment that promoted or expanded one's social interest, the author outlines low participation in religious behaviour meets Adler/s definition of encouragement.

Pedersen, Williams and Kristensen, (2000) in their study tried to find that there might be relation of spiritual self-identity to religious orientation and religious attitude was explored with the WLO An ? scale, the religious Life Inventory, and the Religious Attitude questionnaire, respectively among 315 undergraduates from 4 universities. Those with high scores on spiritual self identity scored significantly higher on the ends orientation and significantly lower on the means & quest orientations. They also manifested higher scores on the effect and conation scales regarding religious matters. Participants manifesting low spiritual self-identity exhibited an opposite pattern of scores. These findings suggest that spiritual self-identity is a salient feature of self-identifications and contributes to the research literature on religiosity. According to Mahalik & Lagan, (2001) it is also a matter for research whether there is any link between religiosity and gender. It was hypothesized that gender role conflict and stress would predict Catholic seminarian and college-aged men's religiosity and spiritual well-being. To test the hypotheses, 151 mostly Caucasian single men (74 Catholic seminarians, 77 Catholic undergraduate men) completed the Gender Role Conflict Scale, Gender Role Stress Scale, Intrinsic–Extrinsic Religious Orientation Scale—Revised, and the Spiritual Well-Being Scale. Separate canonical correlation analyses for the 2 groups revealed significant relationships between the measures assessing gender role conflict and stress and those assessing religiosity and spiritual well-being. The discussion focuses on limitations, future research, and implications for practice (The religiosity may be associated with the health and wellbeing of the community.

The study of Oman and Thoresen (2002) explored that could religion or spirituality cause physical health benefits?' may be given at least four diverging interpretations in terms of causal path diagrams. In common usage, the question may be interpreted to indicate that religion causally influences health by: (1) any mechanism, including well-established factors such as social support and improved health behaviors; (2) additional mechanisms, such as enhanced positive psychological states (e.g. faith, hope, inner peace) acting through psychoneuroimmunologic or psychoneuroendocrinologic pathways; (3) offering psychological strength for acquiring or maintaining positive health behaviors; or (4) causally influencing health by distant healing or intercessory prayer. We review historical confusion between these interpretations, arguing that disentangling them is important for collaborative health care, promotion and research.

The objectives of Krause, (2002) study was to explore the relationship between church-based support and health. In the process, an effort is made to see if the relationships in this model differ for older White and African American people. Interviews were conducted with a national sample of 748 older White and 752 older Black people. The responses of 1,126 of these study participants are used in the analyses presented herein. Survey measures were administered to assess church-based social ties and health. Empirical support was provided for the following theoretical linkages: Older people who attend church often feel their congregations are more cohesive; older people in highly cohesive congregations receive more spiritual and emotional support from their fellow parishioners; older respondents who receive more church-based support have a more personal relationship with God; older people who feel more closely connected with

God are more optimistic; and older people who are more optimistic enjoy better health. Data further reveal that older Black people are more likely than older White people to reap the health-related benefits of religion. The findings contribute to research on religion and health by specifying how the salubrious effects of religion may arise.

The author in this study tries to explain the role of spirituality and religion in mental health. According to him integrating spirituality and religion into clinical practice or psychotherapy has become a significant area of interest in the mental health field today. The present article focuses more specifically on integrating spiritual direction into psychotherapy, discusses ethical issues involved and provides ethical guidelines for the appropriate and helpful use of spiritual direction in the context of psychotherapy and counseling (Tan, 2003). The research of Larson, David, Larson and Susan (2003) gave a longitudinal studies of community samples consistently find links between active spiritual/religious involvement and increased chances for living longer, pointing to the relevance of spirituality/religion as a potential health factor. For a larger proportion of either medically ill or mental health patients, spirituality/religion may provide coping resources, enhance pain management, improve surgical outcomes, protect against depression, and reduce risk of substance abuse and suicide. However, study findings also slow patient spirituality/religion may serve as a source of conflict linked with poorer health outcomes. Whether identifying helps or harms, research elucidates the potential relevance of patient's spirituality/religion, with potential for collaboration with trained champions a part of the health care team to provide spiritual support or deal with spiritual distress for particular patient needs.

According to Ardelt (2003) although religiosity tends to help older people to cope with physical and social losses, not all studies find a significant association between religious involvement and well-being in old age. It might be that primarily the intrinsic rather than the extrinsic aspect of religiosity is responsible for the positive effect of religiosity on well-being. Using a sample of 103 community dwelling older adults (58+), multivariate regression analyses showed that purpose in life rather than extrinsic or intrinsic religious orientation was positively related to elders' subjective well-being and negatively associated with fear of death and death avoidance. Moreover, extrinsic religious orientation had a positive effect on fear of death and death avoidance. Intrinsic religious orientation was positively related to approach acceptance of death. Frequency of shared spiritual activities and religious affiliation were unrelated to subjective well-being but positively related to death avoidance.

Famous researcher Kirby, Coleman, and Dealey (2004) in their previous studies have identified that spiritual beliefs contribute to psychological well-being (PWB) in older people, but limited research has considered the effects of spirituality on PWB when physical health deteriorates and people become frail. We recruited 233 British participants from warden-controlled retirement housing to complete interviewer-administered questionnaires. Results showed that, after we controlled for marital status, age, education, other health problems, and gender, degree of frailty had a negative effect on PWB. Spirituality was also a significant predictor of PWB and moderated the negative effects of frailty on PWB. Therefore, this study suggests that spirituality is a resource in maintaining PWB, and that the use of this resource is more significant for individuals with greater levels of frailty.

The evidence of Fiori (2004) indicates that spirituality and religion are associated with both physical and psychological health. Because a belief that rewards are largely determined by external forces tends to be detrimental to mental health, the idea that God can be equated with such an external force seems contradictory to the proven benefits of religion and spirituality. The purpose of this article is to examine changes in perceived control in the context of spiritual turning points as uncovered in the narrative histories of 30 elderly people. We propose that for many people who derive benefits from religion and spirituality, God may act as a mediator, in the sense that trusting in God provides personal control. In addition to creating a model of God-mediated control, the study's findings suggest a relationship between recall for type of control during a spiritual turning point and the interpretation of that turning point in late life.

The study of Geertsma (2004) tried to describe midlife transition, spirituality, and healing of relationships for members of women's spirituality groups. Ten women completed the Spiritual well-being scale and a 45-minute interview about spirituality, religion, life transitions, relationships, and beneficial aspects of women's spirituality groups. Qualitative analysis found themes to describe spirituality: connection with a Higher Power, personal choice, connectedness with nature and people, healing, and support. The women viewed spirituality and religion as separate, yet connected entities. Benefits of women's spirituality groups include the groups being therapeutic, providing valued relationships, and providing social support. The study of Park (2005) tried to explore how religion, as a meaning system, influences coping with adversity. First, a model emphasizing the role of meaning making in coping is presented. Next, religion as a meaning system is defined, and theory and research on the role of religion in the coping process are summarized. Results from the author's study of 169 bereaved college students are then presented to illustrate some of the pathways through which religious meaning can influence the coping process in the making meaning following loss. Findings indicate that associations between religion and adjustment vary across time since loss, and that these associations are mediated by meaning-making coping. Finally, implications for individual and societal well-being and suggestions for future research are discussed.

The development of social policy related to religion has received increasing focus in recent years, yet psychology continues to play a relatively minor role in this important domain. In the current article, religion's positive and negative influences as a meaning system on individual, community, and societal well-being are delineated. The challenges facing psychology in contributing to public policy development in the religious arena are examined, challenges that stem from profound differences in the meaning system of religion, government, and psychology. These challenges notwithstanding, a number of different pathways in the domains of applied research, community practice, and policy development are delineated through which psychology can help to maximize positive, and minimize negative, outcomes in the religion and social policy arena (Maton, 2005).The increase in attention to religion and spirituality nowadays within psychology is substantial, most notably in the field of psychotherapy and other mental health related issues. Although favorable for the development of the psychology of religion as a sub discipline, there are also reasons for concern. This article addresses some of them by asking whether parts of the contemporary psychological attention to religion and spirituality are not perhaps too focused on questions of mental health, in danger of being transgressive in nature, and biased in their conceptualizations of spirituality (Belzen, 2005).

According to Trede (2006) adults aged in the United States has been increasing steadily for years. Although most would agree that this increased longevity is a remarkable achievement, there is growing concern regarding the resources that will be necessary to provide care and services for this rapidly expanding segment of the population. From a public health perspective, simply increasing longevity is no longer the ultimate outcome sought. A more pertinent goal is increasing the quality of life years, or promoting resilience and successful aging. Strategies that assist adults in delaying the onset of disability or reducing the severity of disabling conditions may serve a vital role in the promotion of resilience and successful aging in older adults. The purpose of this study was to explore the association between religiosity and subjective well-being, commonly identified as a marker of resilience in older adults. In addition, the study sought to determine if that association is mediated by optimism. For this study, subjective well-being was operationalized with measures of depressive symptomatology and life satisfaction. Secondary analyses were conducted on longitudinal data collected for the Florida Retirement Study. Results indicated that religiosity was not significantly associated with future depressive symptomatology, but was significantly associated with future life satisfaction. Dispositional optimism did not mediate the relationships between religiosity and subjective well-being variables. The purpose of Krause, (2008) study was to see whether informal social support from fellow church members sustains an older person's sense of religious meaning in life over time.

Two types of church-based social support were evaluated: spiritual support and emotional support. Data from a nationwide longitudinal survey of older adults suggested that both emotional and spiritual support tend to sustain a sense of religious meaning in life, but of the two, spiritual support appeared to exert the greatest effect. The findings further revealed that older African Americans are more likely than older European Americans to derive a sense of meaning in life through religion. This race difference is largely explained by the fact that older African Americans tend to receive more church-based social support than older European Americans.

Bhasin (2008) through her study put forwarded the Source of Healing of the Gaddis' people, their traditional and folk medicine. Patients seek cures from a variety of medical systems. In the traditional medical systems, medical traditions partly cover other sectors of social life. In contrast to traditional health care system, the official health care system is based on Western science and technology. Gaddis employ different ways in case of sickness. Traditional medical knowledge is coded in to household cooking practices, home remedies; ill health prevention and health maintenance beliefs and routines. Like other rural parts of India, health care in Bharmour among Gaddis is characterized by medical pluralism. Among Gaddis, the health care includes self care, consultation with traditional healers- *chela*; and /or primary health care. Spirit possession is acknowledged as an illness among Gaddis. The cause is a spirit, the effect is spirit possession and the cure is controlled spirit possession. Among Gaddis, deities and evil spirits possess men as well as women. It is believed by Gaddis that traditional medical system is competent of restoring health of the body (herbs) or the mind (*chela*). Modern education, technology, biomedicine has not threatened the traditional therapeutic healing as there are no alternatives. The integration of the two systems is conceptual. These systems just co-exist, side-by-side. To dismiss traditional medical systems as ineffective or weak is to overlook their relevance and benefits in the contexts of their socio-cultural systems. At the same the short comings of modern medical systems: their technical complexity, rising costs, curative rather than preventive focus, and limited accessibility for large population sectors cannot be overlooked.

Goldenberg (2009) explored the existential function of religion and the effect of religious fundamentalism and mortality salience on faith-based medical refusals. Decisions to rely on religious faith over medical treatment for health conditions represent an important but understudied phenomenon. In an effort to understand some of the psychological underpinnings of such decisions, the present research builds from terror management theory to examine whether reminders of death motivate individuals strongly invested in a religious worldview (i.e. fundamentalists) to rely on religious beliefs when making medical decisions. The results showed that heightened concerns about mortality led those high in religious fundamentalism to express greater endorsement of prayer as a medical substitute and to perceive prayer as a more effective medical treatment. Similarly, high fundamentalists were more supportive of religiously motivated medical refusals and reported an increased willingness to rely on faith alone for medical following reminders of death. Finally, affirmations of the legitimacy of divine intervention in health contexts functioned to solidify a sense of existential meaning among fundamentalists who were reminded of personal mortality. The existential importance of religious faith and the health-relevant implications of these findings are discussed. Thakur and Pirta (2009) in their study tried to bring out the mental health and cognitive representations of people experiencing spirit possession. A qualitative method was used to explore the institution of local deity in the villages of Taurjazer Panchayat, Mandi District, of Himachal Pradesh. The focus was on the phenomenon of possession and 30 people experiencing it were selected for quantitative study. A matched group of 30 normal people was taken for making comparisons on measures of mental health and exploration of cognitions. The possession group had lower general well-being than the normal group. Secondly, the possession group indicated a tendency towards neuroticism. Thirdly, continuous controlled association method was used to elicit the memories related to local deities a safe haven, a concept based on Bowlby attachment theory. The possession group recalled greater number of these associations than the comparison group.

In Himachal Pradesh Prof. R. S. Pirta (2010) attempted to find the effect of supernatural elements as context for deliberations on culture and cognition. A unique achievement of human cognition is the invention of supernatural elements having its origin in the shamanistic ceremonies in caves some 30,000 years ago. These elements reside inside and outside the individual, and thus exert two-way control on thinking, feeling and behavior. The paper introduces ten contemporary hypothesis about supernatural elements and while deliberating upon them. In search of the sacred, the paper articulates new paradigm, mind-brain-mind, for psychology. The last section summarizes author's work in context of the religious and cultural ethos prevailing in Himachal Pradesh. Our naturalistic observations on the institution of deity provide evidence for linkages between supernatural elements and coherence in social structure in villages. Case studies at various group levels highlight the role of supernatural elements in the resolution of social conflicts. The human-animal interaction approach, particularly the study of transhumance, introduces one to the complex dynamics of supernatural elements across the verticality of the Himalayas from the Shivaliks to the Tibetan plateau. Using quasi-experimental designs we have been exploring the explicit and implicit memories to study the role of supernatural elements in positive and negative aspects of human well-being.

The objective of Michael (2010) study was to explore how the relationship between religious involvement and mental health varies by gender among the aging population. This article outlines a series of arguments concerning the effects of gender in moderating the effect of religious involvement on mental health and examines them empirically. Using two waves (2001 and 2004) of the Religion, Aging, and Health Survey, this study estimates the differential effect of gender in the religion–mental health connection using multivariate analyses for a nationally representative sample of U.S. adults aged 66–95 years. Results suggest that (a) men obtain more mental health benefits from religious involvement than women, (b) women with higher levels of organizational religious involvement have similar levels of mental health as those with moderate and lower levels of organizational religious involvement, (c) men with very high levels of organizational religious involvement tend to have much higher levels of mental health than all other men. The relationship between organizational religious involvement and mental health is found to be mostly a nonlinear one such that those with the highest levels of religiosity receive all the benefits. The findings suggest a number of promising research directions on the religion–mental health connection among older Americans.

The study of Lima and Putnamb (2010) revealed that although the positive association between religiosity and life satisfaction is well documented, much theoretical and empirical controversy surrounds the question of how religion actually shapes life satisfaction. Using a new panel dataset, this study offers strong evidence for social and participatory mechanisms shaping religion's impact on life satisfaction. Our findings suggest that religious people are more satisfied with their lives because they regularly attend religious services and build social networks in their congregations. The effect of within-congregation friendship is contingent, however, on the presence of a strong religious identity. We find little evidence that other private or subjective aspects of religiosity affect life satisfaction independent of attendance and congregational friendship. Myers (2011) tried to find out the religion paradox. He said if religion makes people happy then why so many people are dropping out. As we estimate here, 68% of human beings – 4.6 billion people- would say that religion is important in their daily lives. Past studies have found that the religious, on average, have higher subjective wellbeing. Yet people are rapidly leaving organized religion in economically developed nations where religious freedom is high. Why would people leave religion if it enhances their happiness? After controlling for circumstances in both United States and world sample, we found that religiosity is associated with slightly higher subjective wellbeing, and similarly so across four major world religions. The associations of religiosity and subjective wellbeing were mediated by social support, feeling respected, and purpose and meaning in life. However there was as interaction underlying the general trend such that the association of religion and wellbeing is conditional on societal circumstances. Nations and states with more difficult life conditions (e.g., widespread hunger and low life expectancy) were much more likely to be highly religious. In these nations, religiosity was associated with greater social support, respect, purpose or meaning, and all three types of subjective wellbeing. In societies with more favorable circumstances, religiosity is less prevalent and religious and nonreligious individuals experience similar levels of subjective wellbeing. There was also a person-culture fit effect such that religious people had higher subjective wellbeing in religious nations but not in non religious nations. Thus, it appears that the benefits of religion for social relationship and subjective wellbeing depend on the characteristics of the society.

The study of Sushine, Terrence and Christopher (2012) aims at to explore religious attendance and loneliness in later life. The study shows that loneliness is a major risk factor for health issues in later life. Although research suggests that religious involvement can protect against loneliness, explanations for this general pattern are underdeveloped. In this paper, we propose and test a theoretical model, which suggests that social integration and social support are key mechanisms that link religious attendance and loneliness. To formally test our theoretical model, we use data from the National Social Life Health and Aging Project (2005/2006), a large national probability sample of older adults aged 57–85 years. We find that religious attendance is associated with higher levels of social integration and social support and that social integration and social support are associated with lower levels of loneliness. A series of mediation tests confirm our theoretical model. Taken together, our results suggest that involvement in religious institutions may protect against loneliness in later life by integrating older adults into larger and more supportive social networks. Future research should test whether these processes are valid across theoretically relevant subgroups. The study of Srivastava (2012) attempted to examine partially the validity of the bio-psychosocial model of health. The study examined the impact of religion-specific culture, life style, belief-systems, and health behavior and practices on physical and psychological health and on responses to illness (i.e. diagnosis of the symptoms, cure-action and adherence, and recovery from illness). The study compared Hindus, Muslims and Christians with regard to the status of their physical health and psychological wellbeing and their responses to illness. The study revealed significant variation in physical as well as psychological health across the religions. Christians were found to manifest significantly lesser symptoms of physical as well as psychological ill health as compared to Hindus and Muslims. Hindus indicated to maintain better physical and psychological health than Muslims did. The results also suggest that religion causes significant variation in diagnosing pattern and cure-action and adherence to the people of different communities. However, no significant difference could be noted in speed of recovery in three religious groups.

3.4 FEAR OF SUCCESS, RELIGIOSITY AND WELLBEING

From the studies it is quite prevalent that the fear of success and religiosity are directly associated with the wellbeing in a positive as well as negative way. The negative affect from guilt and fear associated with religious beliefs is an important topic that has received little research attention. Freud and Ellis, use guilt as the foundation of their arguments that religion is neurotic. However, their views appear to be based more on interpretations of certain cases in their clinical practices than on research. A recent review of research found neither a positive nor a negative relationship between neuroticism and religion. These results do not support the views of the critics, but the results also do not support the strongly beneficial effects of religion that might be expected based on testimonials and case studies reported in the religion literature (Koenig, Smiley, & Gonzales, 1988; Maton & Rappaport, 1984).

The study of Agarwal and Misra (1986) tried to connect causal attribution to the success and failure as a function of locus of internal-external control and contexts were investigated in females. The results indicated that success was attributed to self, motivation and effort by both internal and externals. However, this tendency was dominant in the externals. Internally controlled subjects made consistent attributions across positive and negative outcomes while externally controlled subjects made situation and context based attributions. It was concluded that internally controlled subjects utilize information processing while externally controlled subjects employ self protective motivational processes in attribution. In the study Singh (1989) explored the possible of religion and sex on the personality characteristics of college going students. The sample comprises 380 adolescent students. The average age of the boys was 17 years and for girls 16 years. Two standardized measuring devices were administered. Main finding indicates that the Muslim students and boys are found to be more alienated and more anxious than Hindu students and girls.

The research of Bruce, Ruut, and Alex (1991) addresses issues of causal direction in research on subjective well being. Previous researchers have generally assumed that such variables as domain satisfactions, social support, life events, and levels of expectation and aspiration are causes of SWB. Critics have pointed out that they could just as well be consequences. In some contexts this has been referred to as the top-down versus bottom-up controversy. The main purpose is to propose a general statistical model which holds promise of resolving this controversy. The model can be used when three or more waves of panel data are available. It is used here to assess causal direction between six domain satisfactions (marriage, work, leisure, standard of living, friendship and health) and SWB. Data are drawn from four waves of an Australian Quality of Life panel survey (1981-1987) with an initial sample size of 942. The available evidence suggests that religion can have both beneficial and detrimental effects on well-being. The different effects of religion and the conditions under which they occur have not yet been delineated in research. Several observers have reported anecdotal evidence that members of fundamentalist religions tend to have high levels of religious guilt and fear (e.g., Barr, 1980; Hartz & Everett, 1989; Strozier, 1994). The usual explanation is that guilt and fear of punishment result from an inability to meet the very high, perhaps unrealistically high, standards of conduct and thought set by the religion. However, as Hood, Spilka, Hunsberger, and Gorsuch (1996, p. 427) note, these anecdotal reports have not been investigated with quantitative comparisons of different religious groups. In addition, religion may possibly provide mechanisms to counteract feelings of fear and guilt.

The study of Ruiz (1998) presented the case of 55 yr old Hispanic American women of Cuban descent presented with major depression which she ascribed to "punishment from God". This case provides an illustration of the role of culture in (1) the conceptualization of mental illness, (2) the manifestation of depressive symptoms through somatization, (3) treatment compliance, and (4) the need to integrate the medical and psychiatric care with religious organizations in certain groups. Ellison & Levin (1998) in their research tried on the volume and quality of research on the religion health connection have increased morbidity. This interest in the complex relationships between religion & mental and physical health is being fueled by energetic and innovations research programs in research fields, including sociology, psychology, health behaviour and health education, psychiatry, gerontology, and social epidemiology. This article has 3 main objectives: (1) to briefly review the medical and epidemiologic research on religions factors and both physical health and mental health; (2) to identify the most promising explanatory mechanisms for religious effects on health, giving particular attention to the relationships between religious factors and the central constructs of the life stress paradigm, which guides most current social and behavioral research on health outcomes; and (3) to critique previous work on religion and health, pointing out limitations and promising new research directions.

According to Richards and Bergin (2000), alienation that existed between the mental health professions and religion for most of the 20 k century is ending. The influence of the naturalistic, antireligious assumptions that once gripped the field lane weakened, and there is now a more spiritually often zeitgeist or "spirit of the times". During the 1990's many articles on religious and spiritual issues in mental health and psychotherapy were published in main stream journals. Numerous presentations on these topics were also given at connections of mental health organizations. Topics include a call for greater competency in religious and spiritual diversity; attitudes and skills of spiritually sensitive and competent therapists; and plan of the book. The study of Mahalik, and Lagan (2001) hypothesized that gender role conflict and stress would predict Catholic seminarian and college-aged men's religiosity and spiritual well-being. To test the hypotheses, 151 mostly Caucasian single men (74 Catholic seminarians, 77 Catholic undergraduate men) completed the Gender Role Conflict Scale, Gender Role Stress Scale, Intrinsic–Extrinsic Religious Orientation Scale—Revised, and the Spiritual Well-Being Scale. Separate canonical correlation analyses for the 2 groups revealed significant relationships between the measures assessing gender role conflict and stress and those assessing religiosity and spiritual well-being. The discussion focuses on limitations, future research, and implications for practice.

The article of Beck (2004) is a theoretical and empirical review attempting to describe two modes of religious motivation: defensive versus existential religion. The article begins by seriously considering theoretical and empirical evidence that religion may function as a defense mechanism. It is argued that this description of religious belief is coherent and cannot be ignored by psychology of religion researchers. However, the article goes on to argue for the existence of a non-defensive, existentially aware religious motivation. Theoretical and empirical support for this model, defensive versus existential religion, is presented. Similarly, Mazumdar (2004), in his claimed that religion can play an important role in place attachment and present a conceptualization of it. We provide an understanding of the role of place in the experience of religious place attachment, describing in detail place, design, aesthetics, and special characteristics that facilitate devotion. Next, we describe how attachment to place is learned through a process of socialization involving rituals, use of artifacts, storytelling, and place visits. We argue that there is an active socializing component to religious place attachment in addition to the experimental one. We conclude with a brief discussion integrating the complex issues of religion, place, identity, and attachment.

A growing body of scientific research suggests connections between religion, spirituality, and both mental and physical health. The findings are particularly strong in patients with severe or chronic illnesses who are having stressful psychological and social changes, as well as existential struggles related to meaning and purpose. Recent studies indicate that religious beliefs influence medical decisions, such as the use of chemotherapy and other life-saving treatments, and at times may conflict with medical care. This article addresses the ways physicians can use such information. Spirituality is an area that makes many physicians uncomfortable, since training in medical schools and continuing medical education programs are limited. Not only do most physicians lack the necessary training, they worry about spending additional time with patients and overstepping ethical boundaries. While these concerns are valid, each can be addressed in a sensible way. Taking a spiritual history, supporting the patient's beliefs, and orchestrating the fulfillment of spiritual needs are among the topics this article will address. The goal is to help physicians provide medical care that is sensitive to the way many patients understand and cope with medical illness (Koenig, 2004).

According to Wenger (2005) explicit cognitions are those that occur with intention and conscious awareness; implicit cognitions occur without such intention and awareness.

Whereas some investigations have demonstrated consistencies between beliefs maintained at these two levels of awareness, others have demonstrated inconsistencies. In the present research, participants performed a speeded response task, a variation of the Implicit Association Test (A.G.Greenwald), to evaluate their implicit identification with intrinsic and extrinsic religious motivation. Also, participants completed a self-report measure to evaluate their corresponding tendencies toward explicit motivations. The results provided evidence for consistency between participant's implicit identification and their explicit identification with intrinsic and extrinsic religious motivations. The finding of this consistency has implications for the relationship between intrinsic religiousness and social-desirability effects.

Recent understanding of subjective well-being suggests that it consists of global judgments of life satisfaction, hedonic experiences, and beliefs about facets of one's life. Traditionally, life satisfaction judgments have been the outcome of interest in studies examining the relationship between religiosity and well-being. Two studies were conducted to look at the interactive effects of personal religious beliefs, namely God images, and environmental stimuli, particularly priming the thought of "God". The first study examines hedonic experiences, which is one of the information sources when constructing a well-being judgment. A second study attempts to replicate the findings with life satisfaction ratings. Results of the first study showed that one's image of God as a controlling or non-controlling entity moderated the affective response to being primed to think about God. In particular, those who had a high controlling image of God had a negative affective reaction to the God prime. Results of the second study replicated the pattern of results using life satisfaction ratings as the dependent variable (Wiegand and Weiss, 2006).

In India's hilly state Himachal Pradesh, the paper of R.S.Ranta and R.S.Pirta, (2007) had explored three North Himalayan villages to understand how community involves the divine factor through the institution of deity for its well-being. The institution of Jamlu in Malana of Kullu district has perhaps a unique democratic system for resolving people's problems but at the same time the community isolates itself through social fencing. Second instance is from the far eastern part of Himachal Pradesh, the Mathi of Chhitkul in Kinnaur district. People in this physically remote village show unique achievement in the indicators modern development through abiding with Hindu and Buddhist religious beliefs. Third example is from a comparatively easily accessible place where the modern horticulture has a significant impact. The apple growers of Banchunch in Shimla district, where the institution of Boindra thrive, revive an old cult of Bhunda yajna for their well-being in a unique show of solidarity between villages over an enormous area.

The paper of Campion and Nurse (2007) tried to presents a public health model of mental health which places wellbeing at its centre and illustrates how wellbeing is influenced by the inter-relationship between risk, protective and environmental factors. This model should encourage a more comprehensive approach to wellbeing promotion and will assist in developing appropriate mental health public health initiatives. METHODS: The model considers how different social and individual risk factors impact negatively upon mental health and how these risk factors can be addressed.

It explores the need for active development of protective factors in order to increase an individual's resilience to deal with stresses of life and the additional input required to promote resilience in those with existing mental health problems. This approach to wellbeing balances addressing risk factors with promoting protective factors and uses a public mental health approach to wellbeing promotion within particular settings and the wider environment, supported by both local-level and regional policy. It also suggests that considerable economic savings could be achieved by implementing such integrated management programmes.

Study conducted by Koo and Fishbach (2010) pointed out that pursuing a series of progressive goals that form a goal ladder often leads to a trade-off between moving up to a more advanced level and repeating the same goal level. Study investigates how monitoring one's current goal in terms of remaining actions versus completed actions influences the desire to move up the goal ladder. The authors proposed that a focus on remaining actions increases the motivation to move up to a more advanced level, whereas the focus on completed actions increases the satisfaction derived from the present level. They find support for these predictions across several goals ladders, ranging from academic and professional ladders to simple, experimental tools. They further find that individuals strategically attend to information about remaining actions to prepare to move up the goal ladder.

In the words of Sasaki and Kim (2011) the religion may help people in maintaining a sense of control, particularly secondary control-acceptance of and adjustment to difficult situations-and contributes to strengthening social relationships in a religious community. However, little is known about how culture may influence these effects. The current research examined the interaction of culture and religion on secondary control and social affiliation, comparing people from individualistic cultures, who tend to be more motivated towards personal agency, and people from collectivistic cultures (e.g. east Asians), who tend to be more motivated to maintain social relationships. Studies showed that experimental priming of religion led to acts of secondary control for European Americans but not Asian Americans. Another study showed that religious coping predicted more secondary control for European Americans but not Koreans, and religious coping predicted more social affiliation for Koreans and European Americans. These findings suggest the importance of understanding socio-cultural moderators for the effects of religion.

From the studies it is quite clear that the men and women in general and educated persons in particular may differ in levels of fear of success, religiosity and wellbeing. The fear of success may be associated with religiosity in general and wellbeing in particular. Similarly religiosity may be associated with their wellbeing. Therefore in the present study an attempt has be made to see the relationship between fear of success, religiosity and wellbeing in terms of magnitude and direction of co-relation on the one hand and on the other the present study tries to see the impact of fear of success and religiosity on the wellbeing. Therefore following hypothesis has been framed:-

3.5 HYPOTHESES

1. There will be a significant difference between employed and unemployed men and women of different castes on the measure of fear of success.

2. There will be a significant difference between employed and unemployed men and women of different caste on the measure of spiritual wellbeing.
3. There will be a significant difference between employed and unemployed men and women of different caste on the measure of wellbeing.
4. The employed and unemployed men and women of different castes will significantly differ in magnitude and direction of co-relation.
5. The fear of success will be positively related to the religiosity and negatively to the wellbeing among the employed and unemployed men and women of four different castes.
6. The religiosity will be positively related to the psychological well being among employed and unemployed men and women of four different castes.
7. There will be a significant impact of fear of success and religiosity on the wellbeing among employed and unemployed men and women of four different castes.

FEAR OF SUCCESS SKILL

The objective of the present study is to assess and compare employed and unemployed men and women of different caste on the measure of fear of success, religiosity and wellbeing. Further, the study intends to find out the relationship in terms of magnitude and direction of co-relation between employed and un-employed men and women of different caste on of fear of success, religiosity and wellbeing. In the same tune, the study also attempt to establish the linkage between fear of success to the religiosity and well being among employed and unemployed men and women of four different caste. In the same tune the linkages of religiosity to the psychological well being among employed and unemployed men and women of four different caste has also been established. Finally, the study intends to see the impact of fear of success and religiosity on the wellbeing of the people of Chopal tehsil of district Shimla of Himachal Pradesh whose description has been given as follows:

4.1 STUDY AREA

Himachal Pradesh is a state in Northern India. *Hima* means snow in Sanskrit, and the literal meaning of the state's name is *In the lap of Himalayas.* It was named by one of the great Sanskrit scholars of Himachal Pradesh, Acharya Diwakar Datt Sharma. Its name means "Abode of Snow· For thousands of years Indians, and especially the Hindus, have looked upon the mighty Himalayas with awe and reverence. For them it is the abode of the gods. There Shiva, the great god of destruction (belonging to the holy Trinity of Creator-Preserver-Destroyer), sat in deep meditation until Parvati, the Himalaya-putri (daughter of the mountains), succeeded in winning his love. Temples of Shiva and Parvati abound in these mountains and thousands of pilgrims from the plains make their arduous climb to them each year. Hindus make up 95% of the state population, making it the most Hindu state (proportionally), in India. It is least urbanized state in India with nearly 90% of population living in rural area with Shimla district being highly urbanized with nearly 25% population living in urban area. Himachal Pradesh is divided into 12 districts namely, Kangra, Hamirpur, Mandi, Bilaspur, Una, Chamba, Lahaul and Spiti, Kinnaur, Kullu, Solan and Shimla. The main communities here are Brahmins, Gujjars, Rathis, Saini, Jats, Rajputs, Gaddis, Dhangar, Ghirth, Kanet, Soods, and Kolis. The population of Himachal Pradesh is a mixed one though Hindus are definitely in majority. The Hindu communities residing in Himachal include the Brahmins, Rajputs, Kannets, Rathis and Kolis. There are also tribal population in the state which mainly comprises Gaddis, Kinnars, Gujjars, Pangawals and Lahaulis. Though Hindi is the state language, many people speak Pahari. Pahari itself has many dialects and all of them trace their origin to the Sanskrit language.

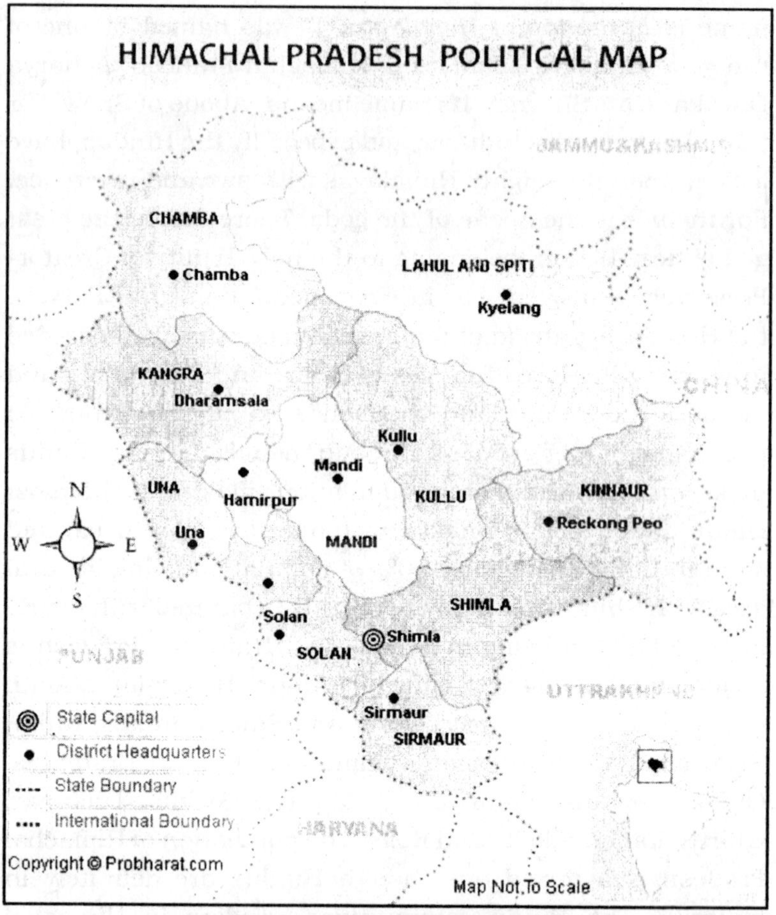

Fig 4.1: Map of Himachal Pradesh

Present study is confined to the Chopal Tehsil of Shimla district of Himachal Pradesh. It is located on the State Highway Number 8. It is approximately 100 km from Shimla and 70 KM from Theog tehsil. It is approachable through road transport buses. The appropriate study site map has also been shown below. More appropriately, the study has been conducted in Ghurla, Khadaran, Bamta, Jhiknipul, Chopal, Deha, Maraog, Devat, Bhabar, and Gagna villages of Chopal tehsil, District Shimla, Himachal Pradesh.

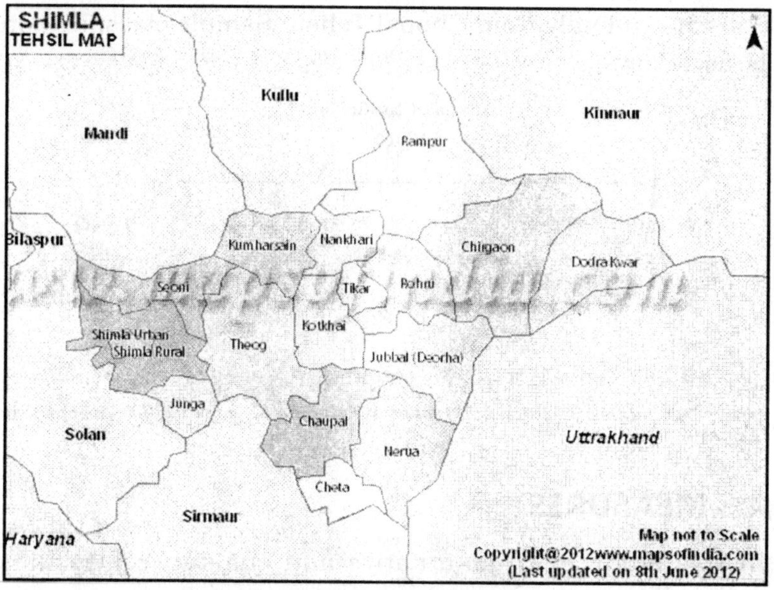

Fig 4.2 Shimla Tehsil map

The boundary of Chopal tehsil is with Theog, Kotkhai, Jubbal and Rohroo. Further the Chopal also touches the boundaries of Uttrakhand.

4.2 SAMPLE

The study has been conducted on a sample of N = 160 people. The sample comprises of equal number of people belonging to Rajput, Thakur, Bhramin, and Harijans castes. More appropriately N = 40 people were taken under each caste those further were subdivided into equal halves based on their employment status. In this manner two groups have been framed that comprises of N = 20 in employment and another N = 20 in un-employment categories. At last these subjects were further subdivided into two more group based on gender that comprises of N = 10 subjects male group and another N = 10 in female group. The sample was chosen randomly from Chopal Tehsil. Sample classification is as follows:

Sample Classification

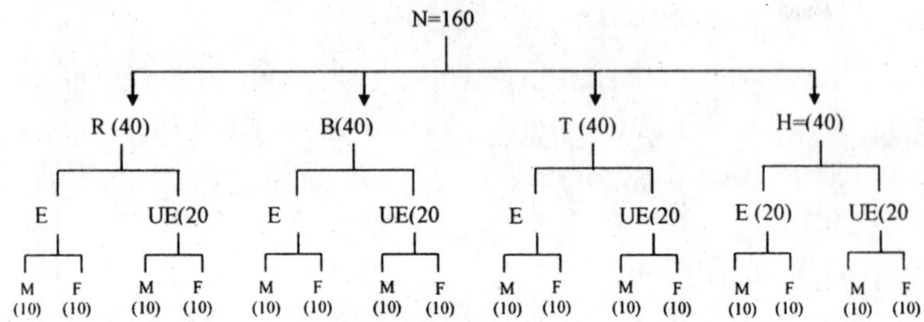

Notations: R=rajput; B=bhramin; T=thakur; H=harigens; E=employed; UE=unemployed; M=males; F=females.

4.3 MEASURES

In this study both quantitative and qualitative measures haves been used. The description is as follows:-

4.3.1 Fear of Success Scale

It was developed by the researcher herself. The items contained in the said scale have been corporate by conducting a pilot study based on the local people. The item that suits to the local people of Chopal district has been incorporated in it. The scale consists of 15 items that has been arranged on a three point scale. The score ranges from minimum of 15 to the maximum of 45.Higher the score more will be fear of success.

4.3.2 Spiritual Well Being Scale

This scale was developed by Craig W. Ellison and F. Raymond in 1982. It is a six point scale that consists of 20 items. It was translated by the researcher herself in Hindi language. The item number 3,4,7,810,11,14,15,17,19 and 20 follow reverse scoring. The score ranges from minimum of 20 to the maximum of 120.Higher the score more will be the spiritual well being.

4.3.3 Satisfaction with Life Scale

It was developed by Diener, Emmons, Loven and Griffin in 1985. It is a short, 5 itemed instrument designed to measure global cognitive judgments on our lives. It was translated into Hindi by Lalit Kumar. It involves 7 point scale that ranges from strongly disagree to strongly agree. More appropriately, it involves the scaling option strongly disagree(1),disagree(2),slightly disagree (3), neither agree nor disagree(4), slightly agree (5),agree (6) and strongly agree (7).The score ranges from minimum of 5 to a maximum of 35.Higher the score more satisfied the people will be in their day to day life.

4.3.4 Short Depression-Happiness Scale

It was developed by Stephan Joseph in 2000. It was translated into Hindi by Dharmander Kumar. It consists of 6 items. It is a 4 point scale. It has three positive items and three negative items. Item number 1, 3 and 6 has reverse scoring. The score ranges from minimum of 0 to maximum of 18.

4.3.5 PGI Health Questionnaire HQ

It was developed by Verma, Wig and Pershad in 1985.It has two sections. Section A consists of 16 questions and section B consists of 22 questions. The score ranges from 0 to 16 in section A and 0 to 22 in section B with a total score of 38.Its reliability ranges from .86 to .88.

4.3.6 Field Observation

It is a fundamental aspect of any science and has been playing an essential part in the development of psychology as a scientific discipline. Observation involves the noting and recording of events and human behavior without formal manipulation of variables operating in the events.

4.3.7 Interview

It is a formal or informal meeting between two or among a group of people for the purpose of obtaining information about something in particular. It is face to face conversation which is always goal directed. It is considered as a successful tool in social sciences research.

4.3.8 Fuzzy Cognitive Mapping (FCM)

Generally the individuals store their own perception in the reality through mental maps. In cognitive maps, the stored concepts are decoded, analyzed and clearly structured through cause and effect relationship, and this is significantly useful both for individual aims (through understanding of complex issues) and in group situations. A cognitive map is constituted by nodes, which represent the concepts and are connected to each other by links (also called edges). The edges are directed to show the direction of cause-effect relationships. The fuzzy cognitive maps developed initially by Kosllo in 1986 and later by Ozesmi in 1999 and 2006 deals with explore cognitive maps of the individuals and groups.

4.3.9 Photography

It is the process of forming stable or permanent visible directly or indirectly by the action of light or other forms of radiation on sensitive surfaces.

4.4 PROCEDURE

Chopal tehsil is located on the state highway number eight. It is approximately 100 km from Shimla. It is approachable only through road transport and personal vehicles. Objective of the present study is to compare employed and unemployed men and women of different caste on the measure of fear of success, religiosity and wellbeing. Further, the study intends to see the relationship between fear of success, religiosity and wellbeing. Finally the study intends to see the impact of both fear of success to the wellbeing. For accomplishing the objective the study has been conducted on sample of 160 people of Chopal tehsil divided into Rajputs, Bhramins, Thakurs, and Harijans (40 in each group). These subjects were further sub-divided into employed and unemployed (20 in each group). Further they were divided into males and females (10) in each group). In all there were sixteen groups in total with 10 subjects in each group that comprising of total sample of 160 people. These sixteen groups were assessed with the help of qualitative and quantitative measures. The qualitative measure include, observation, interview, fuzzy cognitive mapping and photography whereas the quantitative measures include fear of success scale, spiritual well being scale, satisfaction with life scale, short depression-happiness scale and PGI health questionnaire. The quantitative measure is self-report in nature that was administered by the researcher herself by asking open ended questions from the participants. Since the researcher herself belongs to the Chopal tehsil of Shimla district, therefore, it helped her in asking questions to the local people while carrying out descriptive information in a local dialect. Besides this the researcher did her pilot study and asked various people about their experiences and personal feelings about the faith in local deities. The researcher entered in the particular area, by establishing warmth atmosphere with the participants followed with addressing the goal. The ideas elicited by the subjects were welcomed by the researcher and were encouraged to explain more about their experiences, ideas and feelings. A 4 × 2 × 2 way ANOVA has been used besides calculating mean and standard deviation. The score has been tabulated and displayed in the next chapter.

ANALYSIS OF FEAR OF SUCCESS AMONG PEOPLE OF DIFFERENT CASTES

In this chapter an attempt has been made to present the finding based on qualitative and quantitative observation made on the people of Chopal tehsil of district Shimla Himachal Pradesh. In the first section an attempt has been made to present quantitative information whose description is as follows:-

5.1 QUANTITATIVE ANALYSIS

The quantitative analysis has been made by giving various measures to the subjects and the score has been analyzed and interpreted by using appropriate statistics as shown below.

5.1.1 Analysis of Fear of Success among People of Different Castes

Fear of success or success phobia has been studied from classical and relational psychoanalysis to social and cognitive psychology. Psychoanalytic theories believe unconscious forces are at work. Other explanations emphasize conscious and environmental influences. Three major groups that evoked the most interest were students, vocations, gender and sex. Top executive may develop a success neurosis because of the "loneliness of command" brought on by isolation at the top. Feminists argued that women are reacting to stereotypes that inhibit females.

Table 5.1 A 4 × 2 × 2 ANOVA Performed on Fear of Success among Employed and Unemployed Men and Women of Four Different Castes

Source	*SS*	*df*	*Ms*	*F*	*p*
Total	1209927.00	159			
C	4202.819	3	1400.94	28.83	<.01
E	82.656	1	82.656	1.70	n.s.
S	693.056	1	693.056	14.24	<.01
C x E	226.519	3	75.506	1.55	n.s.
C x S	29.519	3	9.840	.203	n.s.
E x S	.056	1	.056	.001	n.s.
C x E x S	16.819	3	5.606	.115	n.s.
Error	6996.500	144			

Notations: C= Caste; E= Employed; S=Sex

From the table 5.1 it is quite clear that the main effect of Caste on the measure of Fear of success was found F (3, 144) = 28.83, p<.01 as statistically significant. The Harijan people reported more fear of success (M = 28.65) as compared to their other three counterparts. *Therefore hypothesis one which states that "There will be a significant difference between employed and unemployed men and women of different castes on the measure of fear of success' is accepted.* But the main effect of Employment on the measure of Fear of success was found F (1, 144) = 1.70, p>.05 as statistically non-significant. The main effect of Sex on the measure of Fear of success was found F (1, 144) = 14.24, p<.01 as statistically significant. The female reported more fear of success as compared to their counterpart that clear from the average score 27.35 as shown in the table 6.1 in the sixth chapter. *Therefore hypothesis one which states that "There will be a significant difference between employed and unemployed men and women of different castes on the measure of fear of successes" is accepted.* The two way interaction between Caste x Employment on the measure of Fear of success was found $F(3, 144) = 1.55$, $p > .05$ as statistically non- significant. Similarly the two way interaction between Caste x Sex on the measure of Fear of success was found $F(3, 144) = .203$, $p > .05$ as statistically non significant. The two way interaction between Employment x Sex on the measure of Fear of success was found $F(1, 144) = .001$, $p > .05$ as statistically non significant. Finally the three way interaction between Caste x Employment x Sex on the measure of Fear of success was found $F(3,144) = .115$, $p > .05$ as statistically non significant.

5.1.2 Analysis of Spiritual Wellbeing among People of Different Castes

The spirituality refers to experience of a deep seated sense of meaning and purpose in life together with a sense of belonging. It is about acceptance, integration and wholeness. The spiritual wellbeing is an integral part of mental, emotional and physical health. It is considered to be a primary coping resource on the journey of recovery and healing. The spirituality and faith provide an opportunity to detach from circumstances and observe life with clarity and integrity. It can either be positive or negative. Similarly, the religiosity refers to the possession by a person or group of some inner spiritual piety that may or may not lead on to attachment to a religious practice or a pre-defined set of beliefs but have some outward social impact. It refers to the numerous aspects of religious activity, dedication, and belief (religious doctrine). In its narrowest sense, religiosity deals more with how religious a person is, and less with how a person is religious (in practicing certain rituals, retelling certain myths, revering certain symbols, or accepting certain doctrines about deities and afterlife). The analysis performed to know spirituality is as follow

Table 5.2 A 4 × 2 × 2 ANOVA Performed on Spiritual Wellbeing among Employed and Unemployed Men and Women of Four Different Castes

Source	*SS*	*df*	*Ms*	*F*	*p*
Total	113493.00	159			
C	487.719	3	162.573	7.389	<.01
E	452.256	1	452.256	20.555	<.01
S	294.306	1	294.306	13.376	<.01
C x E	834.069	3	278.023	12.636	<.01
C x S	34.419	3	11.473	.521	n.s
E x S	.156	1	.156	.007	n.s
C x E x S	9.769	3	3.256	.148	n.s
Error	3168.300	144			

Notations: C=Caste; E=Employment; S=Sex

From the table 5.2 it is quite clear that the main effect of Caste on the measure of Spiritual Wellbeing was found F (3, 144) = 7.39, p<.01 as statistically significant. Thakur reported more wellbeing (M = 90.13) as compared to other caste people counterpart. *Therefore hypothesis two which states that "There will be a significant difference between employed and unemployed men and women of different caste on the measure of spiritual wellbeing" is accepted.* Similarly the main effect of Employment on the measure of Spiritual Wellbeing was found F (1, 144) = 20.56, p<.01 as statistically significant. Employed people reported more spiritual wellbeing (M = 87.24) as compared to their counterpart. *Therefore hypothesis two which states that "There will be a significant difference between employed and unemployed men and women of different caste on the measure of spiritual wellbeing"* got accepted. The main effect of Sex on the measure of Spiritual Wellbeing was found F (1, 144) = 13.38, p<.01 as statistically significant. Male reported more religiosity (M = 88.6) as compared to the female. *Therefore hypothesis two which states that "There will be a significant difference between employed and unemployed men and women of different caste on the measure of spiritual wellbeing" is accepted.* The two way interaction between Caste x Employment on the measure of Spiritual wellbeing was found F (3, 144) =12.636, p<.01 as statistically significant. But the two way interaction between Caste x Sex on the measure of Spiritual Wellbeing was found F (3, 144) =.521, p>.05 as statistically non- significant. Similarly the two way interaction between Employment x Sex on the measure of Spiritual Wellbeing was found F (1, 144) = .007, p>.05 as statistically non-significant. Finally the three way interaction between Caste x Employment x Sex on the measure of Spiritual Wellbeing was found F (3,144) = .148, p>.05 as statistically non significant.

5.1.3 Analysis of Life Satisfaction among People of Different Castes

Life satisfaction refers to how people evaluate their life as a whole rather than their current feelings. It captures a reflective assessment of which life circumstances and conditions are improved for subjective wellbeing. It ranges from positive to negative affect. The satisfaction is a Latin word that means to make or do enough. Satisfaction with one's life implies contentment with or acceptance of one's life circumstances, or the fulfillment of one's wants and needs for one's life as a whole. In essence, life satisfaction is a subjective assessment of the quality of one's life. Because it is inherently an evaluation, judgments of life satisfaction have a large cognitive component. Subjective wellbeing or happiness has both an affective and a cognitive (i.e. for judgmental) component. The affective component consists of how frequently an individual reports experiencing positive and negative affect. It is considered to be the cognitive component of this broader construct. Researchers differentiate between life-domain satisfaction and life as a whole (or global) life satisfaction. Life-domain dealt with specific areas of an individual's life, such as work, marriage, and income, whereas judgments of global life satisfaction are much more broad, consisting of an individual's comprehensive judgment of her life. The analysis is as follows:

Table 5.3 A 4 x 2 x 2 ANOVA Performed on Satisfaction with Life among Employed and Unemployed Men and Women of Four Different Castes

Source	*SS*	*df*	*ms*	*F*	*p*
Total	113006.000	159			
C	283.050	3	94.350	12.39	<.01
E	10.000	1	10.000	1.313	n.s
S	448.900	1	448.900	58.926	<.01
C x E	31.150	3	10.383	1.363	n.s
C x S	22.250	3	7.417	.974	n.s
E x S	16.900	1	16.900	2.218	n.s
C x E x S	5.150	3	1.717	.225	n.s
Error	1097.000	144			

Notations: C=Caste; E=Employment; S=Sex

From the table 5.3 it is quite clear that the main effect of Caste on the measure of Satisfaction with Life was found F (3, 144) = 12.39, p<.01 as statistically significant. Thakur reported more satisfaction with life as compared to other caste. *Therefore hypothesis three which states that "There will be a significant difference between employed and unemployed men and women of different caste on the dimensions of wellbeing" got accepted.* But the main effect of Employment on the measure of Satisfaction with Life was found F (1, 144) = 1.31, p>.05 as statistically non- significant. The main effect of Sex on the measure of Satisfaction with Life was found F (1, 144) = 58.93, p<.01 as statistically significant. *Therefore hypothesis three which states that "There will be a significant difference between employed and unemployed men and women of different caste on the dimensions of wellbeing" got accepted.* Male reported more satisfaction from their life as compared to the female. The two way interaction between Caste x Employment on the measure of Satisfaction with Life was found F (3, 144) =1.36, p>.05 as statistically non- significant. Similarly the two way interaction between Caste x Sex on the measure of Satisfaction with Life was found F (3, 144) =.974, p>.05 as statistically non significant. The two way interaction between Employment x Sex on the measure of Satisfaction with Life was found F (1, 144) = 2.22, p>.05 as statistically non significant. Finally the three way interaction between Caste x Employment x Sex on the measure of Satisfaction with Life was found F (3,144) = .225, p>.05 as statistically non significant.

5.1.4 Analysis of Happiness and Depression among People of Different Castes

Happiness is commonly defined as a state of wellbeing that is commonly associated with feelings good or experiencing pleasure. Understanding happiness and related positive mental states involves the study of contentment with the past, happiness in the present and hope for the future. There is not one key that can lead to happiness and life satisfaction; instead, multiple components are involved in finding happiness. This is similar to having different ingredients in a recipe for happiness. The social relationship can greatly influence your happiness. People who have close relationship with family and friend tend to have greater life satisfaction and happiness. More appropriately, the happiness is not just the absence of depression, but also the presence of number of positive emotional and cognitive states. But the depression deals with severe despondency and dejection, accompanied by feelings of hopelessness and inadequacy. A condition of mental disturbance, typically with lack of energy and difficulty in maintaining concentration or interest in life. The happiness depression analyses have been shown in table 5.4.

Table 5.4 A 4 x 2 x 2 ANOVA Performed on Depression-Happiness Parameters among Employed and Unemployed Men and Women of Four Different Castes

Source	*SS*	*df*	*Ms*	*F*	*p*
Total	30943.000	159			
C	6.119	3	2.040	.573	n.s
E	.506	1	.506	.142	n.s
S	10.506	1	10.506	2.951	<.01
C x E	102.219	3	34.073	9.570	<.01
C x S	25.819	3	8.606	2.417	<.01
E x S	18.906	1	18.906	5.310	<.01
C x E x S	43.719	3	14.573	4.093	<.01
Error	512.700	144			

Notations: C=Caste; E=Employment; S=Sex

From the table 5.4 it is quite clear that the main effect of Caste on the measure of Depression-Happiness Parameters was found F (3, 144) = .573, p>.05 as statistically non-significant. Similarly the main effect of Employment on the measure of Depression-Happiness Parameters was found F (1, 144) = .142, p>.05 as statistically non- significant. The main effect of Sex on the measure of Depression-Happiness Parameters was found F (1, 144) = 2.951, p<.01 as statistically significant. Male reported more depression as compared to the female. *Therefore hypothesis three which states that "There will be a significant difference between employed and unemployed men and women of different caste on the dimensions of wellbeing" got accepted.* The two way interaction between Caste x Employment on the measure of Depression-Happiness Parameters was found F (3, 144) =9.57, p<.01 as statistically significant. *Therefore hypothesis No. 3 which states that "There will be a significant difference between employed and unemployed men and women of different caste on the dimensions of wellbeing" got accepted.* Similarly the two way interaction between Caste x Sex on the measure of Depression-Happiness Parameters was found F (3, 144) =2.42, p<.01 as statistically significant. *Therefore hypothesis three which states that "There will be a significant difference between employed and unemployed men and women of different caste on the dimensions of wellbeing" got accepted.* The two way interaction between Employment x Sex on the measure of Depression-Happiness Parameters was found F (1, 144) = 5.31, p<.01 as statistically significant. Finally the three way interaction between Caste x Employment x Sex on the measure of Depression-Happiness Parameters was found F (3,144) = 4.09, p<.01 as statistically significant. *Therefore hypothesis three which states that "There will be a significant difference between employed and unemployed men and women of different caste on the dimensions of wellbeing" got accepted.*

5.1.5 Appraisal of Health

Health is a state of complete physical, mental and social wellbeing of a person and not merely the absence of disease or infirmity. Mental health describes either a level of cognitive or emotional wellbeing or an absence of a mental disorder. From perspectives of the discipline of positive psychology or holism mental health may include an individual's ability to enjoy life and procure a balance between life activities and efforts to achieve psychological resilience. It is an expression of emotions and signifies a successful adaptation to a range of demands. The World Health Organization defines mental health as "a state of wellbeing in which the individual realizes his or her own abilities, can cope with the normal stresses of life, can work productively and fruitfully, and is able to make a contribution to his or her community". It was previously stated that there was no one "official" definition of mental health. Cultural differences, subjective assessments, and competing professional theories all affect how "mental health" is defined. There are different types of mental health problems, some of which are common, such as depression and anxiety disorders, and some not so common, such as schizophrenia and bipolar disorders. The analysis performed on general health is as follows:

Table 5.5 A 4 x 2 x 2 ANOVA Performed on PGI HQ-health total (area A+ B) among Employed and Unemployed Men and Women of Four Different Castes

Source	*SS*	*df*	*ms*	*F*	*p*
Total	22287.000	159			
C	336.819	3	112.273	8.792	<.01
E	15.006	1	15.006	1.175	n.s
S	1107.756	1	1107.756	86.746	<.01
C x E	38.569	3	12.856	1.007	n.s
C x S	17.319	3	5.773	.452	n.s
E x S	.056	1	.056	.004	n.s
C x E x S	31.819	3	10.606	.831	n.s
Error	1838.900	144			

Notations: C=Caste; E=Employment; S=Sex

From the table 5.5 it is quite clear that the main effect of Caste on the measure of PGI HQ-Total was found F (3, 144) = 8.792, p<.01 as statistically significant. The Harijan people were found poor in health (M = 13.03). *Therefore hypothesis No. 3 which states that "There will be a significant difference between employed and unemployed men and women of different caste on the dimensions of wellbeing" got accepted.* But the main effect of Employment on the measure of PGI HQ-Total was found F (1, 144) = 1.175, p>.05 as statistically non- significant. The main effect of Sex on the measure of PGI HQ-Total was found F (1, 144) = 86.746, p<.01 as statistically significant. *Therefore hypothesis No. 3 which states that "There will be a significant difference between employed and unemployed men and women of different caste on the dimensions of wellbeing" got accepted.* Female reported poor health (12.25) as compared to male. The two way interaction between Caste x Employment on the measure of PGI HQ-Total was found F (3, 144) =1.007, p>.05 as statistically non-significant. Similarly the two way interaction between Caste x Sex on the measure of PGI HQ-Total was found F (3, 144) =.452, p>.05 as statistically non-significant. In the same way the two way interaction between Employment x Sex on the measure of PGI HQ-Total was found F (1, 144) = .004, p>.05 as statistically non-significant. Finally the three way interaction between Caste x Employment x Sex on the measure of PGI HQ-Total was found F (3,144) = .831, p>.05 as statistically non-significant.

Table 5.6 A 4 x 2 x 2 ANOVA Performed on PGI HQ-health questionnaire Area-A among Employed and Unemployed Men and Women of Four Different Castes

Source	***SS***	***df***	***ms***	***F***	***p***
Total	4738.000	159			
C	65.325	3	21.775	4.980	<.01
E	4.225	1	4.225	.966	n.s
S	225.625	1	225.625	51.604	<.01
C x E	36.225	3	12.075	2.762	<.01
C x S	15.725	3	5.242	1.199	n.s
E x S	.625	1	.625	.143	n.s
C x E x S	16.425	3	5.475	1.252	n.s
Error	629.600	144			

Notations: C=Caste; E=Employment; S=Sex

From the table 5.6 it is quite clear that the main effect of Caste on the measure of PGI HQ-A was found F (3, 144) = 4.98, p<.01 as statistically significant. The Brahmin here reported more health problem (M = 5.85) as compared to their counterpart. *Therefore hypothesis three which states that "There will be significant difference between employed and unemployed men and women of different caste on the dimensions of wellbeing" is accepted.* But the main effect of Employment on the measure of PGI HQ-A was found F (1, 144) = .966, p>.05 as statistically non- significant. The main effect of Sex on the measure of PGI HQ-A was found F (1, 144) = 51.604, p<.01 as statistically significant. *Therefore hypothesis three which states that "There will be a significant difference between employed and unemployed men and women of different caste on the dimensions of wellbeing" got accepted.* The female reported more health problem as compared to the male. Similarly the two way interaction between Caste x Employment on the measure of PGI HQ-A was found F (3, 144) =2.76, p<.01 as statistically significant. *Therefore hypothesis three which states that "There will be a significant difference between employed and unemployed men and women of different caste on the dimensions of wellbeing" is accepted.* The two way interaction between Caste x Sex on the measure of PGI HQ-A was found F (3, 144) =1.199, p>.05 as statistically non-significant. In the same way the two way interaction between Employment x Sex on the measure of PGI HQ-A was found F (1, 144)= .143, p>.05 as statistically non-significant. Finally the three way interaction between Caste x Employment x Sex on the measure of PGI HQ-A was found F (3,144) = 1.25, p>.05 as statistically non-significant.

Table 5.7 A 4 x 2 x 2 ANOVA Performed on PGI HQ-health questionnaire Area-B among Employed and Unemployed Men and Women of Four Different Castes

Source	***SS***	***df***	***ms***	***F***	***p***
Total	7407.000	159			
C	163.169	3	54.390	7.907	<.01
E	3.306	1	3.306	.481	n.s
S	333.506	1	333.506	48.486	<.01

Source	SS	df	ms	F	p
C x E	33.619	3	11.206	1.629	n.s
C x S	21.019	3	7.006	1.019	n.s
E x S	.306	1	.306	.045	n.s
C x E x S	41.419	3	13.806	2.007	n.s
Error	990.500	144			

Notations: C=Caste; E=Employment; S=Sex

From the table 5.7 it is quite clear that the main effect of Caste on the measure of PGI HQ-B was found F (3, 144) = 7.907, p<.01 as statistically significant. The Harijan reported more health problem (7.75) as compared to their counterpart. *Therefore hypothesis No. 3 which states that "There will be significant difference between employed and unemployed men and women of different caste on the dimensions of wellbeing" is accepted.* But the main effect of Employment on the measure of PGI HQ-B was found F (1, 144) = .481, p>.05 as statistically non- significant. The main effect of Sex on the measure of PGI HQ-B was found F (1, 144) = 48.486, p<.01 as statistically significant. The female reported more health problem as compared to their counterpart. *Therefore hypothesis No. 3 which states that "There will be a significant difference between employed and unemployed men and women of different caste on the dimensions of wellbeing" is accepted.* The two way interaction between Caste x Employment on the measure of PGI HQ-B was found F (3, 144) =1.629, p>.05 as statistically non-significant. Similarly the two way interaction between Caste x Sex on the measure of PGI HQ-B was found F (3, 144) =1.019, p>.05 as statistically non-significant. In the same way the two way interaction between Employment x Sex on the measure of PGI HQ-B was found F (1, 144) = .045, p>.05 as statistically non-significant. Finally the three way interaction between Caste x Employment x Sex on the measure of PGI HQ-B was found F (3,144) = 2.007, p>.05 as statistically non- significant.

5.1.6 Co-relation of each group among different measures used

Table 5.8 Relationship of Fear of Success, Spiritual Wellbeing to the Dimension of Wellbeing among Rajput Male

	SWL	SDH	GHA	GHB	GHT
FOS	-.192	.428	-.447	-.015	-.441
SW	.010	.364	-.515	.390	-.193

Notations: FOS= fear of success; SW= spiritual wellbeing; SWL= satisfaction with life; SDH= short depression-happiness; GHA= general health A; GHB= general health B; GHT= general health total.

As clearly seen in the table there is no significant difference in any of the measures used.

Table 5.9 Relationship of Fear of Success, Spiritual Wellbeing to the Dimension of Wellbeing among Rajput Female

	SWL	SDH	GHA	GHB	GHT
FOS	.642*	-.041	.437	.012	.293
SW	.523	.167	.593	-.337	.101

Notations: FOS= fear of success; SW= spiritual wellbeing; SWL= satisfaction with life; SDH= short depression-happiness; GHA= general health A; GHB= general health B; GHT= general health total.

It can be seen that fear of success and satisfaction with life measures have positive co-relation among each other as r=.642, p<.05 so they as statistically significant; rest no measure show significant difference. *Therefore hypothesis No 5 which states that "The fear of success will be positively related to the religiosity and negatively to the wellbeing among the employed and unemployed men and women of four different castes" got rejected.*

Table 5.10 Relationship of Fear of Success, Spiritual Wellbeing to the Dimension of Wellbeing among Un-employed Rajput Male

	SWL	SDH	GHA	GHB	GHT
FOS	.055	.114	-.396	.483	.094
SW	-.111	.305	.424	-.156	.260

Notations: FOS= fear of success; SW= spiritual wellbeing; SWL= satisfaction with life; SDH= short depression-happiness; GHA= general health A; GHB= general health B; GHT= general health total.

As clearly seen in the table there is no significant difference in any of the measures used.

Table 5.11 Relationship of Fear of Success, Spiritual Wellbeing to the Dimension of Wellbeing among Un-Employed Rajput Female

	SWL	SDH	GHA	GHB	GHT
FOS	-.152	-.461	-.221	-.778**	-.624
SW	.290	.455	-.222	.101	-.032

Notations: FOS= fear of success; SW= spiritual wellbeing; SWL= satisfaction with life; SDH= short depression-happiness; GHA= general health A; GHB= general health B; GHT= general health total.

From the table it is clear that only there is a negative co-relation between fear of success and general health-b as $r = —.778$, $p<.01$ as statistically significant. *Therefore hypothesis five which states that the fear of success will be positively related to the religiosity and negatively to the wellbeing among the employed and unemployed men and women of four different castes got partially accepted.*

Table 5.12 Relationship of Fear of Success, Spiritual Wellbeing to the Dimension of Wellbeing among Employed Bhramin Male

	SWL	SDH	GHA	GHB	GHT
FOS	.013	-.210	.334	.190	.338
SW	-.074	-.087	-.301	-.488	-.518

Notations: FOS= fear of success; SW= spiritual wellbeing; SWL= satisfaction with life; SDH= short depression-happiness; GHA= general health A; GHB= general health B; GHT= general health total.

As clearly seen in the table there is no significant difference in any of the measures used. *Therefore none of the hypothesis got accepted.*

Table 5.13 Relationship of Fear of Success, Spiritual Wellbeing to the Dimension of Wellbeing among Employed Bhramin Female

	SWL	SDH	GHA	GHB	GHT
FOS	.049	.088	.221	.310	.586
SW	-.677*	.355	.078	.303	.429

Notations: FOS = fear of success; SW = spiritual wellbeing; SWL= satisfaction with life; SDH= short depression-happiness; GHA= general health A; GHB = general health B; GHT = general health total.

It is clear that $r = —.677$, $p<.05$ as statistically significant, therefore spiritual wellbeing and satisfaction with life have are negatively correlated with each other. Rest there is no significant difference between any measures. *Therefore only hypothesis six which states that "The religiosity will be positively related to the psychological well being among employed and unemployed men and women of four different castes" is rejected.*

Table 5.14 Relationship of Fear of Success, Spiritual Wellbeing to the Dimension of Wellbeing among Un-Employed Bhramin Male

	SWL	SDH	GHA	GHB	GHT
FOS	.247	-.310	.357	.064	.249
SW	.325	.191	-.389	-.174	-.335

Notations: FOS= fear of success; SW= spiritual wellbeing; SWL= satisfaction with life; SDH= short depression-happiness; GHA= general health A; GHB= general health B; GHT= general health total.

As clearly seen in the table there is no significant difference in any of the measures used. *Therefore, none of the hypothesis got accepted.*

Table 5.15 Relationship of Fear of Success, Spiritual Wellbeing to the Dimension of Wellbeing among Un-Employed Bhramin Female

	SWL	SDH	GHA	GHB	GHT
FOS	..375	-.777**	.180	.189	271
SW	-.383	.011	-.177	-.118	-.221

Notations: FOS= fear of success; SW= spiritual wellbeing; SWL= satisfaction with life; SDH= short depression-happiness; GHA= general health A; GHB= general health B; GHT= general health total.

It can be seen that there is a negative co-relation between fear of success and short depression-happiness as r= -.777, p <.01 as statistically significant. Rest no measure have significant difference. *Therefore hypothesis five which states that the fear of success will be positively related to the religiosity and negatively to the wellbeing among the employed and unemployed men and women of four different castes got partially accepted.*

Table 5.16 Relationship of Fear of Success, Spiritual Wellbeing to the Dimension of Wellbeing among Employed Thakur Male

	SWL	SDH	GHA	GHB	GHT
FOS	-.718*	.023	-.353	-.109	-.311
SW	-.226	-.626	.214	.356	.330

Notations: FOS= fear of success; SW= spiritual wellbeing; SWL= satisfaction with life; SDH= short depression-happiness; GHA= general health A; GHB= general health B; GHT= general health total.

It is clearly seen that fear of success and satisfaction with life have negative co-relation as r = -.718, p<.05 as statistically significant. Other no measures show positive co-relation. *Therefore hypothesis five which states that "The fear of success will be positively related to the religiosity and negatively to the wellbeing among the employed and unemployed men and women of four different castes" got accepted and other are rejected.*

Table 5.17 Relationship of Fear of Success, Spiritual Wellbeing to the Dimension of Wellbeing among Employed Thakur Female

	SWL	SDH	GHA	GHB	GHT
FOS	-.305	-.471	-.485	.679*	.554
SW	.234	.285	.305	-.090	.011

Notations: FOS= fear of success; SW= spiritual wellbeing; SWL= satisfaction with life; SDH= short depression-happiness; GHA= general health A; GHB= general health B; GHT= general health total.

It can be seen that fear of success and general health-B have positive co-relation as r=.679, p=<.05 as statistically significant and no other measure have significant difference. *Therefore hypothesis five which states that "The fear of success will be positively related to the religiosity and negatively to the wellbeing among the employed and unemployed men and women of four different castes" has been rejected.*

Table 5.18 Relationship of Fear of Success, Spiritual Wellbeing to the Dimension of Wellbeing among Un-Employed Thakur Male

	SWL	SDH	GHA	GHB	GHT
FOS	-.626	.624	-.128	-.364	-.299
SW	-.035	-.290	.196	.650*	.512

Notations: FOS= fear of success; SW= spiritual wellbeing; SWL= satisfaction with life; SDH= short depression-happiness; GHA= general health A; GHB= general health B; GHT= general health total.

There is a positive co-relation between spiritual wellbeing scale and general health-b as r=.650, p<.05 as statistically significant. Rest no other measure show significant difference. *Therefore only hypothesis six which states that "The religiosity will be positively related to the psychological well being among employed and unemployed men and women of four different castes" got accepted while other as rejected.*

Table 5.19 Relationship of Fear of Success, Spiritual Wellbeing to the Dimension of Wellbeing among Un-Employed Thakur Female

	SWL	SDH	GHA	GHB	GHT
FOS	-.441	-.754*	.136	.323	.362
SW	.102	.021	.685*	-.273	.058

Notations: FOS= fear of success; SW= spiritual wellbeing; SWL= satisfaction with life; SDH= short depression-happiness; GHA= general health A; GHB= general health B; GHT= general health total.

It can be seen that fear of success and short depression-happiness have a negative co-relation as r = -.754, p<.05

as statistically significant and spiritual wellbeing and general health-a have a positive co-relation as r=.685, p<.05 as statistically significant. *Therefore hypothesis No. 5 which states that "The fear of success will be positively related to the religiosity and negatively to the wellbeing among the employed and unemployed men and women of four different castes" has been accepted and hypothesis No. 6 which states that "The religiosity will be positively related to the psychological well being among employed and unemployed men and women of four different castes" is also accepted.*

Table 5.20 Relationship of Fear of Success, Spiritual Wellbeing to the Dimension of Wellbeing among Employed Harijan Male

	SWL	SDH	GHA	GHB	GHT
FOS	-.412	-.121	.105	-.039	.041
SW	.372	.000	-.556	-.145	-.474

Notations: FOS= fear of success; SW= spiritual wellbeing; SWL= satisfaction with life; SDH= short depression-happiness; GHA= general health A; GHB= general health B; GHT= general health total.

As clearly seen in the table there is no significant difference in any of the measures used. Here *none of the hypotheses have been accepted.*

Table 5.21 Relationship of Fear of Success, Spiritual Wellbeing to the Dimension of Wellbeing among Employed Harijan Female

	SWL	SDH	GHA	GHB	GHT
FOS	-.088	-.115	-.451	-.300	-.481
SW	.233	.829**	.291	-.034	.143

Notations: FOS= fear of success; SW= spiritual wellbeing; SWL= satisfaction with life; SDH= short depression-happiness; GHA= general health A; GHB= general health B; GHT= general health total.

It can be clearly seen that spiritual wellbeing and short depression-happiness have positive co-relation as r= .829, p <.01 as statistically significant. Rest no other measure have positive co-relation. *Here hypothesis six which states that "The religiosity will be positively related to the psychological well being among employed and unemployed men and women of four different castes" has been accepted.*

Table 5.22 Relationship of Fear of Success, Spiritual Wellbeing to the Dimension of Wellbeing among Un-Employed Harijan Male

	SWL	SDH	GHA	GHB	GHT
FOS	-.673*	-.814**	.379	.374	.550
SW	.569	.453	.143	-.561	-.396

Notations: FOS= fear of success; SW= spiritual wellbeing; SWL= satisfaction with life; SDH= short depression-happiness; GHA= general health A; GHB= general health B; GHT= general health total.

It is clear that fear of success and satisfaction with life have negative co-relation as r= -.673, p<.05 as statistically significant and even fear of success and short depression-happiness have negative co-relation as r = -.814, p<.01 as statistically significant and rest no other measure had positive co-relation. *Here hypothesis five which states that "The fear of success will be positively related to the religiosity and negatively to the wellbeing among the employed and unemployed men and women of four different castes" has been accepted.*

Table 5.23 Relationship of Fear of Success, Spiritual Wellbeing to the Dimension of Wellbeing among Un-Employed Harijan Female

	SWL	SDH	GHA	GHB	GHT
FOS	-.426	-.550	.377	.374	.426
SW	.940**	.918**	-.546	-.567	-.636*

Notations: FOS= fear of success; SW= spiritual wellbeing; SWL= satisfaction with life; SDH= short depression-happiness; GHA= general health A; GHB= general health B; GHT= general health total.

It is clear from the table that spiritual wellbeing and satisfaction with life have positive co-relation as r =.940, p<.01 as statistically significant. Similarly spiritual wellbeing and short depression-happiness have positive co-relation as r=.918, p<.01 as statistically significant *therefore hypothesis No. 6 which states that "The religiosity will be positively related to the psychological well being among employed and unemployed men and women of four different castes" has been accepted.* As spiritual wellbeing and general health-total have negative co-relation as r= -.636, p<.05 as statistically significant, *here hypothesis six which states that "The religiosity will be positively related to the psychological well being among employed and unemployed men and women of four different castes" is rejected.*

Therefore hypothesis four "the employed and un-employed men and women of different castes will significantly differ in magnitude and direction of co-relation" is accepted; as in some cases the co-relation is positive and somewhere negative.

5.1.7 Regression on groups on different measures used

Table 5.24 Regression Analysis performed on Rajput Employed Female in order to see the impact of Fear of Success on Satisfaction with Life

Predictor/ Independent variable	Dependent variable	R (VARIANCE)	R2	R2 Change	R2 Weight	t	F	p
Fear of success	SWL	.642	.413	.413	.642	3.79	5.62	P<.05

Notations: SWL= satisfaction with life

From the table it is quite clear that the main effect of fear of success on the dependent variable satisfaction with life was found as statistically significant F= 5.62, p< .05. The beta weight .642 also supports the same. In this group these factors exerted much influence that is also clearly visible from the higher variance R2 Change= .413. The t-value 3.79, p<.05 also revealed significant difference. *Therefore hypothesis No. 7 which states that "There will be a significant impact of fear of success and religiosity on the wellbeing of employed and unemployed men and women of four different castes" got accepted.*

Table 5.25 Regression Analysis performed on Rajput Un-Employed Female in order to see the impact of Fear of Success on General Health (B)

Predictor/ Independent variable	Dependent variable	R (VARIANCE)	R2	R2 Change	R2 Weight	t	F	p
Fear of success	PGI-B	.778	.605	.605	-.778	4.97	12.27	P<.01

From the table it is quite clear that the main effect of fear of success on the dependent variable PGI-B(general health) was found as statistically significant F= 12.27, p< .01. *The hypothesis seven "There will be a significant impact of fear of success and religiosity on the wellbeing of employed and unemployed men and women of four different castes" got accepted.* The beta weight -.778 also supports the same.

Table 5.26 Regression Analysis performed on Bhramin Employed Female in order to see the impact of Spirituality on Satisfaction with Life

Predictor/ Independent variable	Dependent variable	R (VARIANCE)	R2	R2 Change	R2 Weight	t	F	p
Spiritual wellbeing	SWL	.677	.459	.459	-.677	8.76	6.78	P<.05

Notations: SWL= satisfaction with life

In this group these factors exerted much influence that is also clearly visible from the higher variance R2 Change= .605. The t-value 4.97, p<.01 also revealed significant difference.

From the table it is quite clear that the main effect of spiritual wellbeing on the dependent variable satisfaction with life was found as statistically significant F= 6.78, p< .05. The beta weight -.677 also supports the same. In this group these factors exerted much influence that is also clearly visible from the higher variance R2 Change= .459. The t-value 8.76, p<.05 also revealed significant difference. *So hypothesis seven "There will be a significant impact of fear of success and religiosity on the wellbeing of employed and unemployed men and women of four different castes" got accepted.*

Table 5.27 Regression Analysis performed on Bhramin Un-Employed Female in order to see the impact of Fear of Success on Depression-Happiness Parameter

Predictor/ Independent variable	Dependent variable	R (VARIANCE)	R2	R2 Change	R2 Weight	t	F	p
Fear of success	SDH	.777	.604	.604	-.777	16.23	12.19	P<.01

Notations: SDH= short depression-happiness

From the table it is quite clear that the main effect of fear of success on the dependent variable short depression-happiness was found as statistically significant F= 12.19, p< .01. The beta weight -.777 also supports the same. In this group these factors exerted much influence that is also clearly visible from the higher variance R2 Change= .604. The t-value 16.23, p<.05 also revealed significant difference. *The hypothesis seven "There will be a significant impact of fear of success and religiosity on the wellbeing of employed and unemployed men and women of four different castes" got accepted.*

Table 5.28 Regression Analysis performed on Thakur Employed Male in order to see the impact of Fear of Success on Satisfaction with Life

Predictor/ Independent variable	Dependent variable	R (VARIANCE)	R2	R2 Change	R2 Weight	t	F	p
Fear of success	SWL	.718	.515	.515	-.718	11.04	8.51	P<.01

Notations: SWL = satisfaction with life

From this table it is clear that the main effect of fear of success on the dependent variable satisfaction with life was found as statistically significant F= 8.51, p< .01. The beta weight -.718 also supports the same. In this group these factors exerted much influence that is also clearly visible from the higher variance R2Change= .515. The t-value 11.04, p<.01 also revealed significant difference. *Therefore the hypothesis seven "There will be a significant impact of fear of success and religiosity on the wellbeing of employed and unemployed men and women of four different castes" got accepted.*

Table 5.29 Regression Analysis performed on Thakur Employed Female in order to see the impact of Fear of Success on General Health (B)

Predictor/ Independent variable	Dependent variable	R (VARIANCE)	R2	R2 Change	R2 Weight	t	F	p
Fear of success	PGI-B	.679	.461	.461	.679	-.97	6.84	P<.05

It is clear that the main effect of fear of success on the dependent variable PGI-B (general health) was found as statistically significant F= 6.84, p< .05. The beta weight .679 also supports the same. In this group these factors exerted much influence that is also clearly visible from the higher variance R2 Change= .461. The t-value -.97, p<.05 also revealed significant difference. *Therefore the hypothesis No seven "There will be a significant impact of fear of success and religiosity on the wellbeing of employed and unemployed men and women of four different castes" got accepted.*

Table 5.30 Regression Analysis performed on Thakur Un-Employed Male in order to see the impact of Spirituality on General Health (B)

Predictor/ Independent variable	Dependent variable	R (VARIANCE)	R2	R2 Change	R2 Weight	t	F	p
Spiritual Wellbeing	PGI-B	.650	.422	.422	.650	-2.03	5.84	P<.05

The table shows that the main effect of spiritual wellbeing on the dependent variable PGI-B (general health) was found as statistically significant F= 5.84, p< .05. The beta weight .650 also supports the same. In this group these factors exerted much influence that is also clearly visible from the higher variance R2 Change= .422. The t-value -2.03, p<.05 also revealed significant difference. *The hypothesis seven "There will be a significant impact of fear of success and religiosity on the wellbeing of employed and unemployed men and women of four different castes" got accepted.*

Table 5.31 Regression Analysis performed on Thakur Un-Employed Female in order to see the impact of Fear of Success on Depression- Happiness

Predictor/ Independent variable	Dependent variable	R (VARIANCE)	R2	R2 Change	R2 Weight	t	F	p
Fear of success	SDH	.754	.569	.569	-.754	7.30	10.56	P<.05

Notations: SDH = short depression-happiness

The table shows that the main effect of fear of success on the dependent variable short depression-happiness was found as statistically significant F= 10.56, p< .05. The beta weight -.754 also supports the same. In this group these factors exerted much influence that is also clearly visible from the higher variance R2 Change= .569. The t-value 7.30, p<.05 also revealed significant difference. *"There will be a significant impact of fear of success and religiosity on the wellbeing of employed and unemployed men and women of four different castes" hypothesis seven got accepted.*

Table 5.32 Regression Analysis performed on Harijan Employed Male in order to see the impact of Spirituality on General Health (A)

Predictor/ Independent variable	Dependent variable	R (VARIANCE)	R2	R2 Change	R2 Weight	t	F	p
Spiritual Wellbeing	PGI-A	.685	.469	.469	.685	-2.04	7.06	P<.05

From the table it is quite clear that the main effect of spiritual wellbeing on the dependent variable PGI-A (general health) was found as statistically significant F= 7.06, p< .05. The beta weight .685 also supports the same. In this group these factors exerted much influence that is also clearly visible from the higher variance R2 Change= .469. The t-value -2.04, p<.05 also revealed significant difference. *"There will be a significant impact of fear of success and religiosity on the wellbeing of employed and unemployed men and women of four different castes" hypothesis seven got accepted.*

Table 5.33 Regression Analysis performed on Harijan Employed female in order to see the Impact of Spirituality on Depression-Happiness

Predictor/ Independent variable	Dependent variable	R (VARIANCE)	R2	R2 Change	R2 Weight	t	F	p
Spiritual Wellbeing	SDH	.829	.688	.688	.829	1.08	17.61	P<.05

Notations: SDH = short depression-happiness

The table clearly shows that the main effect of spiritual wellbeing on the dependent variable short depression-happiness was found as statistically significant F= 17.61, p< .05. The beta weight .829 also supports the same. In this group these factors exerted much influence that is also clearly visible from the higher variance R2 Change= .688. The t-value 1.08, p<.05 also revealed significant difference. *Therefore the hypothesis seven "There will be a significant impact of fear of success and religiosity on the wellbeing of employed and unemployed men and women of four different castes" got accepted.*

Table 5.34 Regression Analysis performed on Harijan un-employed male in order to see the impact of Fear of Success on Satisfaction with Life

Predictor/ Independent variable	Dependent variable	R	R2 (VARIANCE)	R2 Change	R2 Weight	t	F	p
Fear of success	SWL	.673	.453	.453	-.673	10.51	6.63	P<.05

Notations: SWL = satisfaction with life

The table clearly shows that the main effect of fear of success on the dependent variable satisfaction with life was found as statistically significant F= 6.63, p< .05. The beta weight -.673 also supports the same. In this group these factors exerted much influence that is also clearly visible

Table 5.35 Regression Analysis performed on Harijan un-employed male in order to see the impact of Fear of Success on Depression-Happiness

Predictor/ Independent variable	Dependent variable	R	R2 (VARIANCE)	R2 Change	R2 Weight	t	F	p
Fear of success	SDH	.814	.663	.663	-.814	9.12	15.74	P<.05

Notations: SDH = short depression happiness

from the higher variance R2 Change= .453. The t-value 10.51, p<.05 also revealed significant difference. *The hypothesis seven "There will be a significant impact of fear of success and religiosity on the wellbeing of employed and unemployed men and women of four different castes" is accepted.*

From the table it is quite clear that the main effect of fear of success on the dependent variable short depression-happiness was found as statistically significant F= 15.74, p< .05. The beta weight -.814 also supports the same. In this group these factors exerted much influence that is also clearly visible from the higher variance R2 Change= .663. The t-value 9.12, p<.05 also revealed significant difference. *Therefore the hypothesis seven "There will be a significant impact of fear of success and religiosity on the wellbeing of employed and unemployed men and women of four different castes" got accepted.*

Table 5.36 Regression Analysis performed on Harijan un-employed female in order to see the impact of Spirituality on Satisfaction with Life

Predictor/ Independent variable	Dependent variable	R (VARIANCE)	R2	R2 Change	R2 Weight	t	F	p
Spiritual Wellbeing	SWL	.940	.883	.883	.940	-3.08	60.49	P<.01

Notations: SWL = satisfaction with life

From the table it is quite clear that the main effect of spiritual wellbeing on the dependent variable satisfaction with life was found as statistically significant F= 60.49, p< .01. The beta weight .940 also supports the same. In this group these factors exerted much influence that is also clearly visible from the higher variance R2 Change= .883. The t-value -3.08, p<.01 also revealed significant difference.

"There will be a significant impact of fear of success and religiosity on the wellbeing of employed and unemployed men and women of four different castes" hypothesis seven is accepted.

Table 5.37 Regression Analysis performed on Harijan un-employed female in order to see the impact of Fear of Success on Depression-Happiness and also of Spirituality on Depression-Happiness

Predictor/ Independent variable	Dependent variable	R (VARIANCE)	R2	R2 Change	R2 Weight	t	F	p
Fear of success	SDH	.968	.937	.094	-.319	-3.24	52.75	P<.01
Spiritual Wellbeing	SDH	.918	.844	.844	.918	-2.45	43.14	P<.01

Notations: SDH = short depression happiness

From the table it is quite clear that the main effect of fear of success on the dependent variable short depression-happiness was found as statistically significant F= 52.75, p < .01. The beta weight -.319 also supports the same. In this group these factors exerted much influence that is also clearly visible from the higher variance R2 Change= .094. The t-value -3.24, p<.01 also revealed significant difference.

Similarly the main effect of spiritual wellbeing on the dependent variable short depression-happiness was found as statistically significant F = 43.14, p < .01. The beta weight .918 also supports the same. In this group these factors exerted much influence that is also clearly visible from the higher variance R2 Change= .844. The t-value -2.45, p<.01 also revealed significant difference. *Therefore the hypothesis seven "There will be a significant impact of fear of success and religiosity on the wellbeing of employed and unemployed men and women of four different castes" is accepted.*

Table 5.38 Regression Analysis performed on Harijan un-employed female in order to see the Impact of Spirituality on General Health (T)

Predictor/ Independent variable	Dependent variable	R (VARIANCE)	R2	R2 Change	R2 Weight	t	F	p
Spiritual Wellbeing	PGI-T	.636	.404	.404	-.636	3.29	5.42	P<.01

The table clearly shows that the main effect of spiritual wellbeing on the dependent variable PGI-Total (general health) was found as statistically significant F= 5.42, p< .01. The beta weight -.636 also supports the same. In this group these factors exerted much influence that is also clearly visible from the higher·variance R2 Change= .404. The t-value 3.29, p<.01 also revealed significant difference. *"There will be a significant impact of fear of success and religiosity on the wellbeing of employed and unemployed men and women of four different castes" hypothesis got accepted.*

5.2 QUALITATIVE ANALYSIS

It can be noticed in the area of Chopal tehsil that the pace of development of the people is slow as compare to their urban areas counterpart. At the same time, its fragile nature and difficulty of taking up conventional development initiatives has not been appreciated. The rural people are living in the interior areas and away from the urban parts. They have to face many physical, psychological and social problems in their daily lives due to difficult geographical area and lack of earnings. The problems can be divided into: physical, psychological, and social.

5.2.1 Physical Problems

Major environmental problems being faced by people are deforestation and soil-erosion, which are leading to the drying up of water resources, flash floods and decline in the yield of food and cash crops, fodder, fuel and other minor forest produce. Intensive human and livestock pressures along with indiscriminate felling of trees for commercial purposes in many areas have already led to loss of soil and rapid depletion and destruction of forest cover. Besides, water retention capacity and productivity of land have been adversely affected. These factors have impaired the ecology significantly and also resulted in deterioration in the economic condition for the hill people. Seemingly harmless activity such as prolonged grazing by livestock, especially goats and sheep, have further exposed many hill areas to serious ecological degradation. There is an urgent need for relating livestock population to the bearing capacity of available land. In order to reduce pressure on land, quality of livestock, including goats, sheep, pigs and poultry birds has to be improved and their numbers reduced.

Development activities like construction of buildings, roads, dams, large and medium industries and mining etc., have aggravated environmental problems. In such hill areas where the population density is low and the villages are small and scattered over long distances, building connectivity through appropriate types of roads including link roads, bridle paths, foot bridges, etc. is a better strategy than concentration on motor able roads. Road construction should be completed in all respects without delays and roads should also be properly maintained. Consequently, perennial sources of water such as springs and small streams have dried up in many areas. The major challenge, therefore, is to devise suitable location-specific solutions, so as to reverse the process and ensure sustainable development of the growing population and ecology of the areas. Proper drainage system is absent in the area and should be developed. Still people in the interiors have to face problem of kaccha houses and don't have proper and appropriate houses to live. Some areas are developed in houses but many people who have less sources of income cannot afford proper houses.

Due to burning of wood as the source of fuel, it leads to air pollution and destruction of forest reserves as well. Lack of availability of sources of fuel people are forced to use natural resources and hence exhaust them. The large majority of the population in the areas depends on agriculture and allied activities. The problems which hamper agricultural production in areas are small and fragmented land holdings, lack of transport and marketing facilities, and inadequacy in availability of appropriate technology. Traditional industries such as handloom products, etc. have lost its charm. It could be made economically viable by introduction of material patterns and designs which have a large market. Tourism is one important industry which is lacking in the area as there are many beautiful and worthwhile places which can be developed as tourist spots. Tourism can be organized as an industry, with due care taken to avoid exploitative use of scarce local resources, especially water and fuel-wood, so that ecology of the areas is preserved and the local traditions; culture and heritage are protected and shown to different people.

For overcoming physical problems local people including educated ones believe in local deities. They ask their local deity for the help of solution of physical problems. They believe that local deity help them in dealing with natural calamities. For this the national programes for fighting diseases endemic to hill areas such as Goiter, Malaria, Respiratory diseases, etc. would be strengthened. The problems of lack of trained medical personnel and lack of proper facility would be mitigated to a certain extent by educating traditional Para-medical practitioners and equipping them with necessary skills and equipments. The children at school and people in general should be made aware of the far reaching implications of environmental degradation and their active participation has to be sought in eco-restoration.

5.2.2 Psychological Problems

Psychological problems greatly affect the health and wellbeing of local people. As physical problems, psychological problems also adversely affect the health and proper functioning of the village people. Due to heard life of the villages, people have to go through many stresses. They have to be every time be care full about their spending so that they are able to meet there expenses and are able to give their children a better life. The local people have anxiety about their adjustment in various weather conditions. The people are apprehensive that there will be environmental hazards if don't believe in devi/devtas. Depression is one of the common problems of the village people. Mainly there are people who have to work for long hours in the day and after that they usually have to stay alone as family is usually shifted to urban areas for their work or education. Due to difficulty in earnings and hard life and lack of facilities people suffer from anxiety, as how to manage their work and live a better life. People suffer from post traumatic stress disorder (PTSD) as always they are fear of the previous loses and problems and they are every time in the same fear of going through the previous loses. Motivation of the people keep decreasing as there is inconsistency in the outcome of the agriculture products as they are mostly dependent on the favorable climatic conditions else there is loss of crops.

Behaviour of people is dependent on the state of their living and how happy they are with the family. Usually people with low income and people living alone have bad temperament and do not mix with people well and cause problems in the workings of the village or any other work of their society. Tension is the major problem people are going through in the villages. Due to the difficulties they have to face in their daily living and problem in earning a better live make their lives full of worries and tension which greatly effect their health and psychological wellbeing.

5.2.3 Social Problems

Some parts of the villages where the production of cash crops is not much and sufficient people are suffering from poverty. Objectively poverty implies a dehumanizing condition in which people are unable to look after the basic needs. Poor people lack the necessary resources and capacity to satisfy basic needs like food, shelter, health and education. They live under difficult conditions which are not conducive for development of their human potential. Poverty interferes with development in many ways. For instance lack of or inadequate nutrition arrests mental development during early childhood. The unavailability of stimulating environment and absence of effective role models decreases the motivation level. A large section of poor children do not go to school. Even if they go they become drop outs and fail to complete education. In this context it may be pointed out that poverty is also related to the social structure. A number of low caste, scheduled tribe and backward communities have been put to discrimination for many centuries. They are socially disadvantaged and are deprived from the experiences necessary for development on account of their membership of specific groups. In this sense they are doubly deprived. Children from the background of poverty, their cognitive development and performance are found to be at a lower level. It has also been found that the poverty condition is demotivating and makes a person more vulnerable. Low level of achievement motivation and greater need for dependence in these people make them less effective in coping with the problems of everyday life. As a result the poor become marginalized and cannot contribute to the mainstream of the society.

Villages consist of people from different linguistic and ethnic back grounds. Efforts have been made to put people on the path of socio-economic development. Traditionally the village society was hierarchically arranged and the different communities and caste groups showed a pattern of social distance in which low caste, tribals and minority groups were discriminated against and looked down upon. Many of the communities were considered as untouchables. Caste-related prejudice and discrimination has also been on rise in many areas. In the course of socialization people acquire negative attitudes and stereotypes. Thus if we have prejudice against someone it may lead to aggression, hostility and harm doing towards the target groups. In recent years inter group conflicts related to caste has moved from the social to the political arena of life. In this context the rise of low caste groups who often call themselves Dalits is becoming a prominent feature in every area.

Women and men are equally important for the growth and development of individual and social live. However, careful analysis of village society indicates that the situation is not good for women folk. The sex ratio of male and female in the population has been changing and becoming unfavorable towards women. We have gods and goddesses both and one of the incarnations of lord Shiva is

Ardhanareeshwar, which is made of half male and half female in its constitution. Unfortunately this equality and prominence tells an incomplete fact. The women are also subjected to discrimination in learning, dowry, deaths and exploitations of various kinds which are very common. The incident of infanticide, early marriage, emphasis on domestic activities and lesser emphasis on education and career have made women's lives full of problems. They are discriminated against from early childhood. The dependence on others (e.g. parents, husbands) becomes fate of the majority of the women folk. The pattern of discrimination against women varies across rural, urban and tribal areas. The girl child is usually burdened with responsibilities that are beyond her capacity. Such exploitations function as obstacles in the process of development and growth of the girl child. They are neither able to realize their potentials nor able to contribute to the mainstream of society. Their contributions are often limited to family and that too are ignored. The illiteracy is another major problem of the upper areas. The lack of these skills renders them deprived of the opportunities for upward social mobility. Such people have to depend on others for various things and are exploited in various ways. The lack of reading and writing skills makes a person incapable of availing the various opportunities to help themselves. Village people suffer from the problem of unemployment. As there are fewer sources of earnings, even there are less opportunities of employment. Large population is unemployed as they are illiterate also. So the first step is to educate people so they are able to get more jobs and are able to seek new opportunities.

Child labour is one of the growing problems of villages. As these are areas far in the interiors, there are no rules and laws followed as such and people are forced to send their child for labour as in order to earn money and fulfill their living. To get rid of their worries people of the areas consume alcohol and use tobacco. After some time they become habitual and are not able to come out of it and they then spend much of their income on it and further reduce their income and get into further problems. The population of the villages is much higher as compare to the urban areas. People are not aware of the problems arising from increase population. They only feel that more people will earn more money and this attitude leads them in wrong direction. Check in the rural areas is of most importance as only then rest of the problems can be solved. The social problems described above deal with different domains of life. You can see that the solutions for these problems require inputs from different disciplines. The role of psychology is prominent as it deals with behaviour. Modification of attitudes, feelings and pattern of behaviour are significant. Psychologists can contribute by providing strategies for achieving these goals.

AVARAGE SCORE OF RAJPUT,BRAHMIN &THAKUR

In this chapter an attempt has been made to compare employed and un-employed people and male and females with each other on different measures used by computing their mean scores. Objective of the present chapter is to compare employed and un-employed males and females of different castes on measures such as fear of success, spirituality wellbeing, and satisfaction with life, happiness-depression and general wellbeing. Since, people are religious in different manners and have their own style and their spirituality beliefs differ from individual to individual; therefore it is important to appraise their psychological vulnerabilities by analyzing their mean score on each psychological measure. In the first table an attempt has been made to compare males and females with each other and employed and un-employed of four different castes with each other on fear of success parameter. The average scores have been shown in table 6.1, description is as follows:-

Table 6.1 Average Score of Rajput, Brahmin, Thakur and Harijan People on Fear of Success

	Rajput			Bhramin			Thakur			Harijan		
	M	F	AV.	M	F	AV.	M	F	AV.	M	F	AV.
E	23.60	27.00	**25.30**	25.70	28.30	**27.00**	22.50	26.00	**24.25**	33.40	35.00	**34.20**
UE	21.10	25.50	**23.30**	24.40	27.60	**26.00**	23.90	25.90	**24.90**	22.60	23.60	**23.10**
AV.	**22.35**	**26.25**	**24.30**	**25.05**	**27.95**	**26.50**	**23.20**	**25.90**	**24.55**	**28.00**	**29.30**	**28.65**

The average score of employed Rajput on Fear of Success was found 25.30 as compared to their un-employed counterpart whose score on their same was found 23.30.it clearly shows that the employed people have more fear of success as compare to their counterpart. Further average score of male in FOS was found 22.35 whereas the average scores of female were found as 26.25. It clearly shows that the females have more fear of success as compared to their counterpart. Average score of Rajput employed male on FOS was found 23.60 whereas the average score of employed female was found 27.00. It shows that the employed female have more FOS as compared to their male counterpart. Similarly the average score of unemployed male on FOS was found 21.10 whereas the mean score of unemployed female was found 25.50. It shows that the unemployed female also showed more FOS as compared to their counterpart. Average score of employed male on FOS was found 23.60 whereas the average score of unemployed male was found 21.10. It shows that the un-employed male have more FOS as compared to their counterpart. Average score of employed female on FOS was found 27.00 whereas the average score of unemployed female was found 25.50. It shows that the employed female have more FOS as compared to their counterpart. Average score of employed male on FOS was found 23.60 whereas the average score of unemployed female was found 25.50. It shows that the unemployed female have more FOS as compared to their counterpart. Average score of unemployed male on FOS was found 21.10 whereas the average score of employed female was found 27.00. It shows that the employed female have more FOS as compared to their counterpart.

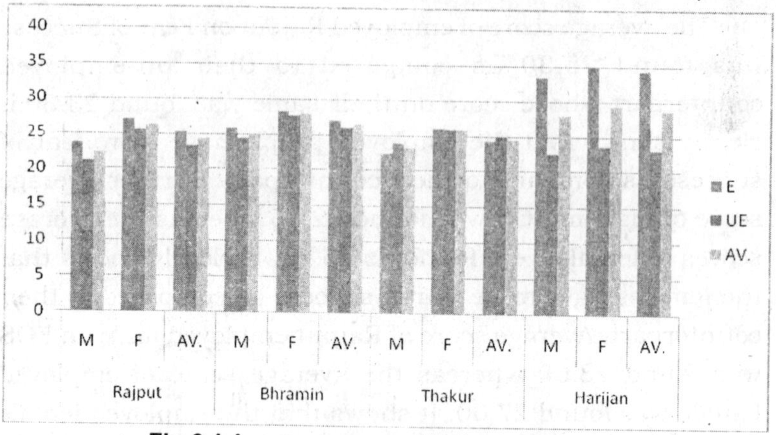

Fig 6.1 Average score of Rajput, Brahmin, Thakur and Harijan people on fear of success

The average score of employed Bhramin on Fear of Success was found 27.00 as compared to their un-employed counterpart whose score on their same was found 26.00.it clearly shows that the employed people have more fear of success as compare to their counterpart. Further average score of male in FOS was found 25.05 whereas the average scores of female were found as 27.95. It clearly shows that the females have more fear of success as compared to their counterpart. Average score of Bhramin employed male on FOS was found 25.70 whereas the average score of employed female was found 28.30. It shows that the employed female have more FOS as compared to their male counterpart. Similarly the average score of unemployed male on FOS was found 224.40 whereas the mean score of unemployed female was found 27.60. It shows that the unemployed female also showed more FOS as compared to their counterpart. Average score of employed male on FOS was found 25.70 whereas the average score of unemployed male was found 24.40. It shows that the employed male have more FOS as compared to their counterpart. Average score of employed female on

FOS was found 28.30 whereas the average score of un-employed female was found 27.60. It shows that then employed female have more FOS as compared to their counterpart. Average score of employed male on FOS was found 25.70 whereas the average score of unemployed female was found 27.60. It shows that the unemployed female have more FOS as compared to their counterpart. Average score of unemployed male on FOS was found 24.40 whereas the average score of employed female was found 28.30. It shows that the employed female have more FOS as compared to their counterpart.

The average score of employed Thakur on Fear of Success was found 24.25 as compared to their un-employed counterpart whose score on their same was found 24.90.it clearly shows that the un-employed people have more fear of success as compare to their counterpart. Further average score of male in FOS was found 23.20 whereas the average scores of female were found as 25.90. It clearly shows that the females have more fear of success as compared to their counterpart. Average score of Thakur employed male on FOS was found 25.50 whereas the average score of employed female was found 26.00. It shows that the employed female have more FOS as compared to their male counterpart. Similarly the average score of unemployed male on FOS was found 23.90 whereas the mean score of unemployed female was found 25.90. It shows that the unemployed female also showed more FOS as compared to their counterpart. Average score of employed male on FOS was found 25.50 whereas the average score of unemployed male was found 23.90. It shows that the employed male have more FOS as compared to their counterpart. Average score of employed female on FOS was found 26.00 whereas the average score of unemployed female was found 25.90. It shows that the employed female have more FOS as compared to their counterpart. Average score of employed male on FOS was found 25.50 whereas the average score of unemployed female was found 25.90. It shows that the unemployed female have more FOS as compared to their counterpart. Average score of unemployed male on FOS was found 23.90 whereas the average score of employed female was found 26.00. It shows that the employed female have more FOS as compared to their counterpart.

The average score of employed Harijan on Fear of Success was found 34.20 as compared to their un-employed counterpart whose score on their same was found 23.10 it clearly shows that the employed people have more fear of success as compare to their counterpart. Further average score of male in FOS was found 28.00 whereas the average scores of female were found as 29.30. It clearly shows that the females have more fear of success as compared to their counterpart. Average score of Harijan employed male on FOS was found 33.40 whereas the average score of employed female was found 35.00. It shows that the employed female have more FOS as compared to their male counterpart. Similarly the average score of unemployed male on FOS was found 22.60 whereas the mean score of unemployed female was found 23.60. It shows that the unemployed female also showed more FOS as compared to their counterpart. Average score of employed male on FOS was found 33.40 whereas the average score of unemployed male was found 22.60. It shows that the employed male have more FOS as compared to their counterpart. Average score of employed female on FOS was found 35.00 whereas the average score of unemployed female was found 23.60. It shows that the employed female have more FOS as compared to their counterpart. Average score of employed male on FOS was found 33.40 whereas the average score of unemployed female was found 23.60. It shows that the unemployed female have more FOS as compared to their counterpart. Average score of unemployed male on FOS was found 22.60 whereas the average score of employed female was found 35.00. It shows that the employed female have more FOS as compared to their counterpart.

There seems to be a very important relationship between fear of success and religiosity. The persons who have fear of failure as well as success both generalize their feeling and expectation of accomplishment to the god and goddess (Taylor, 1978). Religiosity and fear of death were most related and as such religious attitudes did not serve to moderate the effects of induced fear of death. The findings show the influencing on personality and afflictive behavior (Dhawan and Sripat, 1986). Ghazal (2004) in his research tries to explain that it also seems that the family behaviour may mediate the influence of religion on women's labour force activity. Prior research on families has largely overloaded the role of religion in influencing women's labour force decisions, particularly at different stages of the life cycle. In his study, Jonas (2006) made an attempt to find the relation between terror management and religion. Terror management theory suggests that people cope with awareness of death by investing in some kind of literal or symbolic immortality. Study of Pirta and Ranta (2007) tried to bring out the role of reconciliation processes mediated by local deities through possession and solve the social conflicts. The important part of breaking and making of these affectional bonds is the possession of persons by spirits and deities. In his classic study, Kay (2008) proposed that the high levels of support often observed for governmental and religious systems can be explained in part as a means of coping with the threat posed by chronically or situational fluctuating levels of perceived personal control. The study conducted by Kumari and Pirta (2009) provides evidence that God serves as a secure base, which is a generalization of primary infant-mother relationship. Galinsky (2010) says that it has been recently proposed that people can flexibly rely on sources of control that are both internal and external to the self to satisfy the need to believe that their world is under control. Research demonstrates that, when personal control is threatened, people defend external systems of control, such as God and government. According to Sasaki (2011) religion helps people maintain a sense of control, particularly secondary control- acceptance of and adjustment to difficult situations-and contributes to strengthening social relationships in a religious community.

The expectancy that success in achievement-related situations will be followed by negative consequences arouses fear of success in otherwise achievement-motivated women which then inhibits their performance and levels of aspiration. Impairment of the educational and interpersonal functioning of those high in fear of success is noted (Horner, 1972). The findings of Kimball and Leahy (1976) were interpreted as indicating developmental changes in fear of success due to increasing peer affiliation and gender-linked competitive achievement. In their study, Zuckerman, Larrance, Porac, and Blanck, (1980) studied effects of fear of success on intrinsic motivation, causal attribution, and choice behavior. The study of Douglas and Milton (1986) suggest that men and women react differentially to some of the variables involved in the fear-of-success effect. Assessment of Hossein, and Pishe, (2008) on fear of success revealed lack of trust and confidence in one's own personality.

The study of Ivers and Downes, (2011) concluded that fear of success is the key dimension of social class.

Table 6.2 Average Score of Rajput, Brahmin, Thakur and Harijan People on Spiritual Wellbeing

	Rajput			Bhramin			Thakur			Harijan		
	M	F	AV.	M	F	AV.	M	F	AV.	M	F	AV.
E	92.40	87.40	**89.90**	90.40	86.70	**88.55**	92.40	88.40	**90.40**	82.00	78.20	**80.10**
UE	90.50	85.20	**87.85**	91.50	89.00	**90.25**	91.40	88.30	**89.85**	78.20	72.30	**75.25**
AV.	**91.45**	**86.30**	**88.88**	**90.95**	**87.85**	**89.4**	**91.90**	**88.35**	**90.13**	**80.10**	**75.25**	**77.68**

The average score of employed Rajput on spiritual wellbeing was found 89.90as compared to their un-employed counterpart whose score on their same was found 87.85.it clearly shows that the employed people have more spiritual wellbeing as compare to their counterpart. Further average score of male in spiritual wellbeing was found 91.45 whereas the average scores of female were found as 86.30. It clearly shows that the males have more spiritual wellbeing as compared to their counterpart. Average score of Rajput employed male on spiritual wellbeing was found 92.4 whereas the average score of employed female was found 87.4. It shows that the employed male have more spiritual wellbeing as compared to their male counterpart. Similarly the average score of unemployed male on spiritual wellbeing was found 90.5 whereas the mean score of unemployed female was found 85.2. It shows that the unemployed male also showed more spiritual wellbeing as compared to their counterpart. Average score of employed male on spiritual wellbeing was found 92.4 whereas the average score of unemployed male was found 90.5. It shows that the employed male have more spiritual wellbeing as compared to their counterpart. Average score of employed female on spiritual wellbeing was found

87.4 whereas the average score of unemployed female was found 85.2. It shows that the employed female have more spiritual wellbeing as compared to their counterpart. Average score of employed male on spiritual wellbeing was found 92.4 whereas the average score of unemployed female was found 85.2. It shows that the employed male have more spiritual wellbeing as compared to their counterpart. Average score of unemployed male on spiritual wellbeing was found 90.5 whereas the average score of employed female was found 87.4. It shows that the un-employed male have more spiritual wellbeing as compared to their counterpart.

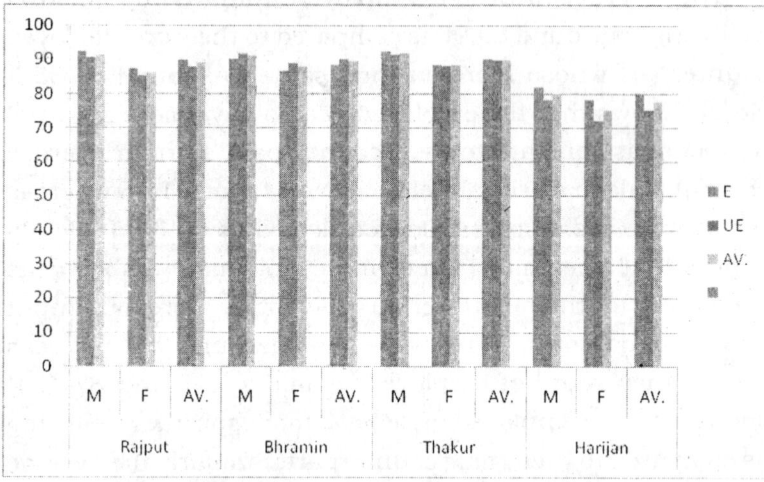

Fig 6.2: Average score of Rajput, Brahmin, Thakur and Harijan people on spiritual wellbeing.

The average score of employed Bhramin on spiritual wellbeing was found 88.55as compared to their un-employed counterpart whose score on their same was found 90.25.it clearly shows that the un- employed people have more spiritual wellbeing as compare to their counterpart. Further average score of male in spiritual wellbeing was found 90.95 whereas the average scores of female were found as 87.85.

It clearly shows that the males have more spiritual wellbeing as compared to their counterpart. Average score of Bhramin employed male on spiritual wellbeing was found 90.40 whereas the average score of employed female was found 86.70. It shows that the employed male have more spiritual wellbeing as compared to their male counterpart. Similarly the average score of unemployed male on spiritual wellbeing was found 91.50 whereas the mean score of unemployed female was found 89.00. It shows that the unemployed male also showed more spiritual wellbeing as compared to their counterpart. Average score of employed male on spiritual wellbeing was found 90.40 whereas the average score of unemployed male was found 91.50. It shows that the un-employed male have more spiritual wellbeing as compared to their counterpart. Average score of employed female on spiritual wellbeing was found 86.70 whereas the average score of unemployed female was found 89.00. It shows that the un- employed female have more spiritual wellbeing as compared to their counterpart. Average score of employed male on spiritual wellbeing was found 90.40 whereas the average score of unemployed female was found 89.00. It shows that the employed male have more spiritual wellbeing as compared to their counterpart. Average score of unemployed male on spiritual wellbeing was found 91.50 whereas the average score of employed female was found 86.70. It shows that the un-employed male have more spiritual wellbeing as compared to their counterpart.

The average score of employed Thakur on spiritual wellbeing was found 90.40 as compared to their un-employed counterpart whose score on their same was found 89.85.it clearly shows that the employed people have more spiritual wellbeing as compare to their counterpart. Further average score of male in spiritual wellbeing was found 91.90 whereas the average scores of female were found as 88.35. It clearly shows that the males have more spiritual wellbeing as compared to their counterpart. Average score of Thakur employed male on spiritual wellbeing was found 92.40 whereas the average score of employed female was found 88.40. It shows that the employed male have more spiritual wellbeing as compared to their male counterpart. Similarly the average score of unemployed male on spiritual wellbeing was found 91.40 whereas the mean score of unemployed female was found 88.30. It shows that the unemployed male also showed more spiritual wellbeing as compared to their counterpart. Average score of employed male on spiritual wellbeing was found 92.40 whereas the average score of unemployed male was found 91.40. It shows that the employed male have more spiritual wellbeing as compared to their counterpart. Average score of employed female on spiritual wellbeing was found 88.40 whereas the average score of unemployed female was found 88.30. It shows that the employed female have more spiritual wellbeing as compared to their counterpart. Average score of employed male on spiritual wellbeing was found 92.40 whereas the average score of unemployed female was found 88.30. It shows that the employed male have more spiritual wellbeing as compared to their counterpart. Average score of unemployed male on spiritual wellbeing was found 91.40 whereas the average score of employed female was found 88.40. It shows that the un-employed male have more spiritual wellbeing as compared to their counterpart.

The average score of employed Harijan on spiritual wellbeing was found 80.10 as compared to their un-employed counterpart whose score on their same was found 75.25.It clearly shows that the employed people have more spiritual wellbeing as compare to their counterpart. Further average score of male in spiritual wellbeing was found 80.10 whereas the average scores of female were found as 75.25. It clearly shows that the males have more spiritual wellbeing as compared to their counterpart. Average score of Harijan employed male on spiritual wellbeing was found 82.00 whereas the average score of employed female was found 78.20. It shows that the employed male have more spiritual wellbeing as compared to their male counterpart. Similarly the average score of unemployed male on spiritual wellbeing was found 78.20 whereas the mean score of unemployed female was found 72.30. It shows that the unemployed male also showed more spiritual wellbeing as compared to their counterpart. Average score of employed male on spiritual wellbeing was found 82.00 whereas the average score of unemployed male was found 78.20. It shows that the employed male have more spiritual wellbeing as compared to their counterpart. Average score of employed female on spiritual wellbeing was found 78.20 whereas the average score of unemployed female was found 72.30. It shows that the employed female have more spiritual wellbeing as compared to their counterpart. Average score of employed male on spiritual wellbeing was found 82.00 whereas the average score of unemployed female was found 72.30. It shows that the employed male have more spiritual wellbeing as compared to their counterpart. Average score of unemployed male on spiritual wellbeing was found 78.20 whereas the average score of employed female was found 78.20. It shows that the both unemployed-male and employed female have equal spiritual wellbeing.

The study of De Vas and Suarez-Orozeo (1987) tried to examine power as it relates to the ritual interaction of sacrifice to explore how the human capacity for coping is psychologically socialized around the inner experience of mechanical and intentional causality. It is suggested that these coping mechanisms are involved in the development of self- consciousness. Pandey (1988) in his study found that intrinsic aspects of religious beliefs were negatively correlated with the extrinsic religious beliefs and positively correlated with social innovativeness. Caste and education were found to have significant relationship with extrinsic belief and social innovativeness. Education was found to have significant relationship with intrinsic beliefs. Scott, Smith, and Davis (1989) in their study found the relationship between religious beliefs, personality and mental health. In his article Bill, (1996) showed that the challenge offered to psychiatry by religions and spiritual values is one encountered by modern society. The study of Christopher and Jeffrey (1998) deals with religion-health connection that have increased markedly in recent years. This interest in the complex relationships between religion and mental and physical health is being fueled by energetic and innovative research programs in several fields, including sociology, psychology, health behavior and health education, psychiatry, gerontology, and social epidemiology.

Studies examining spiritually augmented cognitive–behavioral therapies, forgiveness interventions, different meditation approaches and prayer have provided some evidence of efficacy in improving health under specific conditions (Harris, Thoresen, Mccullough & Larson, 1999). The findings of Pedersen, Williams and Kristensen, (2000) suggest that spiritual self-identity is a salient feature of self-identifications and contributes to the research literature on religiosity. According to Mahalik & Lagan, (2001) it is also a matter for research whether there is any link between religiosity and gender. It was seen that gender role conflict and stress would predict men's religiosity and spiritual wellbeing. Tan, 2003 in this study tries to explain the role of spirituality and religion in mental health. According to him integrating spirituality and religion into clinical practice or psychotherapy has become a significant area of interest in the mental health field today. According to Ardelt (2003) although religiosity tends to help older people to cope with physical and social losses, not all studies find a significant association between religious involvement and well-being in old age. The evidence of Fiori (2004) indicates that spirituality and religion are associated with both physical and psychological health. The study of Park (2005) explored how religion, as a meaning system, influences coping with adversity. Prof. R. S. Pirta (2010) attempted to find the effect of supernatural elements as context for deliberations on culture and cognition. Michael (2010) in his study found that men obtain more mental health benefits from religious involvement than women and women with higher levels of organizational religious involvement have similar levels of mental health as those with moderate and lower levels of organizational religious involvement.

Table 6.3 Average Score of Rajput, Brahmin, Thakur and Harijan People on Satisfaction with Life

	Rajput			Bhramin			Thakur			Harijan		
	M	F	AV.	M	F	AV.	M	F	AV.	M	F	AV.
E	28.20	25.70	**26.95**	26.60	23.40	**25.00**	29.20	27.20	**28.20**	25.80	22.70	**24.25**
UE	30.00	25.90	**27.95**	28.50	24.40	**26.45**	28.50	26.10	**27.30**	27.40	22.00	**24.70**
AV.	**29.10**	**25.80**	**27.45**	**27.55**	**23.90**	**25.73**	**28.85**	**26.65**	**27.75**	**26.60**	**22.35**	**24.48**

The average score of employed Rajput on satisfaction with life was found 26.95 as compared to their un-employed counterpart whose score on their same was found 27.95.It clearly shows that the un-employed people have more satisfaction with life as compare to their counterpart. Further average score of male in satisfaction with life was found 29.10 whereas the average scores of female were found as 25.80. It clearly shows that the males have more satisfaction with life as compared to their counterpart. Average score of Rajput employed male on satisfaction with life was found 28.20 whereas the average score of employed female was found 25.70. It shows that the employed male have more satisfaction with life as compared to their male counterpart. Similarly the average score of unemployed male on satisfaction with life was found 30.00 whereas the mean score of unemployed female was found 25.90. It shows that the unemployed male also showed more satisfaction with life as compared to their counterpart. Average score of employed male on satisfaction with life was found 28.20 whereas the average score of unemployed male was found 30.00. It shows that the un-employed male have more satisfaction with life as compared to their counterpart. Average score of employed female on satisfaction with life was found 25.70 whereas the average score of unemployed female was found 25.90. It shows that the un-employed female have more satisfaction with life as compared to their counterpart. Average score of employed male on satisfaction with life was found 28.20 whereas the average score of unemployed female was found 25.90. It shows that the employed male have more satisfaction with life as compared to their counterpart. Average score of unemployed male on satisfaction with life was found 30.00 whereas the average score of employed female was found 25.70. It shows that the un-employed male have more satisfaction with life as compared to their counterpart.

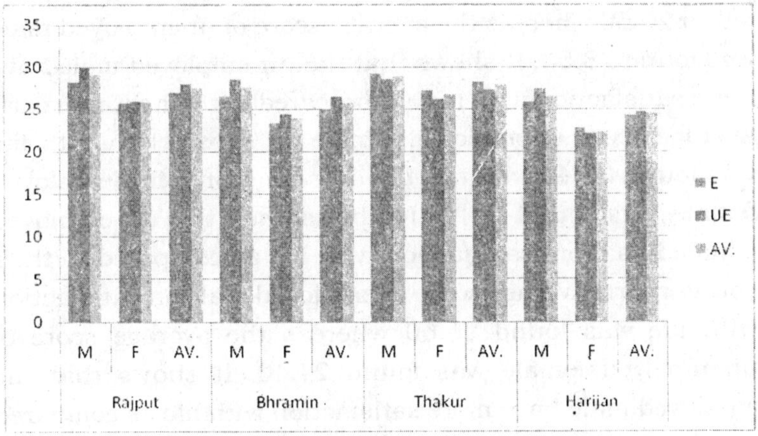

Fig. 6.3 Average score of Rajput, Brahmin, Thakur and Harijan people on satisfaction with life.

The average score of employed Bhramin on satisfaction with life was found 25.00 as compared to their un-employed counterpart whose score on their same was found 26.45.It clearly shows that the un-employed people have more satisfaction with life as compare to their counterpart. Further average score of male in satisfaction with life was found 27.55 whereas the average scores of female were found as 23.90. It clearly shows that the males have more satisfaction with life as compared to their counterpart. Average score of Bhramin employed male on satisfaction with life was found 26.60 whereas the average score of employed female was found 23.40. It shows that the employed male have more satisfaction with life as compared to their male counterpart. Similarly the average score of unemployed male on satisfaction with life was found 28.50 whereas the mean score of unemployed female was found 24.40. It shows that the unemployed male also showed more satisfaction with life as compared to their counterpart. Average score of employed male on satisfaction with life was found 26.60 whereas the average score of unemployed male was found 28.50. It shows that the un-employed male have more satisfaction with life as compared to their counterpart. Average score of employed female on satisfaction with life was found 23.40 whereas the average score of unemployed female was found 24.40.It shows that the un-employed female has more satisfaction with life as compared to their counterpart. Average score of employed male on satisfaction with life was found 26.60 whereas the average score of unemployed female was found 24.40. It shows that the employed male have more satisfaction with life as compared to their counterpart. Average score of unemployed male on satisfaction with life was found 28.50 whereas the average score of employed female was found 23.40. It shows that the un-employed male have more satisfaction with life as compared to their counterpart.

The average score of employed Thakur on satisfaction with life was found 28.20 as compared to their un-employed counterpart whose score on their same was found 27.30.It clearly shows that the employed people have more satisfaction with life as compare to their counterpart. Further average score of male in satisfaction with life was found 28.85 whereas the average scores of female was found as 26.65.It clearly shows that the males have more satisfaction with life as compared to their counterpart. Average score of Thakur employed male on satisfaction with life was found 29.20 whereas the average score of employed female was found 27.20. It shows that the employed male have more satisfaction with life as compared to their male counterpart. Similarly the average score of unemployed male on satisfaction with life was found 28.50 whereas the mean score of unemployed female was found 26.10. It shows that the unemployed male also showed more satisfaction with life as compared to their counterpart. Average score of employed male on satisfaction with life was found 29.20 whereas the average score of unemployed male was found 28.50. It shows that the employed male have more satisfaction with life as compared to their counterpart. Average score of employed female on satisfaction with life was found 27.20 whereas the average score of unemployed female was found 26.10. It shows that the employed female have more satisfaction with life as compared to their counterpart. Average score of employed male on satisfaction with life was found 29.20 whereas the average score of unemployed female was found 26.10. It shows that the employed male have more satisfaction with life as compared to their counterpart. Average score of unemployed male on satisfaction with life was found 28.50 whereas the average score of employed female was found 27.20. It shows that the un-employed male have more satisfaction with life as compared to their counterpart.

The average score of employed Harijan on satisfaction with life was found 24.25 as compared to their un-employed counterpart whose score on their same was found 24.70.It clearly shows that the un-employed people have more satisfaction with life as compare to their counterpart. Further average score of male in spiritual wellbeing was found 26.60 whereas the average scores of female were found as 22.35. It clearly shows that the males have more satisfaction with life as compared to their counterpart. Average score of Harijan employed male on satisfaction with life was found 25.80 whereas the average score of employed female was found 22.70. It shows that the employed male have more satisfaction with life as compared to their male counterpart. Similarly the average score of unemployed male on satisfaction with life was found 27.40 whereas the mean score of unemployed female was found 22.00. It shows that the unemployed male also showed more satisfaction with life as compared to their counterpart. Average score of employed male on satisfaction with life was found 25.80 whereas the average score of unemployed male was found 27.40. It shows that the un-employed male have more satisfaction with life as compared to their counterpart. Average score of employed female on satisfaction with life was found 22.70 whereas the average score of unemployed female was found 22.00. It shows that the employed female have more satisfaction with life as compared to their counterpart. Average score of employed male on satisfaction with life was found 25.80 whereas the average score of unemployed female was found 22.00. It shows that the employed male have more satisfaction with life as compared to their counterpart. Average score of unemployed male on satisfaction with life was found 27.40 whereas the average score of employed female was found 22.70. It shows that the un-employed male have more satisfaction with life as compared to their counterpart.

Galinsky (2010) says that it has been recently proposed that people can flexibly rely on sources of control that are both internal and external to the self to satisfy the need to believe that their world is under control. Consistent with this, past research demonstrates that, when personal control is threatened, people defend external systems of control, such as God and government. The study of Lima and Putnamb (2010) revealed that although the positive association between religiosity and life satisfaction is well documented, much theoretical and empirical controversy surrounds the question of how religion actually shapes life satisfaction. This study offers strong evidence for social and participatory mechanisms shaping religion's impact on life satisfaction. Myers (2011) tried to find out the religion paradox. He said if religion makes people happy then why so many people are drop out. He found that it appears that the benefits of religion for social relationship and subjective wellbeing depend on the characteristics of the society. The research of Bruce, Ruut, and Alex (1991) addresses issues of causal direction in research on subjective well being. Previous researchers have generally assumed that such variables as domain satisfactions, social support, life events, and levels of expectation and aspiration are causes of subjective wellbeing. He have pointed out that they could just as well be consequences. Recent understanding of subjective well-being suggests that it consists of global judgments of life satisfaction, hedonic experiences, and beliefs about facets of one's life. Traditionally, life satisfaction judgments have been the outcome of interest in studies examining the relationship between religiosity and wellbeing (Wiegand and Weiss, 2006).

Table 6.4 Average Score of Rajput, Brahmin, Thakur and Harijan People on Depression-Happiness

	Rajput			Bhramin			Thakur			Harijan		
	M	F	AV.	M	F	AV.	M	F	AV.	M	F	AV.
E	12.40	14.20	**13.30**	12.80	13.80	**13.30**	13.20	13.40	**13.30**	16.00	13.70	**14.85**
UE	15.10	12.50	**13.80**	14.50	14.80	**14.65**	15.30	13.70	**14.50**	12.70	11.80	**12.25**
AV.	**13.75**	**13.35**	**13.55**	**13.65**	**14.30**	**13.98**	**14.25**	**13.55**	**13.90**	**14.35**	**12.75**	**13.55**

The average score of employed Rajput on depression-happiness measure was found 13.30 as compared to their un-employed counterpart whose score on their same was found 13.80.It clearly shows that the un-employed people have more depression-happiness measure as compare to their counterpart. Further average score of male in depression-happiness measure was found 13.75 whereas the average scores of female were found as 13.35. It clearly shows that the males have more depression-happiness measure as compared to their counterpart. Average score of Rajput employed male on depression-happiness measure was found 12.40 whereas the average score of employed female was found 14.20. It shows that the employed female have more depression-happiness measure as compared to their male counterpart. Similarly the average score of unemployed male on depression-happiness measure was found 15.10 whereas the mean score of unemployed female was found 12.50. It shows that the unemployed male also showed more depression-happiness measure as compared to their counterpart. Average score of employed male on depression-happiness measure was found 12.40 whereas the average score of unemployed male was found 15.10. It shows that the un-employed male have more depression-happiness measure as compared to their counterpart. Average score of employed female on depression-happiness measure was found 14.20 whereas the average score of unemployed female was found 12.50. It shows that the employed female have more depression-happiness measure as compared to their counterpart. Average score of employed male on depression-happiness measure was found 12.40 whereas the average score of unemployed female was found 12.50. It shows that the un-employed male have more depression-happiness measure as compared to their counterpart. Average score of unemployed male on depression-happiness measure was found 15.10 whereas the average score of employed female was found 14.20. It shows that the un-employed male have more depression-happiness measure as compared to their counterpart.

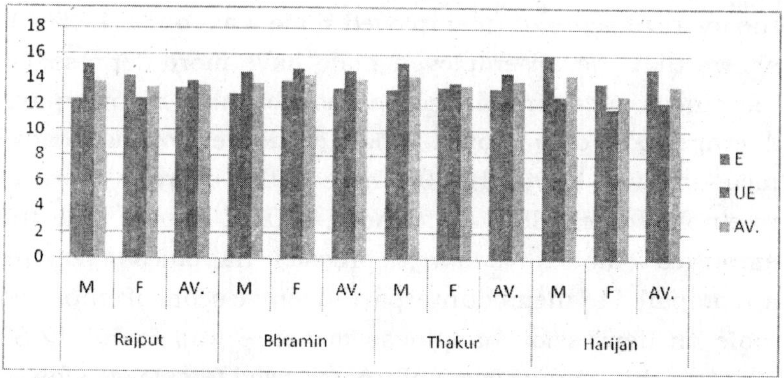

Fig 6.4: Average score of Rajput, Brahmin, Thakur and Harijan people on depression-happiness

The average score of employed Bhramin on depression-happiness measure was found 13.30 as compared to their un-employed counterpart whose score on their same was found 14.65.It clearly shows that the un-employed people have more depression-happiness measure as compare to their counterpart. Further average score of male in depression-happiness measure was found 13.65 whereas the average scores of female were found as 14.30. It clearly shows that the females have more depression-happiness measure as compared to their counterpart. Average score of Bhramin employed male on depression-happiness measure was found 12.80 whereas the average score of employed female was found 13.80. It shows that the employed female have more depression-happiness measure as compared to their male counterpart. Similarly the average score of unemployed male on depression-happiness measure was found 14.50 whereas the mean score of unemployed female was found 14.80. It shows that the unemployed female also showed more depression-happiness measure as compared to their counterpart. Average score of employed male on depression-happiness measure was found 12.80 whereas the average score of unemployed male was found 14.50. It shows that the un-employed male have more depression-happiness measure as compared to their counterpart. Average score of employed female on depression-happiness measure was found 13.80 whereas the average score of unemployed female was found 14.80. It shows that the employed female have more depression-happiness measure as compared to their counterpart. Average score of employed male on depression-happiness measure was found 12.80 whereas the average score of unemployed female was found 14.80. It shows that the un-employed female have more depression-happiness measure as compared to their counterpart. Average score of unemployed male on depression-happiness measure was found 14.50 whereas the average score of employed female was found 13.80. It shows that the un-employed male have more depression-happiness measure as compared to their counterpart.

The average score of employed Thakur on depression-happiness measure was found 13.30 as compared to their un-employed counterpart whose score on their same was found 14.50.It clearly shows that the un-employed people have more depression-happiness measure as compare to their counterpart. Further average score of male in depression-happiness measure was found 14.25 whereas the average scores of female were found as 13.55. It clearly shows that the males have more depression-happiness measure as compared to their counterpart. Average score of Thakur employed male on depression-happiness measure was found 13.20 whereas the average score of employed female was found 13.40. It shows that the employed female have more depression-happiness measure as compared to their male counterpart. Similarly the average score of unemployed male on depression-happiness measure was found 15.30 whereas the mean score of unemployed female was found 13.70. It shows that the unemployed male also showed more depression-happiness measure as compared to their counterpart. Average score of employed male on depression-happiness measure was found 13.20 whereas the average score of unemployed male was found 15.30. It shows that the un-employed male have more depression-happiness measure as compared to their counterpart. Average score of employed female on depression-happiness measure was found 13.40 whereas the average score of unemployed female was found 13.70. It shows that the un-employed female have more depression-happiness measure as compared to their counterpart. Average score of employed male on depression-happiness measure was found 13.20 whereas the average score of unemployed female was found 13.70. It shows that the un-employed female have more depression-happiness measure as compared to their counterpart. Average score of unemployed male on depression-happiness measure was found 15.30 whereas the average score of employed female was found 13.40. It shows that the un-employed male have more depression-happiness measure as compared to their counterpart.

The average score of employed Harijan on depression-happiness measure was found 14.85 as compared to their un-employed counterpart whose score on their same was found 12.25.It clearly shows that the employed people have more depression-happiness measure as compare to their counterpart. Further average score of male in depression-happiness measure was found 14.35 whereas the average scores of female were found as 12.75. It clearly shows that the males have more depression-happiness measure as compared to their counterpart. Average score of Harijan employed male on depression-happiness measure was found

16.00 whereas the average score of employed female was found 13.70. It shows that the employed male have more depression-happiness measure as compared to their male counterpart. Similarly the average score of unemployed male on depression-happiness measure was found 12.70 whereas the mean score of unemployed female was found 11.80. It shows that the unemployed male also showed more depression-happiness measure as compared to their counterpart. Average score of employed male on depression-happiness measure was found 16.00 whereas the average score of unemployed male was found 12.70. It shows that the employed male have more depression-happiness measure as compared to their counterpart. Average score of employed female on depression-happiness measure was found 13.70 whereas the average score of unemployed female was found 11.80. It shows that the employed female have more depression-happiness measure as compared to their counterpart. Average score of employed male on depression-happiness measure was found 16.00 whereas the average score of unemployed female was found 11.80. It shows that the employed male have more depression-happiness measure as compared to their counterpart. Average score of unemployed male on depression-happiness measure was found 12.70 whereas the average score of employed female was found 13.70. It shows that the employed female have more depression-happiness measure as compared to their counterpart.

In his classic study, Kay (2008) proposed that the high levels of support often observed for governmental and religious systems can be explained in part as a means of coping with the threat posed by chronically or situational fluctuating levels of perceived personal control. The study of Ruiz (1998) presented the case of 55 yr old Hispanic

American women of Cuban descent presented with major depression which she ascribed to “punishment from God”. He said that there is a need to integrate the medical and psychiatric care with religious organizations in certain groups.

Table 6.5 Average Score of Rajput, Brahmin, Thakur and Harijan People on PGI HQ- Total General Health

	Rajput			Bhramin			Thakur			Harijan		
	M	F	AV.	M	F	AV.	M	F	AV.	M	F	AV.
E	6.100	11.50	**8.8**	8.200	12.60	**10.4**	6.200	13.20	**6.6**	11.30	15.40	**13.35**
UE	6.600	13.30	**9.95**	9.300	5.300	**7.3**	7.700	11.80	**9.75**	10.50	14.90	**12.7**
AV.	**6.35**	**12.4**	**9.38**	**8.75**	**8.95**	**8.85**	**6.95**	**12.5**	**9.73**	**10.9**	**15.15**	**13.03**

The average score of employed Rajput on PGI HQ-Total was found 8.8 as compared to their un-employed counterpart whose score on their same was found 9.95.It clearly shows that the un-employed people have more PGI HQ-Total as compare to their counterpart. Further average score of male in PGI HQ-Total was found 6.35 whereas the average scores of female were found as 12.4. It clearly shows that the females have more PGI HQ-Total as compared to their counterpart. Average score of Rajput employed male on PGI HQ-Total was found 6.1 whereas the average score of employed female was found 11.50. It shows that the employec females have more PGI HQ-Total measure as compared to their male counterpart. Similarly the average score of unemployed male on PGI HQ-Total was found 6.6 whereas the mean score of unemployed female was found 13.30. It shows that the unemployed female also showed more PGI HQ-Total as compared to their counterpart. Average score of employed male on PGI HQ-Total was found 6.1 whereas the average score of unemployed male was found 6.6. It shows that the un-employed male have more PGI HQ-Total as compared to their counterpart. Average score of employed female on PGI HQ-Total was found 11.50 whereas the average score of unemployed female was found 13.30. It shows that the employed female have more PGI HQ-Total as compared to their counterpart. Average score of employed male on PGI HQ-Total was found 6.1 whereas the average score of unemployed female was found 13.30. It shows that the unemployed female have more PGI HQ-Total as compared to their counterpart. Average score of unemployed male on PGI HQ-Total was found 6.6 whereas the average score of employed female was found 11.50.It shows that the employed females have more PGI HQ-Total as compared to their counterpart.

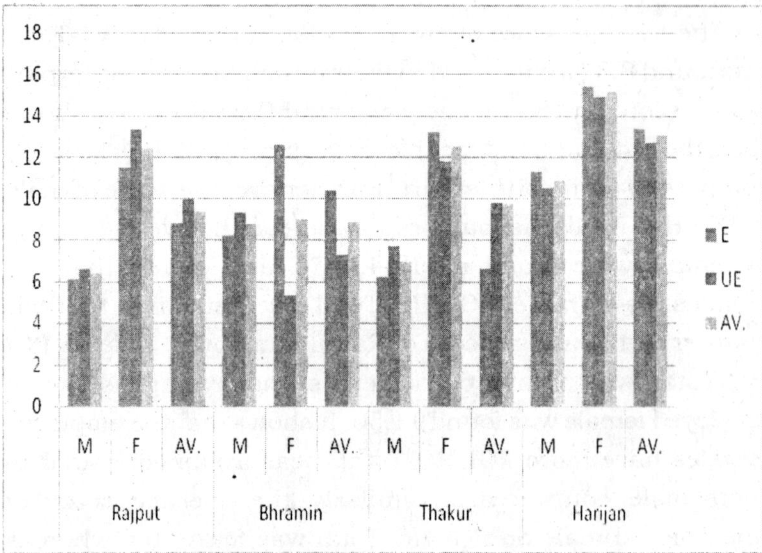

Fig 6.5 Average score of Rajput, Brahmin, Thakur and Harijan people on PGI HQ-total general health.

The average score of employed Bhramin on PGI HQ-Total was found 10.4 as compared to their un-employed counterpart whose score on their same was found 7.3.It clearly shows that the employed people have more PGI HQ-Total as compare to their counterpart. Further average score of male in PGI HQ-Total was found 8.75 whereas the average scores of female were found as 8.95. It clearly shows that the females have more PGI HQ-Total as compared to their counterpart. Average score of Bhramin employed male on PGI HQ-Total was found 8.2 whereas the average score of employed female was found 12.6. It shows that the employed females have more PGI HQ-Total measure as compared to their male counterpart. Similarly the average score of unemployed male on PGI HQ-Total was found 9.3 whereas the mean score of unemployed female was found 5.3. It shows that the unemployed male also showed more PGI HQ-Total as compared to their counterpart. Average score of employed male on PGI HQ-Total was found 8.2 whereas the average score of unemployed male was found 9.3. It shows that the un-employed male have more PGI HQ-Total as compared to their counterpart. Average score of employed female on PGI HQ-Total was found 12.6 whereas the average score of unemployed female was found 5.3. It shows that the employed female have more PGI HQ-Total as compared to their counterpart. Average score of employed male on PGI HQ-Total was found 8.2 whereas the average score of unemployed female was found 5.3It shows that the employed male has more PGI HQ-Total as compared to their counterpart. Average score of unemployed male on PGI HQ-Total was found 9.3 whereas the average score of employed female was found 12.6.It shows that the employed females have more PGI HQ-Total as compared to their counterpart.

The average score of employed Thakur on PGI HQ-Total was found 6.6 as compared to their un-employed counterpart whose score on their same was found 9.75.It clearly shows that the un-employed people have more PGI HQ-Total as compare to their counterpart. Further average score of male in PGI HQ-Total was found 6.95 whereas the average scores of female were found as 12.5. It clearly shows that the females have more PGI HQ-Total as compared to their counterpart. Average score of Thakur employed male on PGI HQ-Total was found 6.2 whereas the average score of employed female was found 13.2. It shows that the employed females have more PGI HQ-Total measure as compared to their male counterpart. Similarly the average score of unemployed male on PGI HQ-Total was found 7.7 whereas the mean score of unemployed female was found 11.8. It shows that the unemployed female also showed more PGI HQ-Total as compared to their counterpart. Average score of employed male on PGI HQ-Total was found 6.2 whereas the average score of unemployed male was found 7.7. It shows that the un-employed male have more PGI HQ-Total as compared to their counterpart. Average score of employed female on PGI HQ-Total was found 13.2 whereas the average score of unemployed female was found 11.8. It shows that the employed female have more PGI HQ-Total as compared to their counterpart. Average score of employed male on PGI HQ-Total was found 6.2 whereas the average score of unemployed female was found 11.8. It shows that the un-employed female have more PGI HQ-Total as compared to their counterpart. Average score of unemployed male on PGI HQ-Total was found 7.7 whereas the average score of employed female was found 13.2.It shows that the employed females have more PGI HQ-Total as compared to their counterpart.

The average score of employed Harijan on PGI HQ-Total was found 13.35 as compared to their un-employed counterpart whose score on their same was found 12.7.It clearly shows that the employed people have more PGI HQ-Total as compare to their counterpart. Further average score of male in PGI HQ-Total was found 10.9 whereas the average scores of female were found as 15.15. It clearly shows that the females have more PGI HQ-Total as compared to their counterpart., Average score of Harijan employed male on PGI HQ-Total was found 11.3 whereas the average score of employed female was found 15.4. It shows that the employed females have more PGI HQ-Total measure as compared to their male counterpart. Similarly the average score of unemployed male on PGI HQ-Total was found 10.5 whereas the mean score of unemployed female was found 14.9. It shows that the unemployed female also showed more PGI HQ-Total as compared to their counterpart. Average score of employed male on PGI HQ-Total was found 11.3 whereas the average score of unemployed male was found 10.5. It shows that the employed male have more PGI HQ-Total as compared to their counterpart. Average score of employed female on PGI HQ-Total was found 15.4 whereas the average score of unemployed female was found 14.9. It shows that the employed female have more PGI HQ-Total as compared to their counterpart. Average score of employed male on PGI HQ-Total was found 11.3 whereas the average score of un-employed female was found 14.9. It shows that the un-employed female have more PGI HQ-Total as compared to their counterpart. Average score of unemployed male on PGI HQ-Total was found 10.5 whereas the average score of employed female was found 15.4.It shows that the employed females have more PGI HQ-Total as compared to their counterpart.

Table 6.6 Average Score of Rajput, Brahmin, Thakur and Harijan People on PGI HQ General Health–A

	Rajput			Bhramin			Thakur			Harijan		
	M	F	AV.	M	F	AV.	M	F	AV.	M	F	AV.
E	2.800	6.100	4.45	3.60	5.800	4.70	3.500	5.300	4.40	4.300	6.000	5.15
UE	3.000	4.90	3.95	4.40	8.800	6.60	3.100	5.000	4.05	4.500	6.300	5.4
AV.	2.90	5.50	4.20	4.00	7.30	5.85	3.30	5.15	4.23	4.40	6.15	5.27

The average score of employed Rajput on PGI HQ-I was found 4.45 as compared to their un-employed counterpart whose score on their same was found 3.95.It clearly shows that the employed people have more PGI HQ-I as compare to their counterpart. Further average score of male in PGI HQ-I was found 2.90 whereas the average scores of female were found as 5.50. It clearly shows that the females have more PGI HQ-I as compared to their counterpart. Average score of Rajput employed male on PGI HQ-I was found 2.80 whereas the average score of employed female was found 6.1. It shows that the employed females have more PGI HQ-I measure as compared to their male counterpart. Similarly the average score of unemployed male on PGI HQ-I was found 3.0 whereas the mean score of unemployed female was found 4.90. It shows that the unemployed female also showed more PGI HQ-I as compared to their counterpart. Average score of employed male on PGI HQ-I was found 2.80 whereas the average score of unemployed male was found 3.0. It shows that the un-employed male have more PGI HQ-I as compared to their counterpart. Average score of employed female on PGI HQ-I was found 6.1 whereas the average score of unemployed female was found 4.90. It shows that the employed female have more PGI HQ-I as compared to their counterpart. Average score of employed male on PGI HQ-I was found 2.80 whereas the average score of unemployed female was found 4.90. It shows that the un-employed female have more PGI HQ-I as compared to their counterpart. Average score of unemployed male on PGI HQ-I was found 3.0 whereas the average score of employed female was found 6.1. It shows that the employed female have more PGI HQ-I as compared to their counterpart.

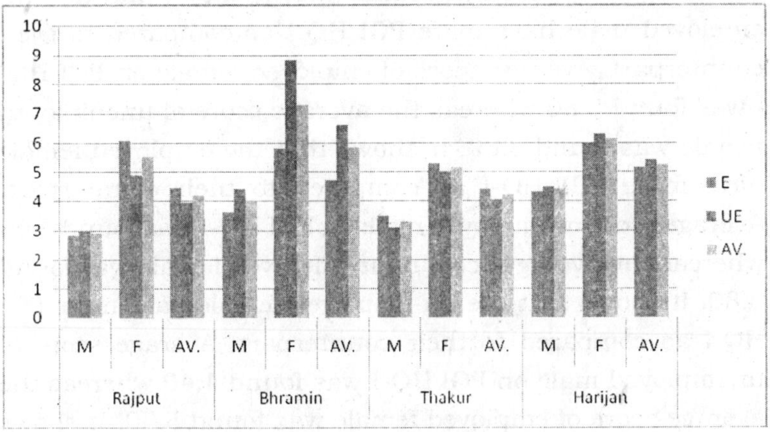

Fig 6.6: Average score of Rajput, Brahmin, Thakur and Harijan people on PGI HQ general health -A

The average score of employed Bhramin on PGI HQ-I was found 4.70 as compared to their un-employed counterpart whose score on their same was found 6.60.It clearly shows that the un-employed people have more PGI HQ-I as compare to their counterpart. Further average score of male in PGI HQ-I was found 4.00 whereas the average scores of female were found as 7.30. It clearly shows that the females have more PGI HQ-I as compared to their counterpart. Average score of Bhramin employed male on PGI HQ-I was found 3.60 whereas the average score of employed female was found 5.80. It shows that the employed females have more PGI HQ-I measure as compared to their male counterpart. Similarly the average score of unemployed male on PGI HQ-I was found 4.40whereas the mean score of unemployed female was found 8.80. It shows that the unemployed female also showed more PGI HQ-I as compared to their counterpart. Average score of employed male on PGI HQ-I was found 3.36 whereas the average score of unemployed male was found 4.40. It shows that the un-employed male have more PGI HQ-I as compared to their counterpart. Average score of employed female on PGI HQ-I was found 5.80 whereas the average score of unemployed female was found 8.80. It shows that the employed female have more PGI HQ-I as compared to their counterpart. Average score of employed male on PGI HQ-I was found 3.60 whereas the average score of unemployed female was found 8.80. It shows that the un-employed female have more PGI HQ-I as compared to their counterpart. Average score of unemployed male on PGI HQ-I was found 4.40 whereas the average score of employed female was found 5.80. It shows that the employed female have more PGI HQ-I as compared to their counterpart.

The average score of employed Thakur on PGI HQ-I was found 4.40 as compared to their un-employed counterpart whose score on their same was found 4.05.It clearly shows that the employed people have more PGI HQ-I as compare to their counterpart. Further average score of male in PGI HQ-I was found 3.3 whereas the average scores of female were found as 5.15. It clearly shows that the females have more PGI HQ-I as compared to their counterpart. Average score of Thakur employed male on PGI HQ-I was found 3.5 whereas the average score of employed female was found 5.3. It shows that the employed females have more PGI HQ-I measure as compared to their male counterpart. Similarly the average score of unemployed male on PGI HQ-I was found 3.1 whereas the mean score of unemployed female was found 5.0. It shows that the unemployed female also showed more PGI HQ-I as compared to their counterpart. Average score of employed male on PGI HQ-I was found 3.5 whereas the average score of unemployed male was found 3.1. It shows that the un-employed male have more PGI HQ-I as compared to their counterpart. Average score of employed female on PGI HQ-I was found 5.3 whereas the average score of unemployed female was found 5.0. It shows that the employed female have more PGI HQ-I as compared to their counterpart. Average score of employed male on PGI HQ-I was found 3.5 whereas the average score of unemployed female was found 5.0. It shows that the un-employed female have more PGI HQ-I as compared to their counterpart. Average score of unemployed male on PGI HQ-I was found 3.1 whereas the average score of employed female was found 5.3. It shows that the employed female have more PGI HQ-I as compared to their counterpart.

The average score of employed Harijan on PGI HQ-I was found 5.15 as compared to their un-employed counterpart whose score on their same was found 5.40.It clearly shows that the un-employed people have more PGI HQ-I as compare to their counterpart. Further average score of male in PGI HQ-I was found 4.4 whereas the average scores of female were found as 6.15. It clearly shows that the females have more PGI HQ-I as compared to their counterpart. Average score of Harijan employed male on PGI HQ-I was found 4.3 whereas the average score of employed female was found 6.0. It shows that the employed females have more PGI HQ-I measure as compared to their male counterpart. Similarly the average score of unemployed male on PGI HQ-I was found 4.5 whereas the mean score of unemployed female was found 6.3. It shows that the unemployed female also showed more PGI HQ-I as compared to their counterpart. Average score of employed male on PGI HQ-I was found 4.3 whereas the average score of unemployed male was found 4.5. It shows that the un-employed male have more PGI HQ-I as compared to their counterpart. Average score of employed female on PGI HQ-I was found 6.0 whereas the average score of unemployed female was found 6.3. It shows that the employed female have more PGI HQ-I as compared to their counterpart. Average score of employed male on PGI HQ-I was found 4.3 whereas the average score of unemployed female was found 6.3. It shows that the un-employed female have more PGI HQ-I as compared to their counterpart. Average score of unemployed male on PGI HQ-I was found 4.5 whereas the average score of employed female was found 6.0.It shows that the employed females have more PGI HQ-I as compared to their counterpart.

Table 6.7 Average Score of Rajput, Brahmin, Thakur and Harijan People on PGI HQ General Health–B

	Rajput			Bhramin			Thakur			Harijan		
	M	F	AV.	M	F	AV.	M	F	AV.	M	F	AV.
E	3.300	5.400	**4.35**	4.600	6.800	**5.70**	2.700	7.900	**5.30**	7.000	9.400	**8.20**
UE	3.600	8.400	**6.00**	4.900	6.500	**2.48**	4.600	6.800	**5.70**	6.000	8.600	**7.25**
AV.	**3.45**	**6.90**	**5.18**	**4.75**	**6.65**	**5.70**	**3.65**	**7.35**	**5.50**	**6.50**	**9.00**	**7.75**

The average score of employed Rajput on PGI HQ-II was found 4.35 as compared to their un-employed counterpart whose score on their same was found 6.00.It clearly shows that the un-employed people have more PGI HQ-II as compare to their counterpart. Further average score of male in PGI HQ-II was found 3.45 whereas the average scores of female were found as 6.90. It clearly shows that the females have more PGI HQ-II as compared to their counterpart. Average score of Rajput employed male on PGI HQ-II was found 3.3 whereas the average score of employed female was found 5.4. It shows that the employed females have more PGI HQ-II measure as compared to their male counterpart. Similarly the average score of unemployed male on PGI HQ-II was found 3.6 whereas the mean score of unemployed female was found 8.4. It shows that the unemployed female also showed more PGI HQ-II as compared to their counterpart. Average score of employed male on PGI HQ-II was found 3.3 whereas the average score of unemployed male was found 3.6. It shows that the un-employed male have more PGI HQ-II as compared to their counterpart. Average score of employed female on PGI HQ-II was found 5.4 whereas the average score of unemployed female was found 8.4. It shows that the employed female have more PGI HQ-II as compared to their counterpart. Average score of employed male on PGI HQ-II was found 3.3 whereas the average score

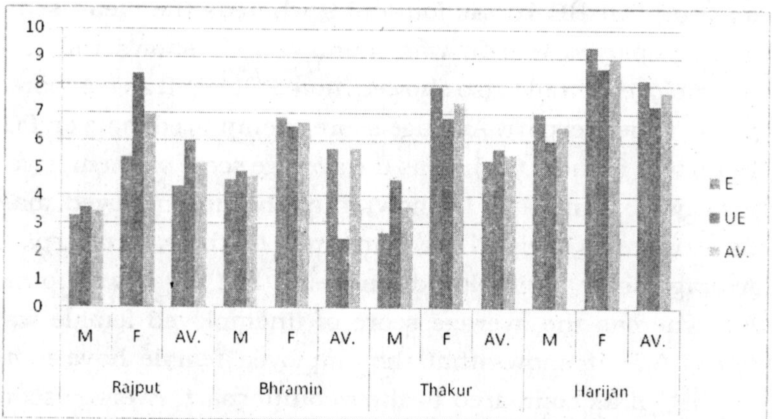

Fig 6.7 Average score of Rajput, Brahmin, Thakur and Harijan people on PGI HQ general health-B

of unemployed female was found 8.4. It shows that the unemployed female have more PGI HQ-II as compared to their counterpart. Average score of unemployed male on PGI HQ-II was found 3.6 whereas the average score of employed female was found 5.4.It shows that the employed females have more PGI HQ-II as compared to their counterpart.

The average score of employed Bhramin on PGI HQ-II was found 5.70 as compared to their un-employed counterpart whose score on their same was found 2.48.It clearly shows that the employed people have more PGI HQ-II as compare to their counterpart. Further average score of male in PGI HQ-II was found 4.75 whereas the average scores of female were found as 6.65. It clearly shows that the females have more PGI HQ-II as compared to their counterpart. Average score of Bhramin employed male on PGI HQ-II was found 4.6 whereas the average score of employed female was found 6.8. It shows that the employed females have more PGI HQ-II measure as compared to their male counterpart. Similarly the average score of unemployed male on PGI HQ-II was found 4.9 whereas the mean score of unemployed female was found 6.5. It shows that the unemployed female also showed more PGI HQ-II as compared to their counterpart. Average score of employed male on PGI HQ-II was found 4.6 whereas the average score of unemployed male was found 4.9. It shows that the un-employed male have more PGI HQ-II as compared to their counterpart. Average score of employed female on PGI HQ-II was found 6.8 whereas the average score of unemployed female was found 6.5. It shows that the employed female have more PGI HQ-II as compared to their counterpart. Average score of employed male on PGI HQ-II was found 4.6 whereas the average score of unemployed female was found 6.5. It shows

that the un-employed female have more PGI HQ-II as compared to their counterpart. Average score of unemployed male on PGI HQ-II was found 4.9 whereas the average score of employed female was found 6.8.It shows that the employed females have more PGI HQ-II as compared to their counterpart.

The average score of employed Thakur on PGI HQ-II was found 5.30 as compared to their un-employed counterpart whose score on their same was found 5.70.It clearly shows that the un-employed people have more PGI HQ-II as compare to their counterpart. Further average score of male in PGI HQ-II was found 3.65 whereas the average scores of female were found as 7.35. It clearly shows that the females have more PGI HQ-II as compared to their counterpart. Average score of Thakur employed male on PGI HQ-II was found 2.7 whereas the average score of employed female was found 7.9. It shows that the employed females have more PGI HQ-II measure as compared to their male counterpart. Similarly the average score of unemployed male on PGI HQ-II was found 4.6 whereas the mean score of unemployed female was found 6.8. It shows that the unemployed female also showed more PGI HQ-II as compared to their counterpart. Average score of employed male on PGI HQ-II was found 2.7 whereas the average score of unemployed male was found 4.6. It shows that the un-employed male have more PGI HQ-II as compared to their counterpart. Average score of employed female on PGI HQ-II was found 7.0 whereas the average score of unemployed female was found 6.8. It shows that the employed female have more PGI HQ-II as compared to their counterpart. Average score of employed male on PGI HQ-II was found 2.7 whereas the average score of unemployed female was found 6.8. It shows

that the un-employed female have more PGI HQ-II as compared to their counterpart. Average score of unemployed male on PGI HQ-II was found 4.6 whereas the average score of employed female was found 7.9.It shows that the employed females have more PGI HQ-II as compared to their counterpart.

The average score of employed Harijan on PGI HQ-II was found 8.20 as compared to their un-employed counterpart whose score on their same was found 7.25.It clearly shows that the employed people have more PGI HQ-II as compare to their counterpart. Further average score of male in PGI HQ-II was found 6.50 whereas the average scores of female were found as 9.00. It clearly shows that the females have more PGI HQ-II as compared to their counterpart. Average score of Harijan employed male on PGI HQ-II was found 7.0 whereas the average score of employed female was found 9.4. It shows that the employed females have more PGI HQ-II measure as compared to their male counterpart. Similarly the average score of unemployed male on PGI HQ-II was found 6.0 whereas the mean score of unemployed female was found 8.6. It shows that the unemployed female also showed more PGI HQ-II as compared to their counterpart. Average score of employed male on PGI HQ-II was found 7.0 whereas the average score of unemployed male was found 6.0. It shows that the un-employed male have more PGI HQ-II as compared to their counterpart. Average score of employed female on PGI HQ-II was found 9.4 whereas the average score of unemployed female was found 8.6. It shows that the employed female have more PGI HQ-II as compared to their counterpart. Average score of employed male on PGI HQ-II was found 7.0 whereas the average score of unemployed female was found 8.6. It shows

that the un-employed female have more PGI HQ-II as compared to their counterpart. Average score of unemployed male on PGI HQ-II was found 6.0 whereas the average score of employed female was found 9.4.It shows that the employed females have more PGI HQ-II as compared to their counterpart.

Most of the studies as quoted by different philosophers and psychologists reveals that the religious person is physically, socially and psychological better as compared to their counterpart. The study of Duhrssen (1978) described similarities between religious practices and psychotherapeutic methods. The study of Alex, Carl, Michael, and David (1999) gave the controlled intervention studies offer considerable promisc to better understand relationships and possible mechanisms between spiritual and religious factors and health. The study of Oman and Thoresen (2002) explored that could religion or spirituality cause physical health benefits to individuals. The article of Tan, 2003 focuses specifically on integrating spiritual direction into psychotherapy, discusses ethical issues involved and provides ethical guidelines for the appropriate and helpful use of spiritual direction in the context of psychotherapy and counseling. Larson and Susan (2003) gave a longitudinal studies of community samples consistently find links between active religious involvement and increased chances for living longer, pointing to the relevance of religion as a potential health factor. Ardelt (2003) in his study said that although religiosity tends to help older people to cope with physical and social losses, not all studies find a significant association between religious involvement and well-being in old age. The study of Geertsma (2004) tried to describe midlife transition, spirituality, and healing of relationships for members of women's spirituality groups. Benefits of women's spirituality groups include the groups being therapeutic, providing valued relationships, and providing social support. Bhasin (2008) through her study put forwarded the Source of Healing of the Gaddis' people, their traditional and folk medicine. Patients seek cures from a variety of medical systems. In the traditional medical systems, medical traditions partly cover other sectors of social life. The study of Michael (2010) explored how the relationship between religious involvement and mental health varies by gender among the aging population.

SPIRITUAL WELLEING

Objective of the present study is to compare employed and unemployed men and women of different caste on the measure of fear of success, religiosity and wellbeing. The study also intends to seek the relationship between the variable under study. Finally the study intends to see the impact of fear of success and religiosity on wellbeing. For accomplishing the objective, the study has been conducted on sample of 160 people of Chopal tehsil divided into Rajputs, Bhramins, Thakurs, and Harijans (40 in each group). These subjects were further sub-divided into employed and unemployed (20 in each group). Further they were divided into males and females (10 in each group). In all there were sixteen groups in total with 10 subjects in each group comprising of total sample of 160 people. The aforesaid groups were also assessed with the help of qualitative and quantitative measures. The qualitative measure include, observation, interview, fuzzy cognitive mapping and photography whereas the quantitative measures include fear of success scale, spiritual well being scale, satisfaction with life scale, short depression-happiness scale and PGI health questionnaire. The result based on mean, SD, A 4 x 2 x 2 ANOVA has been displaced in the below mentioned section in a more synchronized way. The description is as follows:-

7.1 FEAR OF SUCCESS

From the table 5.1 it is quite clear that the main effect of Caste on the measure of Fear of success was found F (3, 144) = 28.83, p<.01 as statistically significant. But the main effect of Employment on the measure of Fear of success was found F (1, 144) = 1.70, p>.05 as statistically non-significant. The main effect of Sex on the measure of Fear of success was found F (1, 144) = 14.24, p<.01 as statistically significant. The two way interaction between Caste x Employment on the measure of Fear of success was found F (3, 144) =1.55, p>.05 as statistically non- significant. Similarly the two way interaction between Caste x Sex on the measure of Fear of success was found F (3, 144) =.203, p>.05 as statistically non significant. The two way interaction between Employment x Sex on the measure of Fear of success was found F (1, 144) = .001, p>.05 as statistically non significant. Finally the three way interaction between Caste x Employment x Sex on the measure of Fear of success was found F (3,144) = .115, p>.05 as statistically non significant. The average score of employed Rajput on Fear of Success was found 25.30 as compared to their un-employed counterpart whose score on their same was found 23.30.it clearly shows that the employed people have more fear of success as compare to their counterpart. Further average score of male in FOS was found 22.35 whereas the average scores of female were found as 26.25. It clearly shows that the females have more fear of success as compared to their counterpart. Average score of Rajput employed male on FOS was found 23.60 whereas the average score of employed female was found 27.00. It shows that the employed female have more FOS as compared to their male counterpart. Similarly the average score of unemployed male on FOS was found 21.10 whereas the mean score of unemployed female was found 25.50. It shows that the unemployed female also showed more FOS as compared to their counterpart. Average score of employed male on FOS was found 23.60 whereas the average score of unemployed male was found 21.10. It shows that the un-employed male have more FOS as compared to their counterpart. Average score of employed female on FOS was found 27.00 whereas the average score of unemployed female was found 25.50. It shows that the employed female have more FOS as compared to their counterpart. Average score of employed male on FOS was found 23.60 whereas the average score of unemployed female was found 25.50. It shows that the unemployed female have more FOS as compared to their counterpart. Average score of unemployed male on FOS was found 21.10 whereas the average score of employed female was found 27.00. It shows that the employed female have more FOS as compared to their counterpart.

The average score of employed Bhramin on Fear of Success was found 27.00 as compared to their un-employed counterpart whose score on their same was found 26.00.it clearly shows that the employed people have more fear of success as compare to their counterpart. Further average score of male in FOS was found 25.05 whereas the average scores of female were found as 27.95. It clearly shows that the females have more fear of success as compared to their counterpart. Average score of Bhramin employed male on FOS was found 25.70 whereas the average score of employed female was found 28.30. It shows that the employed female have more FOS as compared to their male counterpart. Similarly the average score of unemployed male on FOS was found 224.40 whereas the mean score of unemployed female was found 27.60. It shows that the unemployed female also showed more FOS as compared to their counterpart. Average score of employed male on FOS was found 25.70 whereas the average score of unemployed male was found 24.40. It shows that the employed male have more FOS as compared to their counterpart. Average score of employed female on FOS was found 28.30 whereas the average score of un-employed female was found 27.60. It shows that then employed female have more FOS as compared to their counterpart. Average score of employed male on FOS was found 25.70 whereas the average score of unemployed female was found 27.60. It shows that the unemployed female have more FOS as compared to their counterpart. Average score of unemployed male on FOS was found 24.40 whereas the average score of employed female was found 28.30. It shows that the employed female have more FOS as compared to their counterpart.

The average score of employed Thakur on Fear of Success was found 24.25 as compared to their un-employed counterpart whose score on their same was found 24.90.it clearly shows that the un-employed people have more fear of success as compare to their counterpart. Further average score of male in FOS was found 23.20 whereas the average scores of female were found as 25.90. It clearly shows that the females have more fear of success as compared to their counterpart. Average score of Thakur employed male on FOS was found 25.50 whereas the average score of employed female was found 26.00. It shows that the employed female have more FOS as compared to their male counterpart. Similarly the average score of unemployed male on FOS was found 23.90 whereas the mean score of unemployed female was found 25.90. It shows that the unemployed female also showed more FOS as compared to their counterpart. Average score of employed male on FOS was found 25.50 whereas the average score of unemployed male was found 23.90. It shows that the employed male have more FOS as compared to their counterpart. Average score of employed female on FOS was found 26.00 whereas the average score of unemployed female was found 25.90. It shows that the employed female have more FOS as compared to their counterpart. Average score of employed male on FOS was found 25.50 whereas the average score of unemployed female was found 25.90. It shows that the unemployed female have more FOS as compared to their counterpart. Average score of unemployed male on FOS was found 23.90 whereas the average score of employed female was found 26.00. It shows that the employed female have more FOS as compared to their counterpart.

The average score of employed Harijan on Fear of Success was found 34.20 as compared to their un-employed counterpart whose score on their same was found 23.10 it clearly shows that the employed people have more fear of success as compare to their counterpart. Further average score of male in FOS was found 28.00 whereas the average scores of female were found as 29.30. It clearly shows that the females have more fear of success as compared to their counterpart. Average score of Harijan employed male on FOS was found 33.40 whereas the average score of employed female was found 35.00. It shows that the employed female have more FOS as compared to their male counterpart. Similarly the average score of unemployed male on FOS was found 22.60 whereas the mean score of unemployed female was found 23.60. It shows that the unemployed female also showed more FOS as compared to their counterpart. Average score of employed male on FOS was found 33.40 whereas the average score of unemployed male was found 22.60. It shows that the employed male have more FOS as compared to their counterpart. Average score of employed female on FOS was found 35.00 whereas the average score of unemployed female was found 23.60. It shows that the employed female have more FOS as compared to their counterpart. Average score of employed male on FOS was found 33.40 whereas the average score of unemployed female was found 23.60. It shows that the unemployed female have more FOS as compared to their counterpart. Average score of unemployed male on FOS was found 22.60 whereas the average score of employed female was found 35.00. It shows that the employed female have more FOS as compared to their counterpart.

7.2 SPIRITUAL WELLBEING

From the table 5.2 it is quite clear that the main effect of Caste on the measure of Spiritual Wellbeing was found $F(3, 144) = 7.39$, $p<.01$ as statistically significant. Similarly the main effect of Employment on the measure of Spiritual Wellbeing was found $F(1, 144) = 20.56$, $p<.01$ as statistically significant. The main effect of Sex on the measure of Spiritual Wellbeing was found $F(1, 144) = 13.38$, $p<.01$ as statistically significant. The two way interaction between Caste x Employment on the measure of Spiritual wellbeing was found $F(3, 144) = 12.636$, $p<.01$ as statistically significant. But the two way interaction between Caste x Sex on the measure of Spiritual Wellbeing was found $F(3, 144) = .521$, $p>.05$ as statistically non- significant. Similarly the two way interaction between Employment x Sex on the measure of Spiritual Wellbeing was found $F(1, 144) = .007$, $p>.05$ as statistically non-significant. Finally the three way interaction between Caste x Employment x Sex on the measure of Spiritual Wellbeing was found $F(3,144) = .148$, $p>.05$ as statistically non significant.

The average score of employed Rajput on spiritual wellbeing was found 89.90as compared to their un-employed counterpart whose score on their same was found 87.85.it clearly shows that the employed people have more spiritual wellbeing as compare to their counterpart. Further average score of male in spiritual wellbeing was found 91.45 whereas the average scores of female were found as 86.30. It clearly shows that the males have more spiritual wellbeing as compared to their counterpart. Average score of Rajput employed male on spiritual wellbeing was found 92.4 whereas the average score of employed female was found 87.4. It shows that the employed male have more spiritual wellbeing as compared to their male counterpart. Similarly the average score of unemployed male on spiritual wellbeing was found 90.5 whereas the mean score of unemployed female was found 85.2. It shows that the unemployed male also showed more spiritual wellbeing as compared to their counterpart. Average score of employed male on spiritual wellbeing was found 92.4 whereas the average score of unemployed male was found 90.5. It shows that the employed male have more spiritual wellbeing as compared to their counterpart. Average score of employed female on spiritual wellbeing was found 87.4 whereas the average score of unemployed female was found 85.2. It shows that the employed female have more spiritual wellbeing as compared to their counterpart. Average score of employed male on spiritual wellbeing was found 92.4 whereas the average score of unemployed female was found 85.2. It shows that the employed male have more spiritual wellbeing as compared to their counterpart. Average score of unemployed male on spiritual wellbeing was found 90.5 whereas the average score of employed female was found 87.4. It shows that the un-employed male have more spiritual wellbeing as compared to their counterpart.

The average score of employed Bhramin on spiritual wellbeing was found 88.55as compared to their un-employed counterpart whose score on their same was found 90.25.it clearly shows that the un- employed people have more spiritual wellbeing as compare to their counterpart. Further average score of male in spiritual wellbeing was found 90.95 whereas the average scores of female were found as 87.85. It clearly shows that the males have more spiritual wellbeing as compared to their counterpart. Average score of Bhramin employed male on spiritual wellbeing was found 90.40 whereas the average score of employed female was found 86.70. It shows that the employed male have more spiritual wellbeing as compared to their male counterpart. Similarly the average score of unemployed male on spiritual wellbeing was found 91.50 whereas the mean score of unemployed female was found 89.00. It shows that the unemployed male also showed more spiritual wellbeing as compared to their counterpart. Average score of employed male on spiritual wellbeing was found 90.40 whereas the average score of unemployed male was found 91.50. It shows that the un-employed male have more spiritual wellbeing as compared to their counterpart. Average score of employed female on spiritual wellbeing was found 86.70 whereas the average score of unemployed female was found 89.00. It shows that the un- employed female have more spiritual wellbeing as compared to their counterpart. Average score of employed male on spiritual wellbeing was found 90.40 whereas the average score of unemployed female was found 89.00. It shows that the employed male have more spiritual wellbeing as compared to their counterpart. Average score of unemployed male on spiritual wellbeing was found 91.50 whereas the average score of employed female was found

86.70. It shows that the un-employed male have more spiritual wellbeing as compared to their counterpart.

The average score of employed Thakur on spiritual wellbeing was found 90.40 as compared to their un-employed counterpart whose score on their same was found 89.85.it clearly shows that the employed people have more spiritual wellbeing as compare to their counterpart. Further average score of male in spiritual wellbeing was found 91.90 whereas the average scores of female were found as 88.35. It clearly shows that the males have more spiritual wellbeing as compared to their counterpart. Average score of Thakur employed male on spiritual wellbeing was found 92.40 whereas the average score of employed female was found 88.40. It shows that the employed male have more spiritual wellbeing as compared to their male counterpart. Similarly the average score of unemployed male on spiritual wellbeing was found 91.40 whereas the mean score of unemployed female was found 88.30. It shows that the unemployed male also showed more spiritual wellbeing as compared to their counterpart. Average score of employed male on spiritual wellbeing was found 92.40 whereas the average score of unemployed male was found 91.40. It shows that the employed male have more spiritual wellbeing as compared to their counterpart. Average score of employed female on spiritual wellbeing was found 88.40 whereas the average score of unemployed female was found 88.30. It shows that the employed female have more spiritual wellbeing as compared to their counterpart. Average score of employed male on spiritual wellbeing was found 92.40 whereas the average score of unemployed female was found 88.30. It shows that the employed male have more spiritual wellbeing as compared to their counterpart. Average score of unemployed male on spiritual wellbeing was found 91.40 whereas the average score of employed female was found 88.40. It shows that the un-employed male have more spiritual wellbeing as compared to their counterpart.

The average score of employed Harijan on spiritual wellbeing was found 80.10 as compared to their un-employed counterpart whose score on their same was found 75.25.It clearly shows that the employed people have more spiritual wellbeing as compare to their counterpart. Further average score of male in spiritual wellbeing was found 80.10 whereas the average scores of female were found as 75.25. It clearly shows that the males have more spiritual wellbeing as compared to their counterpart. Average score of Harijan employed male on spiritual wellbeing was found 82.00 whereas the average score of employed female was found 78.20. It shows that the employed male have more spiritual wellbeing as compared to their male counterpart. Similarly the average score of unemployed male on spiritual wellbeing was found 78.20 whereas the mean score of unemployed female was found 72.30. It shows that the unemployed male also showed more spiritual wellbeing as compared to their counterpart. Average score of employed male on spiritual wellbeing was found 82.00 whereas the average score of unemployed male was found 78.20. It shows that the employed male have more spiritual wellbeing as compared to their counterpart. Average score of employed female on spiritual wellbeing was found 78.20 whereas the average score of unemployed female was found 72.30. It shows that the employed female have more spiritual wellbeing as compared to their counterpart. Average score of employed male on spiritual wellbeing was found 82.00 whereas the average score of unemployed female was found 72.30. It shows that the employed male have more spiritual wellbeing as compared to their counterpart. Average score of unemployed male on spiritual wellbeing was found 78.20 whereas the average score of employed female was found 78.20. It shows that the both unemployed-male and employed female have equal spiritual wellbeing.

7.3 ANALYSIS OF LIFE SATISFACTION

From the table 5.3 it is quite clear that the main effect of Caste on the measure of Satisfaction with Life was found F (3, 144) = 12.39, p<.01 as statistically significant. But the main effect of Employment on the measure of Satisfaction with Life was found F (1, 144) = 1.31, p>.05 as statistically non- significant. The main effect of Sex on the measure of Satisfaction with Life was found F (1, 144) = 58.93, p<.01 as statistically significant. The two way interaction between Caste x Employment on the measure of Satisfaction with Life was found F (3, 144) =1.36, p>.05 as statistically non-significant. Similarly the two way interaction between Caste x Sex on the measure of Satisfaction with Life was found F (3, 144) =.974, p>.05 as statistically non significant. The two way interaction between Employment x Sex on the measure of Satisfaction with Life was found F (1, 144) = 2.22, p>.05 as statistically non significant. Finally the three way interaction between Caste x Employment x Sex on the measure of Satisfaction with Life was found F (3,144) = .225, p>.05 as statistically non significant.

The average score of employed Rajput on satisfaction with life was found 26.95 as compared to their un-employed counterpart whose score on their same was found 27.95.It clearly shows that the un-employed people have more satisfaction with life as compare to their counterpart. Further average score of male in satisfaction with life was found 29.10 whereas the average scores of female were found as 25.80. It clearly shows that the males have more satisfaction with life as compared to their counterpart. Average score of Rajput employed male on satisfaction with life was found 28.20 whereas the average score of employed female was found 25.70. It shows that the employed male have more satisfaction with life as compared to their male counterpart. Similarly the average score of unemployed male on satisfaction with life was found 30.00 whereas the mean score of unemployed female was found 25.90. It shows that the unemployed male also showed more satisfaction with life as compared to their counterpart. Average score of employed male on satisfaction with life was found 28.20 whereas the average score of unemployed male was found 30.00. It shows that the un-employed male have more satisfaction with life as compared to their counterpart. Average score of employed female on satisfaction with life was found 25.70 whereas the average score of unemployed female was found 25.90. It shows that the un-employed female have more satisfaction with life as compared to their counterpart. Average score of employed male on satisfaction with life was found 28.20 whereas the average score of unemployed female was found 25.90. It shows that the employed male have more satisfaction with life as compared to their counterpart. Average score of unemployed male on satisfaction with life was found 30.00 whereas the average score of employed female was found 25.70. It shows that the un-employed male have more satisfaction with life as compared to their counterpart.

The average score of employed Bhramin on satisfaction with life was found 25.00 as compared to their un-employed counterpart whose score on their same was found 26.45.It clearly shows that the un-employed people have more satisfaction with life as compare to their counterpart. Further average score of male in satisfaction with life was found 27.55 whereas the average scores of female were found as 23.90. It clearly shows that the males have more satisfaction with life as compared to their counterpart. Average score of Bhramin employed male on satisfaction with life was found 26.60 whereas the average score of employed female was found 23.40. It shows that the employed male have more satisfaction with life as compared to their male counterpart. Similarly the average score of unemployed male on satisfaction with life was found 28.50 whereas the mean score of unemployed female was found 24.40. It shows that the unemployed male also showed more satisfaction with life as compared to their counterpart. Average score of employed male on satisfaction with life was found 26.60 whereas the average score of unemployed male was found 28.50. It shows that the un-employed male have more satisfaction with life as compared to their counterpart. Average score of employed female on satisfaction with life was found 23.40 whereas the average score of unemployed female was found 24.40.It shows that the un-employed female has more satisfaction with life as compared to their counterpart. Average score of employed male on satisfaction with life was found 26.60 whereas the average score of unemployed female was found 24.40. It shows that the employed male have more satisfaction with life as compared to their counterpart. Average score of unemployed male on satisfaction with life was found 28.50 whereas the average score of employed female was found 23.40. It shows that the un-employed male have more satisfaction with life as compared to their counterpart.

The average score of employed Thakur on satisfaction with life was found 28.20 as compared to their un-employed counterpart whose score on their same was found 27.30.It clearly shows that the employed people have more satisfaction with life as compare to their counterpart. Further average score of male in satisfaction with life was found 28.85 whereas the average scores of female was found as 26.65.It clearly shows that the males have more satisfaction with life as compared to their counterpart. Average score of Thakur employed male on satisfaction with life was found 29.20 whereas the average score of employed female was found 27.20. It shows that the employed male have more satisfaction with life as compared to their male counterpart. Similarly the average score of unemployed male on satisfaction with life was found 28.50 whereas the mean score of unemployed female was found 26.10. It shows that the unemployed male also showed more satisfaction with life as compared to their counterpart. Average score of employed male on satisfaction with life was found 29.20 whereas the average score of unemployed male was found 28.50. It shows that the employed male have more satisfaction with life as compared to their counterpart. Average score of employed female on satisfaction with life was found 27.20 whereas the average score of unemployed female was found 26.10. It shows that the employed female have more satisfaction with life as compared to their counterpart. Average score of employed male on satisfaction with life was found 29.20 whereas the average score of unemployed female was found 26.10. It shows that the employed male have more satisfaction with life as compared to their counterpart. Average score of unemployed male on satisfaction with life was found 28.50 whereas the average score of employed female was found 27.20. It shows that the un-employed male have more satisfaction with life as compared to their counterpart.

The average score of employed Harijan on satisfaction with life was found 24.25 as compared to their un-employed counterpart whose score on their same was found 24.70.It clearly shows that the un-employed people have more satisfaction with life as compare to their counterpart. Further average score of male in spiritual wellbeing was found 26.60 whereas the average scores of female were found as 22.35. It clearly shows that the males have more satisfaction with life as compared to their counterpart. Average score of Harijan employed male on satisfaction with life was found 25.80 whereas the average score of employed female was found 22.70. It shows that the employed male have more satisfaction with life as compared to their male counterpart. Similarly the average score of unemployed male on satisfaction with life was found 27.40 whereas the mean score of unemployed female was found 22.00. It shows that the unemployed male also showed more satisfaction with life as compared to their counterpart. Average score of employed male on satisfaction with life was found 25.80 whereas the average score of unemployed male was found 27.40. It shows that the un-employed male have more satisfaction with life as compared to their counterpart. Average score of employed female on satisfaction with life was found 22.70 whereas the average score of unemployed female was found 22.00. It shows that the employed female have more satisfaction with life as compared to their counterpart. Average score of employed male on satisfaction with life was found 25.80 whereas the average score of unemployed female was found 22.00. It shows that the employed male have more satisfaction with life as compared to their counterpart. Average score of unemployed male on satisfaction with life was found 27.40 whereas the average score of employed female was found 22.70. It shows that the un-employed male have more satisfaction with life as compared to their counterpart.

7.4 ANALYSIS OF HAPPINESS AND DEPRESSION

From the table 5.4 it is quite clear that the main effect of Caste on the measure of Depression-Happiness Parameters was found F (3, 144) = .573, p>.05 as statistically non-significant. Similarly the main effect of Employment on the measure of Depression-Happiness Parameters was found F (1, 144) = .142, p>.05 as statistically non- significant. The main effect of Sex on the measure of Depression-Happiness Parameters was found F (1, 144) = 2.951, p<.01 as statistically significant. The two way interaction between Caste x Employment on the measure of Depression-Happiness Parameters was found F (3, 144) =9.57, p<.01 as statistically significant. Similarly the two way interaction between Caste x Sex on the measure of Depression-Happiness Parameters was found F (3, 144) =2.46, p<.01 as statistically significant. The two way interaction between Employment x Sex on the measure of Depression-Happiness Parameters was found F (1, 144) = 5.31, p<.01 as statistically significant. Finally the three way interaction between Caste x Employment x Sex on the measure of Depression-Happiness Parameters was found F (3,144) = 4.09, p<.01 as statistically significant.

The average score of employed Rajput on depression-happiness measure was found 13.30 as compared to their un-employed counterpart whose score on their same was found 13.80.It clearly shows that the un-employed people have more depression-happiness measure as compare to their counterpart. Further average score of male in depression-happiness measure was found 13.75 whereas the average scores of female were found as 13.35. It clearly shows that the males have more depression-happiness measure as compared to their counterpart. Average score of Rajput employed male on depression-happiness measure was found 12.40 whereas the average score of employed female was found 14.20. It shows that the employed female have more depression-happiness measure as compared to their male counterpart. Similarly the average score of unemployed male on depression-happiness measure was found 15.10 whereas the mean score of unemployed female was found 12.50. It shows that the unemployed male also showed more depression-happiness measure as compared to their counterpart. Average score of employed male on depression-happiness measure was found 12.40 whereas the average score of unemployed male was found 15.10. It shows that the un-employed male have more depression-happiness measure as compared to their counterpart. Average score of employed female on depression-happiness measure was found 14.20 whereas the average score of unemployed female was found 12.50. It shows that the employed female have more depression-happiness measure as compared to their counterpart. Average score of employed male on depression-happiness measure was found 12.40 whereas the average score of unemployed female was found 12.50. It shows that the un-employed male have more depression-happiness measure as compared to their counterpart. Average score of unemployed male on depression-happiness measure was found 15.10 whereas the average score of employed female was found 14.20. It shows that the un-employed male have more depression-happiness measure as compared to their counterpart.

The average score of employed Bhramin on depression-happiness measure was found 13.30 as compared to their un-employed counterpart whose score on their same was found 14.65.It clearly shows that the un-employed people have more depression-happiness measure as compare to their counterpart. Further average score of male in depression-happiness measure was found 13.65 whereas the average scores of female were found as 14.30. It clearly shows that the females have more depression-happiness measure as compared to their counterpart. Average score of Bhramin employed male on depression-happiness measure was found 12.80 whereas the average score of employed female was found 13.80. It shows that the employed female have more depression-happiness measure as compared to their male counterpart. Similarly the average score of unemployed male on depression-happiness measure was found 14.50 whereas the mean score of unemployed female was found 14.80. It shows that the unemployed female also showed more depression-happiness measure as compared to their counterpart. Average score of employed male on depression-happiness measure was found 12.80 whereas the average score of unemployed male was found 14.50. It shows that the un-employed male have more depression-happiness measure as compared to their counterpart. Average score of employed female on depression-happiness measure was found 13.80 whereas the average score of unemployed female was found 14.80. It shows that the employed female have more depression-happiness measure as compared to their counterpart. Average score of employed male on depression-happiness measure was found 12.80 whereas the average score of unemployed female was found 14.80. It shows that the un-employed female have more depression-happiness measure as compared to their counterpart. Average score of unemployed male on depression-happiness measure was found 14.50 whereas the average score of employed female was found 13.80. It shows that the un-employed male have more depression-happiness measure as compared to their counterpart.

The average score of employed Thakur on depression-happiness measure was found 13.30 as compared to their un-employed counterpart whose score on their same was found 14.50.It clearly shows that the un-employed people have more depression-happiness measure as compare to their counterpart. Further average score of male in depression-happiness measure was found 14.25 whereas the average scores of female were found as 13.55. It clearly shows that the males have more depression-happiness measure as compared to their counterpart. Average score of Thakur employed male on depression-happiness measure was found 13.20 whereas the average score of employed female was found 13.40. It shows that the employed female have more depression-happiness measure as compared to their male counterpart. Similarly the average score of unemployed male on depression-happiness measure was found 15.30 whereas the mean score of unemployed female was found 13.70. It shows that the unemployed male also showed more depression-happiness measure as compared to their counterpart. Average score of employed male on depression-happiness measure was found 13.20 whereas the average score of unemployed male was found 15.30. It shows that the un-employed male have more depression-happiness measure as compared to their counterpart. Average score of employed female on depression-happiness measure was found 13.40 whereas the average score of unemployed female was found 13.70. It shows that the un-employed female have more depression-happiness measure as compared to their counterpart. Average score of employed male on depression-happiness measure was found 13.20 whereas the average score of unemployed female was found 13.70. It shows that the un-employed female have more depression-happiness measure as compared to their counterpart. Average score of unemployed male on depression-happiness measure was found 15.30 whereas the average score of employed female was found 13.40. It shows that the un-employed male have more depression-happiness measure as compared to their counterpart.

The average score of employed Harijan on depression-happiness measure was found 14.85 as compared to their un-employed counterpart whose score on their same was found 12.25.It clearly shows that the employed people have more depression-happiness measure as compare to their counterpart. Further average score of male in depression-happiness measure was found 14.35 whereas the average scores of female were found as 12.75. It clearly shows that the males have more depression-happiness measure as compared to their counterpart. Average score of Harijan employed male on depression-happiness measure was found 16.00 whereas the average score of employed female was found 13.70. It shows that the employed male have more depression-happiness measure as compared to their male counterpart. Similarly the average score of unemployed male on depression-happiness measure was found 12.70 whereas the mean score of unemployed female was found 11.80. It shows that the unemployed male also showed more depression-happiness measure as compared to their counterpart. Average score of employed male on depression-happiness measure was found 16.00 whereas the average score of unemployed male was found 12.70. It shows that the employed male have more depression-happiness measure as compared to their counterpart. Average score of employed female on depression-happiness measure was found 13.70 whereas the average score of unemployed female was found 11.80. It shows that the employed female have more depression-happiness measure as compared to their counterpart. Average score of employed male on depression-happiness measure was found 16.00 whereas the average score of unemployed female was found 11.80. It shows that the employed male have more depression-happincss measure as compared to their counterpart. Average score of unemployed male on depression-happiness measure was found 12.70 whereas the average score of employed female was found 13.70. It shows that the employed female have more depression-happiness measure as compared to their counterpart.

7.5 APPRAISAL OF HEALTH

From the table 5.5 it is quite clear that the main effect of Caste on the measure of PGI HQ-Total was found F (3, 144) = 8.792, p<.01 as statistically significant. But the main effect of Employment on the measure of PGI HQ-Total was found F (1, 144) = 1.175, p>.05 as statistically non-significant. The main effect of Sex on the measure of PGI HQ-Total was found F (1, 144) = 86.746, p<.01 as statistically significant. The two way interaction between Caste x Employment on the measure of PGI HQ-Total was found F (3, 144) =1.007, p>.05 as statistically non-significant. Similarly the two way interaction between Caste x Sex on the measure of PGI HQ-Total was found F (3, 144) =.452, p>.05 as statistically non-significant. In the same way the two way interaction between Employment x Sex on the measure of PGI HQ-Total was found F (1, 144) = .004, p>.05 as statistically non-significant. Finally the three way interaction between Caste x Employment x Sex on the measure of PGI HQ-Total was found $F (3,144) = .831, p>.05$ as statistically non-significant.

The average score of employed Rajput on PGI HQ-Total was found 8.8 as compared to their un-employed counterpart whose score on their same was found 9.95.It clearly shows that the un-employed people have more PGI HQ-Total as compare to their counterpart. Further average score of male in PGI HQ-Total was found 6.35 whereas the average scores of female were found as 12.4. It clearly shows that the females have more PGI HQ-Total as compared to their counterpart. Average score of Rajput employed male on PGI HQ-Total was found 6.1 whereas the average score of employed female was found 11.50. It shows that the employed females have more PGI HQ-Total measure as compared to their male counterpart. Similarly the average score of unemployed male on PGI HQ-Total was found 6.6 whereas the mean score of unemployed female was found 13.30. It shows that the unemployed female also showed more PGI HQ-Total as compared to their counterpart. Average score of employed male on PGI HQ-Total was found 6.1 whereas the average score of unemployed male was found 6.6. It shows that the un-employed male have more PGI HQ-Total as compared to their counterpart. Average score of employed female on PGI HQ-Total was found 11.50 whereas the average score of unemployed female was found 13.30. It shows that the employed female have more PGI HQ-Total as compared to their counterpart. Average score of employed male on PGI HQ-Total was found 6.1 whereas the average score of unemployed female was found 13.30. It shows that the un-employed female have more PGI HQ-Total as compared to their counterpart. Average score of unemployed male on PGI HQ-Total was found 6.6 whereas the average score of employed female was found 11.50.It shows that the employed females have more PGI HQ-Total as compared to their counterpart.

The average score of employed Bhramin on PGI HQ-Total was found 10.4 as compared to their un-employed counterpart whose score on their same was found 7.3.It clearly shows that the employed people have more PGI HQ-Total as compare to their counterpart. Further average score of male in PGI HQ-Total was found 8.75 whereas the average scores of female were found as 8.95. It clearly shows that the females have more PGI HQ-Total as compared to their counterpart. Average score of Bhramin employed male on PGI HQ-Total was found 8.2 whereas the average score of employed female was found 12.6. It shows that the employed females have more PGI HQ-Total measure as compared to their male counterpart. Similarly the average score of unemployed male on PGI HQ-Total was found 9.3 whereas the mean score of unemployed female was found 5.3. It shows that the unemployed male also showed more PGI HQ-Total as compared to their counterpart. Average score of employed male on PGI HQ-Total was found 8.2 whereas the average score of unemployed male was found 9.3. It shows that the un-employed male have more PGI HQ-Total as compared to their counterpart. Average score of employed female on PGI HQ-Total was found 12.6 whereas the average score of unemployed female was found 5.3. It shows that the employed female have more PGI HQ-Total as compared to their counterpart. Average score of employed male on PGI HQ-Total was found 8.2 whereas the average score of unemployed female was found 5.3It shows that the employed male has more PGI HQ-Total as compared to their counterpart. Average score of unemployed male on PGI HQ-Total was found 9.3 whereas the average score of employed female was found 12.6.It shows that the employed females have more PGI HQ-Total as compared to their counterpart.

The average score of employed Thakur on PGI HQ-Total was found 6.6 as compared to their un-employed counterpart whose score on their same was found 9.75.It clearly shows that the un-employed people have more PGI HQ-Total as compare to their counterpart. Further average score of male in PGI HQ-Total was found 6.95 whereas the average scores of female were found as 12.5. It clearly shows that the females have more PGI HQ-Total as compared to their counterpart. Average score of Thakur employed male on PGI HQ-Total was found 6.2 whereas the average score of employed female was found 13.2. It shows that the employed females have more PGI HQ-Total measure as compared to their male counterpart. Similarly the average score of unemployed male on PGI HQ-Total was found 7.7 whereas the mean score of unemployed female was found 11.8. It shows that the unemployed female also showed more PGI HQ-Total as compared to their counterpart. Average score of employed male on PGI HQ-Total was found 6.2 whereas the average score of unemployed male was found 7.7. It shows that the un-employed male have more PGI HQ-Total as compared to their counterpart. Average score of employed female on PGI HQ-Total was found 13.2 whereas the average score of unemployed female was found 11.8. It shows that the employed female have more PGI HQ-Total as compared to their counterpart. Average score of employed male on PGI HQ-Total was found 6.2 whereas the average score of unemployed female was found 11.8. It shows that the un-employed female have more PGI HQ-Total as compared to their counterpart. Average score of unemployed male on PGI HQ-Total was found 7.7 whereas the average score of employed female was found 13.2.It shows that the employed females have more PGI HQ-Total as compared to their counterpart.

The average score of employed Harijan on PGI HQ-Total was found 13.35 as compared to their un-employed counterpart whose score on their same was found 12.7.It clearly shows that the employed people have more PGI HQ-Total as compare to their counterpart. Further average score of male in PGI HQ-Total was found 10.9 whereas the average scores of female were found as 15.15. It clearly shows that the females have more PGI HQ-Total as compared to their counterpart. Average score of Harijan employed male on PGI HQ-Total was found 11.3 whereas the average score of employed female was found 15.4. It shows that the employed females have more PGI HQ-Total measure as compared to their male counterpart. Similarly the average score of unemployed male on PGI HQ-Total was found 10.5 whereas the mean score of unemployed female was found 14.9. It shows that the unemployed female also showed more PGI HQ-Total as compared to their counterpart. Average score of employed male on PGI HQ-Total was found 11.3 whereas the average score of unemployed male was found 10.5. It shows that the employed male have more PGI HQ-Total as compared to their counterpart. Average score of employed female on PGI HQ-Total was found 15.4 whereas the average score of unemployed female was found 14.9. It shows that the employed female have more PGI HQ-Total as compared to their counterpart. Average score of employed male on PGI HQ-Total was found 11.3 whereas the average score of un-employed female was found 14.9. It shows that the un-employed female have more PGI HQ-Total as compared to their counterpart. Average score of unemployed male on PGI HQ-Total was found 10.5 whereas the average score of employed female was found 15.4.It shows that the employed females have more PGI HQ-Total as compared to their counterpart.

From the table 5.6 it is quite clear that the main effect of Caste on the measure of PGI HQ-I was found F (3, 144) = 4.98, p<.01 as statistically significant. But the main effect of Employment on the measure of PGI HQ-I was found F (1, 144) = .966, p>.05 as statistically non- significant. The main effect of Sex on the measure of PGI HQ-I was found F (1, 144) = 51.604, p<.01 as statistically significant. Similarly the two way interaction between Caste x Employment on the measure of PGI HQ-I was found F (3, 144) =2.76, p<.01 as statistically significant. The two way interaction between Caste x Sex on the measure of PGI HQ-I was found F (3, 144) =1.199, p>.05 as statistically non-significant. In the same way the two way interaction between Employment x Sex on the measure of PGI HQ-I was found F (1, 144) = .143, p>.05 as statistically non-significant. Finally the three way interaction between Caste x Employment x Sex on the measure of PGI HQ-I was found F (3,144) = 1.25, p>.05 as statistically non-significant.

The average score of employed Rajput on PGI HQ-I was found 4.45 as compared to their un-employed counterpart whose score on their same was found 3.95.It clearly shows that the employed people have more PGI HQ-I as compare to their counterpart. Further average score of male in PGI HQ-I was found 2.90 whereas the average scores of female were found as 5.50. It clearly shows that the females have more PGI HQ-I as compared to their counterpart. Average score of Rajput employed male on PGI HQ-I was found 2.80 whereas the average score of employed female was found 6.1. It shows that the employed females have more PGI HQ-I measure as compared to their male counterpart. Similarly the average score of unemployed male on PGI HQ-I was found 3.0 whereas the mean score of unemployed female was found 4.90. It shows that the unemployed female also showed more PGI HQ-I as compared to their counterpart. Average score of employed male on PGI HQ-I was found 2.80 whereas the average score of unemployed male was found 3.0. It shows that the un-employed male have more PGI HQ-I as compared to their counterpart. Average score of employed female on PGI HQ-I was found 6.1 whereas the average score of unemployed female was found 4.90. It shows that the employed female have more PGI HQ-I as compared to their counterpart. Average score of employed male on PGI HQ-I was found 2.80 whereas the average score of unemployed female was found 4.90. It shows that the un-employed female have more PGI HQ-I as compared to their counterpart. Average score of unemployed male on PGI HQ-I was found 3.0 whereas the average score of employed female was found 6.1. It shows that the employed female have more PGI HQ-I as compared to their counterpart.

The average score of employed Bhramin on PGI HQ-I was found 4.70 as compared to their un-employed counterpart whose score on their same was found 6.60.It clearly shows that the un-employed people have more PGI HQ-I as compare to their counterpart. Further average score of male in PGI HQ-I was found 4.00 whereas the average scores of female were found as 7.30. It clearly shows that the females have more PGI HQ-I as compared to their counterpart. Average score of Bhramin employed male on PGI HQ-I was found 3.60 whereas the average score of employed female was found 5.80. It shows that the employed females have more PGI HQ-I measure as compared to their male counterpart. Similarly the average score of unemployed male on PGI HQ-I was found 4.40whereas the mean score of unemployed female was found 8.80. It shows that the unemployed female also showed more PGI HQ-I as compared to their counterpart. Average score of employed male on PGI HQ-I was found 3.36 whereas the average score of unemployed male was found 4.40. It shows that the un-employed male have more PGI HQ-I as compared to their counterpart. Average score of employed female on PGI HQ-I was found 5.80 whereas the average score of unemployed female was found 8.80. It shows that the employed female have more PGI HQ-I as compared to their counterpart. Average score of employed male on PGI HQ-I was found 3.60 whereas the average score of unemployed female was found 8.80. It shows that the un-employed female have more PGI HQ-I as compared to their counterpart. Average score of unemployed male on PGI HQ-I was found 4.40 whereas the average score of employed female was found 5.80. It shows that the employed female have more PGI HQ-I as compared to their counterpart.

The average score of employed Thakur on PGI HQ-I was found 4.40 as compared to their un-employed counterpart whose score on their same was found 4.05.It clearly shows that the employed people have more PGI HQ-I as compare to their counterpart. Further average score of male in PGI HQ-I was found 3.3 whereas the average scores of female were found as 5.15. It clearly shows that the females have more PGI HQ-I as compared to their counterpart. Average score of Thakur employed male on PGI HQ-I was found 3.5 whereas the average score of employed female was found 5.3. It shows that the employed females have more PGI HQ-I measure as compared to their male counterpart. Similarly the average score of unemployed male on PGI HQ-I was found 3.1 whereas the mean score of unemployed female was found 5.0. It shows that the unemployed female also showed more PGI HQ-I as compared to their counterpart.

Average score of employed male on PGI HQ-I was found 3.5 whereas the average score of unemployed male was found 3.1. It shows that the un-employed male have more PGI HQ-I as compared to their counterpart. Average score of employed female on PGI HQ-I was found 5.3 whereas the average score of unemployed female was found 5.0. It shows that the employed female have more PGI HQ-I as compared to their counterpart. Average score of employed male on PGI HQ-I was found 3.5 whereas the average score of unemployed female was found 5.0. It shows that the un-employed female have more PGI HQ-I as compared to their counterpart. Average score of unemployed male on PGI HQ-I was found 3.1 whereas the average score of employed female was found 5.3. It shows that the employed female have more PGI HQ-I as compared to their counterpart.

The average score of employed Harijan on PGI HQ-I was found 5.15 as compared to their un-employed counterpart whose score on their same was found 5.40.It clearly shows that the un-employed people have more PGI HQ-I as compare to their counterpart. Further average score of male in PGI HQ-I was found 4.4 whereas the average scores of female were found as 6.15. It clearly shows that the females have more PGI HQ-I as compared to their counterpart. Average score of Harijan employed male on PGI HQ-I was found 4.3 whereas the average score of employed female was found 6.0. It shows that the employed females have more PGI HQ-I measure as compared to their male counterpart. Similarly the average score of unemployed male on PGI HQ-I was found 4.5 whereas the mean score of unemployed female was found 6.3. It shows that the unemployed female also showed more PGI HQ-I as compared to their counterpart. Average score of employed male on PGI HQ-I was found 4.3 whereas the average score of unemployed male was found

4.5. It shows that the un-employed male have more PGI HQ-I as compared to their counterpart. Average score of employed female on PGI HQ-I was found 6.0 whereas the average score of unemployed female was found 6.3. It shows that the employed female have more PGI HQ-I as compared to their counterpart. Average score of employed male on PGI HQ-I was found 4.3 whereas the average score of unemployed female was found 6.3. It shows that the un-employed female have more PGI HQ-I as compared to their counterpart. Average score of unemployed male on PGI HQ-I was found 4.5 whereas the average score of employed female was found 6.0.It shows that the employed females have more PGI HQ-I as compared to their counterpart.

From the table 5.7 it is quite clear that the main effect of Caste on the measure of PGI HQ-II was found $F(3, 144) = 7.907$, $p<.01$ as statistically significant. But the main effect of Employment on the measure of PGI HQ-II was found $F(1, 144) = .481$, $p>.05$ as statistically non- significant. The main effect of Sex on the measure of PGI HQ-II was found $F(1, 144) = 48.486$, $p<.01$ as statistically significant. The two way interaction between Caste x Employment on the measure of PGI HQ-II was found $F(3, 144) = 1.629$, $p>.05$ as statistically non-significant. Similarly the two way interaction between Caste x Sex on the measure of PGI HQ-II was found $F(3, 144) = 1.019$, $p>.05$ as statistically non-significant. In the same way the two way interaction between Employment x Sex on the measure of PGI HQ-II was found $F(1, 144) = .045$, $p>.05$ as statistically non-significant. Finally the three way interaction between Caste x Employment x Sex on the measure of PGI HQ-II was found $F(3,144) = 2.007$, $p>.05$ as statistically non- significant.

The average score of employed Rajput on PGI HQ-II was found 4.35 as compared to their un-employed counterpart whose score on their same was found 6.00.It clearly shows that the un-employed people have more PGI HQ-II as compare to their counterpart. Further average score of male in PGI HQ-II was found 3.45 whereas the average scores of female were found as 6.90. It clearly shows that the females have more PGI HQ-II as compared to their counterpart. Average score of Rajput employed male on PGI HQ-II was found 3.3 whereas the average score of employed female was found 5.4. It shows that the employed females have more PGI HQ-II measure as compared to their male counterpart. Similarly the average score of unemployed male on PGI HQ-II was found 3.6 whereas the mean score of unemployed female was found 8.4. It shows that the unemployed female also showed more PGI HQ-II as compared to their counterpart. Average score of employed male on PGI HQ-II was found 3.3 whereas the average score of unemployed male was found 3.6. It shows that the un-employed male have more PGI HQ-II as compared to their counterpart. Average score of employed female on PGI HQ-II was found 5.4 whereas the average score of unemployed female was found 8.4. It shows that the employed female have more PGI HQ-II as compared to their counterpart. Average score of employed male on PGI HQ-II was found 3.3 whereas the average score of unemployed female was found 8.4. It shows that the un-employed female have more PGI HQ-II as compared to their counterpart. Average score of unemployed male on PGI HQ-II was found 3.6 whereas the average score of employed female was found 5.4.It shows that the employed females have more PGI HQ-II as compared to their counterpart.

The average score of employed Bhramin on PGI HQ-II was found 5.70 as compared to their un-employed counterpart whose score on their same was found 2.48.It clearly shows that the employed people have more PGI HQ-

II as compare to their counterpart. Further average score of male in PGI HQ-II was found 4.75 whereas the average scores of female were found as 6.65. It clearly shows that the females have more PGI HQ-II as compared to their counterpart. Average score of Bhramin employed male on PGI HQ-II was found 4.6 whereas the average score of employed female was found 6.8. It shows that the employed females have more PGI HQ-II measure as compared to their male counterpart. Similarly the average score of unemployed male on PGI HQ-II was found 4.9 whereas the mean score of unemployed female was found 6.5. It shows that the unemployed female also showed more PGI HQ-II as compared to their counterpart. Average score of employed male on PGI HQ-II was found 4.6 whereas the average score of unemployed male was found 4.9. It shows that the un-employed male have more PGI HQ-II as compared to their counterpart. Average score of employed female on PGI HQ-II was found 6.8 whereas the average score of unemployed female was found 6.5. It shows that the employed female have more PGI HQ-II as compared to their counterpart. Average score of employed male on PGI HQ-II was found 4.6 whereas the average score of unemployed female was found 6.5. It shows that the un-employed female have more PGI HQ-II as compared to their counterpart. Average score of unemployed male on PGI HQ-II was found 4.9 whereas the average score of employed female was found 6.8.It shows that the employed females have more PGI HQ-II as compared to their counterpart.

The average score of employed Thakur on PGI HQ-II was found 5.30 as compared to their un-employed counterpart whose score on their same was found 5.70.It clearly shows that the un-employed people have more PGI HQ-II as compare to their counterpart. Further average score of male in PGI HQ-II was found 3.65 whereas the average scores of female were found as 7.35. It clearly shows that the females have more PGI HQ-II as compared to their counterpart. Average score of Thakur employed male on PGI HQ-II was found 2.7 whereas the average score of employed female was found 7.9. It shows that the employed females have more PGI HQ-II measure as compared to their male counterpart. Similarly the average score of unemployed male on PGI HQ-II was found 4.6 whereas the mean score of unemployed female was found 6.8. It shows that the unemployed female also showed more PGI HQ-II as compared to their counterpart. Average score of employed male on PGI HQ-II was found 2.7 whereas the average score of unemployed male was found 4.6. It shows that the un-employed male have more PGI HQ-II as compared to their counterpart. Average score of employed female on PGI HQ-II was found 7.0 whereas the average score of unemployed female was found 6.8. It shows that the employed female have more PGI HQ-II as compared to their counterpart. Average score of employed male on PGI HQ-II was found 2.7 whereas the average score of unemployed female was found 6.8. It shows that the un-employed female have more PGI HQ-II as compared to their counterpart. Average score of unemployed male on PGI HQ-II was found 4.6 whereas the average score of employed female was found 7.9.It shows that the employed females have more PGI HQ-II as compared to their counterpart.

The average score of employed Harijan on PGI HQ-II was found 8.20 as compared to their un-employed counterpart whose score on their same was found 7.25.It clearly shows that the employed people have more PGI HQ-II as compare to their counterpart. Further average score of male in PGI HQ-II was found 6.50 whereas the average scores of female were found as 9.00. It clearly shows that the females have more PGI HQ-II as compared to their counterpart. Average score of Harijan employed male on PGI HQ-II was found 7.0 whereas the average score of employed female was found 9.4. It shows that the employed females have more PGI HQ-II measure as compared to their male counterpart. Similarly the average score of unemployed male on PGI HQ-II was found 6.0 whereas the mean score of unemployed female was found 8.6. It shows that the unemployed female also showed more PGI HQ-II as compared to their counterpart. Average score of employed male on PGI HQ-II was found 7.0 whereas the average score of unemployed male was found 6.0. It shows that the un-employed male have more PGI HQ-II as compared to their counterpart. Average score of employed female on PGI HQ-II was found 9.4 whereas the average score of unemployed female was found 8.6. It shows that the employed female have more PGI HQ-II as compared to their counterpart. Average score of employed male on PGI HQ-II was found 7.0 whereas the average score of unemployed female was found 8.6. It shows that the un-employed female have more PGI HQ-II as compared to their counterpart. Average score of unemployed male on PGI HQ-II was found 6.0 whereas the average score of employed female was found 9.4.It shows that the employed females have more PGI HQ-II as compared to their counterpart.

SUGGESTIONS

1. The institutions of deities seems to play vital role in social discrimination therefore the temple of each deity be opened for all people including socially disadvantaged people and women.
2. Although religiosity is better for health however excessive religiosity followed with ancestral stereotype may affect the life of unprivileged people by unnecessary impose their conditioned belief and norms.
3. For overcoming the fear Education in general and technological education in particular is needed to maintain their wellbeing.
4. Favorable policies to maintain socio-cultural heritage be put forth and while forming the same the right of socially disadvantaged people be kept in mind.
5. People should be made psychological strong by imparting different counseling and psychotherapeutic programs.
6. Better infrastructure and medical facilities should be provided for better wellbeing.
7. More media connectivity followed with transport facilities should be provided so that people reable

to reach to the important places and have more connectivity with other people.

8. People should be encouraged to try new techniques and more advanced agricultural products for improvement in their growth and earnings.
9. People should be taught to be more realistic and practical way through physically, mentally, socially and spiritually to maintain their resilience.
10. People should be given more support by the administration whenever needed and to improve their life quality.
11. Environmental aspects can be suitably woven into the curriculum of primary and high school classes. Emphasis should be on effective use of traditional technology, and to develop appropriate technology at the scale required for the hill areas.

REFERENCES

Agarwal, R. & Misra, G. (1986). Locus of control and attribution for achievement outcomes. *Psychological studies, 31 (1).*

Alex, H. S., Carl, E. T., Michael, E. M. & David, B. L. (1999). Spiritually and Religiously Oriented Health Interventions. *Journal of Health Psychology, 4 (3), 413-433.*

Alkire, S., & Black, R. (1997). A practical reasoning theory of development ethics: furthering the capabilities approach. *JID* 9 (2), 262–80.

Allport, G. W. & Ross J.M. (1967). Personal religious orientation and prejudice" *Journal of Personality & Social Psychology, 5, (4), 432 - 443.*

Ardelt, M. (2003). Effects of Religion and Purpose in Life on Elders' Subjective Well-Being and Attitudes toward Death. *Journal of Religious Gerontology, 14 (4), 55-70.*

Ashwini, Y.(2012). *Role of Guru In Your Life. Times Of India, second july.*

Atkinson, S, & Haran, D. (2005). Individual and district determinants of users' satisfaction with primary health care in developing countries. *Social Science and Medicine* 60, 501–13.

August, M. (2000). Overcoming fears of financial success. Retrieved 15 March 2004, from *http://www.planetlightworker .com/ articles/ marilynaugust/ article3.htm/)*

Australian Unity & Deakin University, (2008). *The Australian Unity Index Report* – What makes Australian Happy?

Bagget, B. (2000). How to overcome the fear of success. Retrieved 20 February 2004, from *http://www.handwrgtinguniversity.com /newsletterssamples/fear-of-success.*

Bandura, A. (1993). Perceived self-efficacy in cognitive development and functioning. *Educational Psychologist, 28, 117-148.*

Bandura, A. (1982). Self-efficacy mechanism in human agency. *American Psychologist, 37, 122-147.*

Bowlby, J. (1973). *Attachment and loss: Vol.2. Separation.* New York: Basic books.

Brown, I., Friefeld, S. and Schiller, C. (1993). *Quality of life for persons with development disabilities.* Toronto: Centre for Health Promotion, University of Toronto.

Banton, R., Clifford, P., Frosh, S., Lusada, J. & Rosenthall, J. (1985). *The politics of mental health.* London: Macmillan.

Barr, J. (1980). *The Scope and Authority of the Bible.* Philidelphia: Westminister Press.

Basham, K. & Miehls, D. (2004). *Transforming the legacy: Couple therapy with survivors of child trauma.* New York: Columbia University.

Beck, R. (2004). The function of religious belief: Defensive versus Existential Religion. *Journal of psychology and Christianity, 23 (3), 208-218.*

Belss, A. (1998). *Psychology of laziness.* (Gharachedaghy, M., trans.). Tehran. (Original work published 1991).

Belzen, 2005. In defense of the object: On trends and directions psychology of religion. *International journal of the Psychology of Religion, 15 (1), 1-16.*

Bhasin, V. (1997). "The human settlements and health status in Sikkim", in K. C. Mahantam (ed.), *People of the Himalayas.* Delhi: Kamla-Raj Enterprises.

Bhasin, V. (2008). Gaddis' Folk Medicine: A Source of Healing. *Ethno-Med., 2 (1): 1-27.*

Bill, B. et.al. (1996). Religion, spirituality and psychiatry: conceptual, cultural and personal challenges. *Australian and New Zealand journal of psychiatry, 30 (6), 728-729.*

Boisen, A.T. (1994). Personality changes and upheavals arising out of the sense of personal failure. *American journal of psychiatry, 151 (6), 125-133.*

Bowlley, J. (1969). *Attachment and loss.* Vol 1: Attachment. New York: Basic Books.

Bradburn , N.M. & Caplovitz, P. (1965). Reports on happiness: *A pilot study of behavior related to mental health.* Chicago: Aldine.

Brooks, T. (2005). Understanding the fear of success. Retrieved 5 February 2006, from

http://www.black-collegian-com/ news/fearofsuccess507.5html)

Broota, K.D. (1987). Beliefs and their functional significance. *Trends in social science research, 4 (1). 134-136.*

Bruce, H., Ruut, V. & Alex, W. (1991). Top-down versus Bottom-up theories of subjective wellbeing. *Published in: Social Indicators Research, 1991, vol. 24. pp. 81-100*

Campbell A., Converse, P.E. & Rodgers, W.Z. (1976) .*The quality of American life. Perceptions, evaluations & Satisfactions.* New York: Russell Sage foundation.

Campion, J. & Nurse, J. (2007) A dynamic model for wellbeing. *Australas, Psychiatry, 15, 1, 24-28.*

Chambers, R. (1997). *Whose Reality Counts? Putting the First Last.* Intermediate Technology Publications, London.

Cheston, S. E. (2000). Spirituality of encouragement. *Journal of Individual Psychology, 56 (3),* 296-304.

Christopher, G. E. & Jeffrey, S. L. (1998). The Religion-Health Connection: Evidence, Theory, and Future Directions. *Health Education and Behavior December, 25 (6), 700-720.*

Clark, W.H. (1958). *The psychology of religion:an introduction to religious experiences and behavior.* New York: Macmillan.

Cohen, A.B. (2005). Social versus Individual Motivation: Implication for normative definitions of religious orientation. *International journal for the psychology of religion, 15 (1).*

Compton,W., (2005). *Introduction to Positive Psychology.* Australia: Thompson: Wadsworth.

Cote,D. (2007). Les rites de possession chez les Gaddis du Dhauladhar (Himachal, Inde): spiritualite, guerison, societe. *Ph. D. thesis, Department of Anthropology,Universite de Montreal (Quebec, Canada).*

Daver, B.V. (Ed.) (2001). *Mental health from a gender perspective.* New Delhi: Sage.

David, N. (1999). *A History of the World's Religions,* 10 Th Ed. Upper Saddle River, N.J.: Prentice Hall, 1999.).

Dein, S. (2007). Religion, spirituality and depression: implications for research and treatment. *Primary Care Community Psychiatry, 11 (2), 61 – 72.*

De Vas, G.A. & Suarez-Orozeo, M.M. (1987). Sacrifice and the experience of power. *Journal of psychoanalytic anthropology, 10 (4), 309-340.*

Dew, R; Daniel, S; Goldston, D; Kuchibhatla, M; Scheifler, C; Triplett, M & Koenig, H (2009) "Prospective study of religion/ spirituality and depressive symptoms among adolescent psychiatric patients" *Journal of Affective Disorders Eprint*

Dhaleta, S. (2012). *Devta on pilgrimage, festivities on hold. Times Of India, thirteenth November.*

Dhawan, N. &Sripat, K. (1986). Fear of death and religiosity as related to need for affiliation. *Psychological studies, 31.*

Diener, E. & Diener, C. (1995). Factors predicting the subjective well-being of Nations. *Journal of Personality and Social Psychology, 5,* 851-864.

Diener & Lucas (2000). Explaining differences in societal levels of happiness: relative standards need fulfillment, culture, and evaluation theory. *Journal of Happiness Studies* **1**, 41–78.

Diener, E., Sandvik, E., & Pavot, W. (1989). Happiness in the frequency, not intensity of positive versus negative affect. In F.Sttrack, M.Argyle, & N. Schwarz (Eds.), *The social psychology of subjective well-being, USA.*

Douglas L. R. & Milton F. S. (1986). A test of two hypotheses of fear of success. *Sex Roles,* 14, (3-4), 163-180.

Donelson & Elaine. (1999). Psychology of religion and adolescents in the United States: Past to present. *Journal of Adolescence, 22 (2), 187-204.*

Duhrssen, A. (1978). Religious practices and psychotherapeutic methods. *Zeitschrift fur psychosomatische medizinund psychoanalyse, 24 (3), 201-208.*

Ellis A. (1980). Psychotherapy and atheistic values: a response to A. E. Bergin's "Psychotherapy and religious values."*Journal of Consulting Clinical Psychology.* 48 (5):635-9.

Ellison, C. G. & Levin, I. S. (1998). The religion-health connection: Evidence, theory and future directions. *Health Education and Behaviour, 25 (6), 700-720.*

Eme, R., & Lawrence, L. (1976). Fear of success and academic underachievement. *Sex Roles, 2 (3),* 269-271.

Emmons, R.A. (2005). Striving for the sacred: Personal goals, life meaning, and religion. *Journal of social issues, 61 (4), 731-745.*

Epstein, Y.M. (1981). *Effects of crowding on cognitive performance and social behavior,* Rugter University.

Farahani, M. (1999). *Psychology of personality.* Tehran, Iran: Teacher Training University.

Fetzer Institute, National Institute on Aging Working Group (1999). *Multidimensional measurement of religiousness/ spirituality for use in health research.* A report of a national working group supported by the Fetzer institute in collaboration with the national institute on aging Kalamazoo.

Fiori, K.L. (2004). Spiritual turning points and perceived control over the life course. *International journal of aging and human development, 59 (4), 391-420.*

Fisher, and Crandle (1997). Complex attachment: Pattern of relating in the couples. *Sexual and Marital Therapy, 12 (3), 211-233.*

Fonagy, P. (2001). *Attachment theory and psychoanalysis.* New York: Other Press.

Freeney, B. & Collins, N. (2004). Interpersonal safe heavens and secure base care giving processes in adulthood. In S. Rholes, & J. Simsons Eds., *Adult attachment: Theory, research and clinical implications (pp. 330-338).* New York: Guilford.

Gasper, D. (1997). Sen's capability approach and Nussbaum's capabilities ethic. *JID 9 (2), 281–302.)*

Galinsky, D.A. et al. (2010). For God (or) Country: the hydraulic relation between government instability and belief in religious sources of control. *Journal of personality and social psychology, 99 (5), 725-739.*

Geertsma, E.J. (2004). Midlife transition and Women's spirituality groups: A preliminary investigation. *Counseling and Values, 49 (1), 27-36.*

George, C., & Solomon, J. (1999). Loss and bereavement: Attachment theory and recent controversies concerning "grief work" and the nature of detachment. In J. C assidy, & P. Shavers (Eds.), *Handbook of attachment. Theory, research and clinical applications (pp. 735-759).* New York: Guilford.

Ghazal, J. (2004). Family, religion, and work among Arab American Women. *Journal of marriage and family, 66 (4), 1042-1050.*

Goldenberg, J. L. (2009). Exploring the existential function of religion: The effect of religious fundamentalism and mortality salience on faith-based medical refusals. *Journal of personality and social psychology, 97 (2), 334-350.*

James, W. (1902). *The varieties of religious experience.* Modern library edition. New York: random house.

Jonas, E & Fischer, P. (2006). Terror management and religion: evidence that intrinsic religiousness mitigates worldview defense following mortality salience. *Journal of personality and social psychology, 553-567.*

Haber, J; Jacob, T and Spangler (2007) "Dimensions of Religion/ Spirituality and Relevance to Health Research". *The*

International Journal for the Psychology of Religion, 17 (4), pp 265 – 288.

Hart, J. et al. (2005). Attachment, self-esteem, worldviews and terror management: evidence for a tripartite security system. *Journal of personality and social psychology, 88 (6), 999-1013.*

Harris,A. H., Thoresen, C. E., Mccullough, M. E., & Larson, D. B. (1999). Spiritually and Religiously Oriented Health Interventions. *Journal of Health Psychology, 4 (3), 413-433.*

Hartz, G.W, & Everett, H.C. (1989) Fundamentalist religion and its effect on mental health. *Journal of Religion and Health*, 28, 207-217.

Hazan, C., Gur-Yaish, N., & Campa, M. (2004). What does it means to be attached? In S. Rholes, & J. Simson's (Eds), *Adult attachment; Theory, research and clinical implications (pp. 55-85).* New York: Guilford.

Heintzman, P. (2002). A conceptual model of leisurc and spiritual well-being. *Journal of Park & Recreation Administration, 20, 4, 147-169.*

Hesse, E. (1999). The adult attachment interview: Historical and current perspective. In J. Cassidy & P. Shaver (Eds.), *Handbook of attachment, theory, research and clinical applications (pp. 394-433).* New York: Guilford.

Hide, J. (2001). *Psychology of women.* (Rahmaty, B., trans.). Tehran: Jihon Publication. (Original work published 1998).

Hood, R.W., Spilka, B., Hunsberger, B., & Gorsuch, R. (1996). *The psychology of religion.* New York: Gilford Press.

Horner, M.S. (1972). Toward an understanding of achievement-related conflicts in women. *Journal of Social Issues, 28 (2),* 157-175.

Horner, M. S. (1968). *"Sex Differences in Achievement Motivation and Performance in Competitive and Noncompetitive Situations.* Doctoral dissertation. University of Michigan.

Hosscin, M. & Pishe, M. (2008). A study of the relationship between fear of success and burnout among working women in Iranian public schools. *Asian Academy of Management Journal, 13 (1), 1–14.*

House, A. (2006). The earliest recorded theories of the future are mythological and religious. *"Ancient Myth, Religion, and Philosophy"* in Lombardo, Thomas. The Evolution of Future Consciousness. Bloomington, Indiana.

Hungsberger, B. (2005). Religion, meaning, and prejudice. *Journal of Social Issues, 61 (4), 807-826.*

Ivers & Downes, P. (2011). A phenomenological reinterpretation of Horner's fear of success in terms of social class. *Instituto Superior de Psicologia Aplicada, Lisboa, Portugal and Springer Science+Business Media BV.*

Jackaway, R., & Teevan, R. (1976). Fear of failure and fear of success: Two dimensions of the same motive. *Sex Roles, 2 (3),* 283-293.

Jacobsson, L. & Merdasa, F. (1991). Traditional perceptions and treatment of mental disorders in western Ethiopia before the 1974 revolution. *Acta Psychiatric Scandinavica, 84 (5), 475-481.*

Jones,E. (2006). Terror Management and Religion: Evidence that intrinsic religiousness mitigates worldview defense following mortality salience. *Journal of personality and social psychology, 91, pp. 553-567.*

Kakar, S. (1982). *Shamans, mystics and doctors: a psychological enquiry into India and its healing tradition.* New Delhi: Oxford university press.

Kamat, S. (2012). *The sum of all fears: When in trouble, what better escape than to cause more trouble? Times Of India, second July.*

Kasek, R. B. (1999). Adaptation of the Big Give as a hermeneutic instrument for religious constructs. *Personality & Individual Differences,* 27 (2), 229-237.

Kay, C.A. et al. (2008). God and the government: testing a compensatory control mechanism for the support of external systems. *Journal of personality and social sciences. 95 (1).*

Kelly, G. A. (1955). *The psychology of personal constructs.* New York: Norton.

Khan, M. (2012). *Civilisation and Spiritual Evolution. Times Of India, fourteenth June.*

Kimball, B., & Leahy, R.L. (1976). Fear of success in males and females: Effects of developmental level and sex-linked course of study. *Sex Roles 2 (3),* 273-281.

Kirby, S. E., Coleman, P. G. & Dealey, D. (2004). Spirituality and Well-Being in Frail and Nonfrail Older Adults. *J Gerontol B Psychol Sci Soc Sci (2004) 59 (3): P123-P129.*

Koenig, H.G., Smiley, M., & Gonzales, J. (1988). *Religion, health, and aging.* Westport, CT: Greenwood Press.

Koenig, H. G. (2004). *Religion, Spirituality, and Medicine:* Research Findings and Implications for Clinical Practice. Southern Medical Association, Durham

Kohlberg, L. (1968). A cognitive developmental analysis of children's sex role concepts and attitudes. *The development of sex differences, 82-173.*

Koo, M. & Fishbach, A. (2010). Climbing the goal ladder: how upcoming actions increase level of aspiration. *Journal of personality and social psychology, 99 (1), 1-13.*

Krause, N. (2002). Church-Based Social Support and Health in Old Age Exploring Variations by Race. *Journal of Gerontol B Psychol Sci Soc Sci, 57 (6), S332-S347.*

Krause, N. (2008) .The Social Foundation of Religious Meaning in Life. *Research on Aging, 30, 4, 395-427.*

Kumari, A & Pirta, R. S. (2009). Exploring Human Relationship with God as a Secure Base. *Journal of the Indian Academy of Applied Psychology.*

Kureshi, A., Khan, A.R., & Singh, J.C. (1980). Fear of failure (FF) among Indian and non- Indian students at Aligarh: A cross-cultural study. *Psychological studies, 25 (2).*

Larson, David B. & Larson, & Susan S. (2003). Spirituality's potential relevance to physical and emotional health: A review of quantitative research. *Journal of Psychology & Theology, 31(1), 37-51.*

Layard R (2005). *Happiness: Lessons from a New Science.* Penguin, London.

Lee, B & Newberg, L. (2005). Religion and health: A review and critical analysis. *Zygon, 40, (2), 443 – 468.*

Lima, C. & Putnamb, R. D. (2010). Religion, Social Networks, and Life Satisfaction. *American Sociological Review, 75, (6), 914-933.*

Mahalik & Lagan (2001). Examining masculine gender role conflict and stress in relation to religious orientation and spiritual well-being. *Psychology of Men & Masculinity, l 2 (1), 24-33.*

Maton, K.I., & Rappaport, J. (1984). Empowerment in a religious setting: A multivariate investigation. *Prevention in human services*, 3, 37-72.

Marano, H. (2004). Fear of success. Retrieved 5 February 2006, from *http://cms.psychologyday.com/articles/index.php?Term=PTO-20031224-0.00001.xml.*

Marvin, R., Cooper, G., Hoffman, K., & Powell, B. (2002). The circle of security project: Attachment based intervention with care-giver pre-schools child's days. *Attachment &Human Development, 4, 107-124.*

Maton, K.I. (2005). Religion as a meaning system: Policy implications for the new millennium. *Journal of social issues, 61 (4), 847-867.*

Mazumdar, 2004. Religion and place attachment: A study of sacred places. *Journal of environmental psychology, 24 (3), 385-397.*

McKinney, Paul and McKinsey, Kathleen (1999) . Prayer in the lives of late adolescents. *Journal of Adolescence, 22 (2)*, 279-290.

Meadow, M.J. et al. (1979). Dealing with religious issues in counseling and psychotherapy: a symposium. *Journal of religion & health, 18 (3), 176-202.*

Mc Latchie, L.R. & Draguns, J.G. (1984). Mental health concepts of evangelical protestants. *Journal of psychology, 118 (2), 147-159.*

Michael, J. M. (2010) .Religion and Mental Health Among Older Adults: Do the Effects of Religious Involvement Vary by Gender? *J Gerontol B Psychol Sci Soc Sci,* 65B (5): 621-630.

Mikulicer, M. et.al. (2002). Activation of the attachment system in adulthood: Threat-related primes increase the accessibility of mental representations of attachment figures. *Journal of personality and social psychology, 83 (4), 881-895.*

Motaghi, M. H., Mosapor, N., & Arjomand, S. H. (2004). Reasons related to fear of success in working women. *Women Studies, 5, 40–63.*

Myers, D. G. (2011). The Religion Paradox: If Religion Makes People Happy, Why Are So Many Dropping Out? *Journal of personality and social psychology. 101 (6).1278-1290.*

Nathawat, S.S. (1988). Factors influencing social well-being in research students in India. *Abstracts of XXIV international congress of Psychology. Abstract No., F 40.* Sydney, Australia.

Nathawat, S.S., & Rathore, S. (1996). Influence of hardiness and social support on well-being in elderly men & women. *Indian Journal of Clinical Psychology, 23,* 92-101.

Neal, Chatters, Meltzer, Tina & Morgan, David (2000). Using focus groups to explore the nature of prayer in late life. *Journal of aging studies, 14 (2), 191-212.*

Olsen, N.J., & Willemsen, E.W. (1978). Fear of success: Fact or artifact? *Journal of Psychology, 98,* 65-70.

Oman, D. & Thoresen, E. E. (2002). 'Does Religion Cause Health?': Differing Interpretations and Diverse Meanings. *Journal of Health Psychology, 7 (4), 365-380*

Pappo. M. (1972). *"Fear of Success: A Theoretical Analysis and the Construction and Validation of a Measuring Instrument."* Doctoral dissertation, Columbia University.

Pandey, D.U. (1988). A study of religious beliefs and social innovativeness. *Journal of psychological researches, 33 (1&2), pp. 41-44.*

Pargament, K.I. (2005). The sacred and the search for significance: Religion as a unique process. *Journal of social issues, 61 (4), 665-687.*

Park, C.L. (2005). Religion as a meaning-making framework in coping with life stress. *Journal of social issues, 61 (4), 707-729.*

Pedersen, D. M., Williams, R. N. & Kristensen, K. B. (2000). The relation of spiritual self-identity to religious orientations and attitudes. *Journal of Psychology & Theology, 28 (2),* 138-148.

Peteet, J.R. (1994). Approaching spiritual problems in psychotherapy: a conceptual framework. *Journal of psychotherapy practice and research, 3 (3), 237-245.*

Piedmont, R.L. (1988). An interactional model of achievement motivation and fear of success. *Sex Roles, 19 (7/8),* 467-490.

Piedmont, R.L. (1995). Another look at fear of success, fear of failure, and test anxiety: A motivational analysis using the five-factor model. *Sex Roles, 32 (3/4),* 139-158.

Pirta , R. S. & Ranta, R. S. (2007). Social Conflicts and Possession: The Role of Reconciliation Processes Mediated by Local Deities. *Journal of the Indian Academy of Applied Psychology, 33 (2), 201-212.*

Pirta, R. s., Ranta, R. S. & Vashisht, V. (2008). Folk psychology: The role of little traditonin mental health. *Journal of Psychological Researches, 3, 47-70.*

Pirta, R. S. (2010). Supernatural elements as context for deliberations on culture and cognition. *A revised version of invited presentation at the National Symposium. ISSN, 1 (1).*

Poll by global research company *Ipsos-"Indians among happiest on this planet".* Hidustan Times, twelfth February.

Powers, R. L. (2003). Robert L. Powers's original contribution to spirituality in the alderian forum. *Journal of Industrial Psychology,* 50 (1), 84-85.

Pyszczynski, T. et.al. (2003). *Freedom versus fear: on the defense, growth and expansion of the self.* Handbook of self and identity. Guilford Press: New York.

Pyysiainen, I (2003). True fiction: Philosophy and psychology of religious belief. *Philosophical psychology,* 16 (1), 109-125.

Quizilbash, M. (1997). A weakness of the capability approach with respect to gender justice. *JID 9 (2), 251–63.*

Rao, V. (2004). Which type of fear might be holding you back from success in business?

Retrieved from http://r144.com/hbnorticle036.htm/.

Richard (2006). Communion and complaint- attachment, object-relations, and triangular love perspectives on relationship with God. *Journal of psychology and theology.34 (1), 43-52.*

Richards, P. S. & Bergin, A. E. (2000). *Handbook of psychotherapy and religious diversity.* American psychological Association: Washington, DC.

Ruiz, P. (1998). The role of culture in psychiatric care. *American Journal of Psychiatry, 1555 (12), 1763-1765.*

Ryan, R. M., & Deci, E L. (2001). On happiness and human potentials : A review of research on hedonic and eudaimonic well-being. *Annual Review of Psychology, 52,* 141-166

Sasaki, J. Y. (2011). At the intersection of culture and religion: a cultural analysis of religion's implications for secondary control and social affiliation. *Journal of personatity and social psychology, 101 (2), 401-414.*

Sasaki,Y.J. &Kim, S.H. (2011). At the intersection of culture and religion: a cultural analysis of religion's implications for secondary control and social affiliation. *Journal of personality and social psychology,101 (2), 401-414.*

Schumaker J.F. (1992). *Religion and Mental Health.* New York: Oxford University Press.

Schyns, P. (1998). Crossnational differences in happiness: economic and cultural factors explored? *Social Indicators Research* 43,3–26.

Scott, P.R., Smith, S.A. & Davis, L.F. (1989). Healthy and unhealthy forms of religiousness manifested by psychotherapy clients: an empirical investigation. *Journal of research in personality, 23 (4), 506-524.*

Sethi, M.V. (2012). *From the Material to God-Consciousness. Times Of India, twenty seventh September.*

Sharma, S. (1999). *Encyclopedia of Himalayas (2).* New Delhi: anmol publications pvt. Ltd.

Singh, A.K. (1989). Gender and Religion related differences in alienation and anxiety. *Indian journal of current psychology research, 4 (1), 57-61.*

Singhal, S. (1988).Children's attributions of perceived school success and failure. *Journal of psychological researches, 32 (1&2), pp. 5-8.*

Srivastava, A.R.N. (1992). *What is Anthropology?* Allahabad: horizon publishers.

Srivastava, A.K. (2012). Religion and Health: An inquiry into the relationship. *Journal of Indian health psychology, 6 (2), 113-120.*

Srivastava, S. (2012). *Of Sex-Goddesses and Godmen. Times Of India, twenty second May.*

Strozier, C.B. (1994) *Apocalypse: On the psychology of fundamentalism in America.* Boston: Beacon Press.

Sushine, R., Terrence, D.H. & Christopher, G. E. (2012). Religious Attendance and Loneliness in Later Life. *The Gerontologist, 10, 1093-96.*

Tan, S. X. (2003). Integrating spiritual direction into psychotherapy: ethical isssues and guidelines. *Journal of Psychology and Theorlogy,* 31 (1), 14-23..

Taylor,E.I. (1978). Psychology of religion and Asian studies: The William James legacy. *Journal of transpersonal psychology, 10(1), 67-79.*

Thakur,M.R. (1997). *Myths, rituals and beliefs in himachal Pradesh.* New Delhi Indus publishing Company.

Thakur, S. & Pirta, R. S. (2009). Mental health and cognitive representations of people experiencing spirit possession. *Journal of the Indian Academy of Applied Psychology. 35 (2), 203-209.*

Thouless, R.H. (1971). *An introduction to the psychology of religion.* Third edition. London: Cambridge university press.

Trede, T. A. (2006). *An investigation of the relationship between religiosity and subjective well-being in older adults: The mediating role of optimism.* PhD thesis and dissertation.

Tresemer, D. (1976b). The cumulative record of research on "fear of success". *Sex Roles, 2 (3),* 217-236.

Umoren, U.E. (1990). Religion and traditional medicine: an anthropological case study of a Nigerian treatment of mental illness. *Medical anthropology, 12 (4), 389-400.*

Verma, M.A. & Verma, S.K. (1989). A co-relationship study of two well-being scales. *Journal of personality and clinical studies, 5, (1) 93-95.*

Verma, R.K. & Ghadially, R. (1985). Effect of mother's sex role attitudes on need for achievement and expectancy for success in children. *Psychological studies, 30.*

Vess, M. et al. (2009). Blowing in the (social) wind: implications of extrinsic esteem contingencies of terror management and health. *Journal of personality and social psychology, 96 (6), 1191-1205.*

Victor, F. et.al. (1997). Fear of personal death in adulthood: the impact of early and recent losses. *Death studies, 21 (1), 1-24.*

Victor, T. (1983). Body, brain and culture. *Journal of religion and science, 18 (3), 221-245.*

Vidyarthi, P.B. (1978). *Knowledge, self and God in Ramanuja.* Oriental publishers & distributors, New Delhi.

Watson, P.J. (1999). Religion and the experimental system: Relationships of constructive thinking with religious orientation. *International journal for the psychology of religion, 9 (3), 195-207.*

Wenger, J.L. (2005). Religious individuals: Evaluating their intrinsic and extrinsic motivation at the implicit level of awareness. *Journal of social psychology, 145 (1), 5-16.*

Whitehead, H. (1976). *The village gods of south India.* Delhi: Sumit publications.

Wiegand, K.E. & Weiss, H.M.,2006. Affective reactions to the thought of "God": moderating effects of image of God. *Journal of happiness studies, 7 (1), 23-40.*

Wilkins, W.J. (1972). *Hindu mythology. Vedic and puranic.* Delhi, Delhi Book Store.

Zinta, R.L. (2006). Is guided mastery helpful in problem solving. *Psychological Studies, 51(4), 323-325.*

Zou, Z. (2010). Know thyself: misperceptions of actual performance undermine achievement motivation, future performance and subjective wellbeing. *Journal of personality and social psychology, 99 (3), 395-409.*

Zuckerman, M., Larrance, D.T., Porac, J.F.A., & Blanck, P.D. (1980). Effects of fear o f success on intrinsic motivation, causal attribution, and choice behavior. *Journal ofPersonality and Social Psychology,* 39 (3), 503-513.

APPENDICES

Bothe Mahsu devta

Worshiped in a village Ghurla and some other parts of chopal area. The Bothe Mahsu has a palanquin made of gold and silver. He is of a calm nature but punishment is eminent if someone displeases him. No one accept the main priest of the temple touches the scripture.

The palanquin of Mahadev

People in the Choor Dhar region, Chaupal, Himachal Pradesh worship him. He is another incarnation of lord Shiva, supposed to be very kind, generous and calm in nature

Shirgul Devta

People in the Choor Dhar region, Chaupal, Himachal Pradesh worship him.

Duindar Kali Temple, chopal

Devat deity arrives at khilla festival

Temple of Devat Devta

Devta coming out of the Temple

Bijjat Maharaj Temple/ Sarain: it is situated in Hambal Valley and 26 Km away from Chopal Town and is well

known for its centuries old Bijjat Maharaj Temple. Sarain is surrounded by the fields, apple orchards, small villages and forest of deodar. This is one of the starting points of the trek to the Churdhar Peak. Temple complex has two parallel tall building houses the Bijjat Maharaj Devta "The God Of Lightening". There are many building in the complex and all are doublestoryed except for the two tall towers, which rise almost four times higher. The twin temple of Bijjat Maharaj at Sarahan is one of the most remarkable monument of Himachal Pradesh. This is the main deity in the area and is identified as the ‘God of prosperity and good health'. In the month of April; the Bishu Fair is organized here, which attracts thousand of pilgrims from all over the state and out of state.